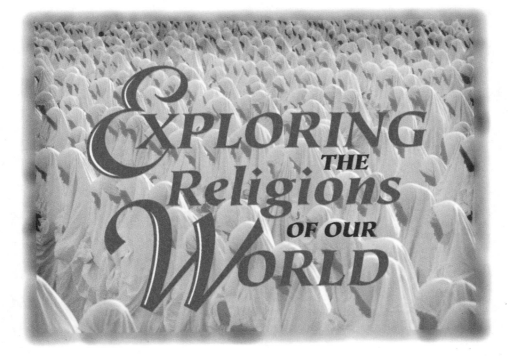

Exploring the Religions of our World

Nancy Clemmons, SNJM

ave maria press   Notre Dame, Indiana

Nihil Obstat:
Reverend John P. Brennan
Censor Deputatus

Imprimatur:
His Eminence Cardinal Roger Mahony
Archbishop of Los Angeles

Given on 20 January 1999

The *Nihil Obstat* and *Imprimatur* are official declarations that the work contains nothing contrary to Faith and Morals. It is not implied thereby that those granting the *Nihil Obstat* and *Imprimatur* agree with the contents, statements, or opinions expressed. The *Nihil Obstat* applies specifically to Chapter 1, "Beginning the Journey" and chapter 3, "Christianity."

Passages from Jewish Holy Scriptures taken from *The Holy Scriptures According to the Masoretic Text* (2 vols.) Philadelphia: The Jewish Publication Society of America, 1955.

Christian scripture passages are taken from *The New American Bible with Revised New Testament*, copyright ©1988 by the Confraternity of Christian Doctrine, Washington, D.C. All rights reserved.

International Standard Book Number:
0-87793-674-9

Project Editor: Michael Amodei

Cover/text design: Katherine Robinson Coleman

Photography credits:

Anthony Dalton: 104 upper right and left, 107, 116, 124, 129 right.

Galyn C. Hammond: 23, 28, 44, 55 upper right, left, and middle, 56 left, 66, 84, 99 left, 100 right, 102, 126, 129 lower left, 130-131, 163 lower right, 181 left.

Diane C. Lyell: 133, 155, 174, 177 top, 180.

Paul A. Pavlik: 55 middle right, 58.

Rocky Bullen Images: 111.

AP/Wide World Photos: 31, 33, 35, 50, 73, 95, 157, 188, 189-190, 192, 195, 198, 202.

Bill Wittman, cover stain-glass photo, 13, 49, 59.

Printed and bound in the United States of America.

Contents

Chapter 1

BEGINNING

THE JOURNEY

his is not just another religion book. This is a book about religion itself. In other religion classes you have taken, you learned about one particular religion. In studying Catholic Christianity, you most likely had classes on such topics as Jesus of Nazareth, the Bible, sacraments, morality, justice and peace, and church history.

A class on the world's religions is different. Instead of in-depth studies about one religion, this class is an overview of religions other than and including your own. One thing that helps people practice their own religion is understanding religions practiced by others. Some awareness of other religions has a two-fold benefit. First, in learning about other religions you can gain a clearer understanding of your own. The more you understand your own religion, the more benefit you gain in practicing it. Second, better compre-

hension of other religions assists you in being more open and accepting of people who, on the surface, seem very different.

In the United States, the first amendment grants all human beings the inalienable right to practice their religion. We know from American history that people have left their home countries because they were persecuted for practicing what they believed. The importance of practicing their religion was so great that people were willing to risk everything to come to a foreign land in order to worship freely. Though the United States was "discovered" by predominantly Catholic explorers, predominantly Protestant settlers established it as a nation. In addition to Christians, the new nation also included Jews and some African slaves who were Muslims in their native countries, but were denied the right of practicing Islam in this country. In the nineteenth century Japanese and Chinese immigrants brought their religions with them. Nonetheless, Protestant Christians were, and still are, the dominant religious group in the United States. Not until about the time of the election of John F. Kennedy as president did Catholic Christians enter mainstream American society. At the beginning of the third millennium, other religious traditions are dotting the religious landscape of America. The following excerpt from the *Los Angeles Times* reports on the growing religious diversity in the United States:

> With almost no fanfare, the United States is experiencing its most dramatic religious transformation this century. What has been a nation steeped in the Judeo-Christian tradition is fast becoming the most spiritually diverse country in the world. . . .
>
> The United States is now home to almost four million Muslims, five times as many as there were in 1970. Close to half of them are African-Americans. At this rate, by 2000 Islam is likely to outpace Judaism, which has leveled off at 5.5 million members.
>
> Two million Americans identify themselves as Buddhists, a ten-fold increase since 1970. Hindus have grown from 100,000 to 950,000 in the same period, Sikhs from 1,000 to 220,000. . . .
>
> While the United States remains predominantly Christian—85 percent of Americans claim this faith—the same forces that have broadened the nation's religious base are remaking many of Christianity's institutions. . . .
>
> During the last quarter of the twentieth century, the country's fastest growing religious communities have been Pentecostal, Mormon, and Jehovah's Witnesses.

Once the churches that served the rural South or remote West, they are now outstripping such mainstream Protestant congregations as the Presbyterians, Episcopalians and United Methodists, whose numbers continue to drop.

Losses for the United Methodist and the Presbyterian USA church would be even greater if not for the

recent addition of Asian immigrants. Korean Americans now account for close to one percent of the Methodist and two percent of the Presbyterian USA church.

With 60 million adherents, Roman Catholicism remains the country's largest denomination, but there too, expansion has been largely dependent on immigration. Latinos make up more than thirty percent of the membership. At the same time, the Southern Baptist Convention, the country's second largest denomination with 16 million members, has seen its ethnic congregations, particularly Asian and Latino, grow by more than fifty percent. They make up about three million members of the church.

None of this accounts for the most startling challenge to America's oldest religious structures: the rise of the nondenominational megachurch. In 1970, there were ten. Now, there are close to 400, with California home to seventy-nine more than any other state.

"The old-line churches, by that I mean Presbyterian, Episcopal and Congregationalist, won't disappear soon," said Wade Clark Roof, a religion professor at UC Santa Barbara. "But their position of dominance won't hold. The old line is becoming the sideline. The direction is away from history and doctrine, toward a generic form of religion."

Quoted from "Redefining Religion in America" (*The Los Angeles Times*, June 21, 1998)

You are probably familiar with the term "world religions." To be specific, this term refers to religions that are worldwide, such as Christianity and Islam. In this class we will study worldwide religions. But we will also study religions that are significant, but not found all over the world. For example, Hinduism has a very large number of adherents due to its seminal location in south Asia. However, 95 percent of Hindus live in India while the other 5 percent are spread across the other continents.

What religious diversity are you aware of in your geographical region?

Defining Religion

Though we glibly use the word "religion," the vast majority of scriptures used by the various religions, including the Bible, do not even have the word "religion" in them. Until modern times, religion was not separated from the rest of life. In birth and death, work and play, relationships with people, and connections with nature, what we now call religion was once—and for many cultures still is— all wrapped up in the fabric of life.

Even now a definition of religion is illusive. It is derived from the Latin word religio, meaning "to bind." Under the name of religion a person or community "bound" itself to something that was worthy of reverence or respect. Generally, certain obligations came along with this willingness to have strong ties with that which was over and beyond them. Asking people to define religion, we hear phrases like "worshipping God," "living a moral life," or "one's belief system." Religion is not just one thing. Imagining the many aspects of the world's religions, the spectrum of religious expression is boundless.

Why Study the World's Religions?

You may wonder, "If religion cannot be definitively defined and if religious expression is boundless, why study the various religions?" This is a fair question. Until very recently, the study of religion was a peculiarly western discipline. At first glance, it may seem impossible to get a handle on what has already been described above as illusive. On the other hand, there are some patterns or elements that could be included in a systematic study of religion. Reasons to study the world's religions include the following:

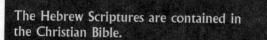

The Hebrew Scriptures are contained in the Christian Bible.

❖ To gain a better understanding of the present world.

❖ To gain insight into other human beings by understanding their religious activities.

❖ To gain understanding about one's own religion.

❖ To seek those things that are universal among the world's various cultures.

❖ To learn from some of the world's great sources of wisdom.

Which of the listed reasons best describe why you are studying the world's religions?

A Different Religion Class

As you no doubt have already experienced, religion classes are different from any other class. Putting it succinctly, a religion class calls upon learning in both the head and the heart. More than any other class, religion classes call upon one to deal with facts *and* experiences. Like other subjects, religion does deal with the rational. Unlike other subjects, topics such as life and death, good and evil, love and hate, joy and sorrow, and questions like where we came from, why we are here, and where we are going are integral to religion classes. What is unique about studying the world's religions as compared to studying one's own religion is that each religious tradition addresses and interprets these, and other experiences, differently.

A Certain Attitude

As students of the world's religions we are asked not to pass judgment upon the various religious traditions. As the documents of the Second Vatican Council state:

The Catholic church rejects nothing which is true and holy in these religions. She looks with sincere respect upon those ways of conduct and of life, those rules and teaching which, though differing in many particulars from what she holds and sets forth, nevertheless often reflect a ray of that Truth which enlightens all (*Nostra Aetate*, #2).

We are asked to suspend judgment as to the truth claims of a religious tradition and accept the tradition on its own terms. All of the religious traditions we will study have something to teach us. We are asked to engender an attitude of *empathy*. The word "empathy" means to identify and understand the situation of another. In other words, we are asked to "walk in the moccasins of another" as we study some of the world's religions.

When our journey is completed we are able to return with more insight into our holy Catholic faith, which "proclaims and must ever proclaim Christ, 'the way, the truth, and the life' (John 14:6), in whom we find the fullness of religious life, and in whom God has reconciled all things to Himself (cf. 2 Corinthians 5:18-19).[1]

Some Common Elements or Patterns

Though a definition of "religion" is rather illusive, there are some common elements or patterns that can broadly be categorized as elements of a religious tradition. Though not every religious tradition gives the same importance to every element, nor does every religious tradition have all of the elements, some tendencies are strong enough to categorize traditions we are studying as religious.

Sacred Stories, Sacred Scriptures, and Community

Most religious traditions have stories that tell how the world began, how humans were created, and why. These sacred stories are commonly called *myths*. They are not false stories but truth stories—they are intended to convey sacred truths. For some religious traditions, these sacred stories are part of sacred history. Certain core historical events—for example, the birth of Muhammed or the Exodus of the Jews—have become part of that religion's sacred history. These events are known as empirical history, that is, history that is verifiable or provable from other sources. Generally, these stories were first passed on orally. Later some sacred stories became part of the collective memory of the adherents of a religious tradition and have often defined them as a community.

So, the history of a particular religious community often involves myths, sacred history, and empirical history. For example, the story of the Jews includes creation myth stories, the sacred history of the patriarchs, prophets, and a nomadic tribe, and the centuries of empirical history up to the establishment of the State of Israel in the twentieth century.

Name a sacred or holy story that tells of your own family's religious experience.

Beliefs and Actions

Though not all religious traditions have a formal set of beliefs, there are certain truths held by each that separate one religious tradition from another. Buddhism and Christianity have well formulated doctrines. The Four Noble Truths and the Noble Eight-Fold Path are clearly delineated Buddhist doctrines. The Apostles' Creed is a formal statement of Christian beliefs. Though the *Sh'ma* is the one formal doctrine of Judaism and does not include commentary about human nature, sin, and how to relate to widows and orphans, this does not mean Judaism has nothing to say about those topics. Often an individual or group communicates the beliefs of a particular religious community through how they act when faced with those issues or how they explain their actions. The experiences and explanations are passed down orally from one generation to the next. Eventually they are recounted in written form and become important writings within the community. Some of these writings are even considered sacred.

Observing a person's behavior is a way to detect his or her beliefs. For example, witnessing a Muslim neighbor facing toward Mecca in Saudi Arabia in daily prayer tells us that prayer and the city of Mecca are very important to Muslims. Or knowing that Catholics feed and house the poor at neighborhood Catholic Worker Hospitality Houses tells us that the dignity of every human person is important to Catholic Christians. Of course, these are ideal behaviors. Each religious tradition has some sort of moral code—written and unwritten—that guides adherents in the conduct expected. It is through proper behavior that one can be a good Buddhist or a good Muslim. For many religious traditions, these behaviors also determine how one will spend the next life or eternal life.

Which of your personal behaviors clearly reflect your religious beliefs?

Sacred Time

Though most religious traditions consider all time sacred, there are particular times when certain actions or attitudes give greater focus to the sacred. Whether these times occur daily, weekly, monthly, yearly, or even every seven years, observers are able to comment, "That time is holy for them." Though

Muslims praying

times for personal devotions are often at the discretion of the individual, communal observances are more formal. Muslims have Friday, Jews have Saturday, and Christians have Sunday as their days for weekly observances. Muslims have Ramadan, Jews have Yom Kippur, and most Christians have Lent as annual times of fasting for spiritual renewal and growth. Festivals mark times of celebration for the respective religious traditions; for example, Buddhists celebrate Bodhi Day, Sikhs celebrate Guru Gobind Singh's birthday, and Jews celebrate Passover. Festivals and observances give members of a religious tradition a sense of belonging and are opportunities for personal and communal recommitment and renewal.

Rites of passage are also sacred times. In particular, rites of birth, coming of age, marriage, and death are observed as sacred times in many religious traditions.

What times are sacred to you?

Sacred Space

Generally, sacred time can be observed and celebrated anywhere. However, sacred time often takes place in a sacred space. Places where the religion began or where the founder traveled become sacred spaces. Thus, Mecca and Medina are holy ground for Muslims. The Galilee region in the State of Israel is sacred space for Christians. Shrines, temples, churches, mosques, and synagogues are all sacred spaces. Others find places in nature such as mountains and rivers to be sacred. The Jordan River for Christians and the Ganges River for Hindus come to mind. The Mount of Olives is sacred to Christians while Mount Fuji is sacred to Shintos. Unfortunately, there are times when sacred spaces are sources of conflict. For example, Muslims, Christians, and Jews all claim Jerusalem as sacred space. Two or more groups claiming the same space as sacred have the potential of raising the level of conflict.

What spaces are sacred to you?

Beginning the Journey

You now have the basic tools necessary to begin this very special study of some of the world's religions. You have:

❖ the understanding that the term "religion" has many meanings;

❖ thought about your own reason(s) for studying the world's religions;

❖ knowledge that this religion class is different from the others;

❖ considered the attitude of empathy and began to develop it;

❖ learned some elements or patterns needed in this systematic study of the world's religions.

This course can be merely a systematic investigation of some of the world's religions. Or it can be the beginning of your growth in understanding your neighbor and *vice versa*. There is a section in each chapter called, "Who Is My

The Ganges River

Neighbor?" This section is an opportunity for each of you to begin to think about, and perhaps even engage in conversation with, people who participate in a different religious tradition than you yet live nearby. The classroom learning is just the beginning. The rest is up to you.

CHAPTER 1 IN BRIEF

❖ Awareness of different religions has a two-fold benefit: first, one gains a clearer understanding of his or her own religion; second, it creates an openness and acceptance of many other people.

❖ In the United States, non-traditional religions have recently sported the greatest percentage increases in membership.

❖ Though difficult to define, *religion* traditionally means "to bind." A person or community may be bound to God, or something else they consider over and beyond themselves.

❖ In describing a religious tradition, there are some common patterns or elements to look at, including sacred stories, sacred scriptures, community, beliefs and actions, sacred time, and sacred places.

CHAPTER 1 REVIEW QUESTIONS

1. Summarize the religious diversity in the United States at the present time according to the *Los Angeles Times* article on page 8-9.

2. Why use the term "world's religions" rather than "world religions" in studying the various religious traditions?

3. Where did the word religion originate? Why do you think it is so difficult to define "religion?"

4. What are some reasons for studying the world's religions?

5. What are the common elements or patterns we will be using in studying the world's religions?

6. What attitude is asked of us when studying the world's religions? Explain.

7. What makes a class on the world's religions different from other religion classes?

RESEARCH & ACTIVITIES

1. Use at least three English dictionaries—a collegiate or concise dictionary, a very large dictionary and a multi-volume dictionary—to look up the word *religion*. After writing *all* the definitions you find, write your own definition of the word *religion*.

2. Write the common elements or patterns found in religious traditions. Using your own tradition, write down what you already know about each.

SELECTED VOCABULARY

Catholic	Islam	*religio*
Christian	Judaism	religion
empathy	myth	sacred
Hinduism	Protestant	Shinto

Chapter 2

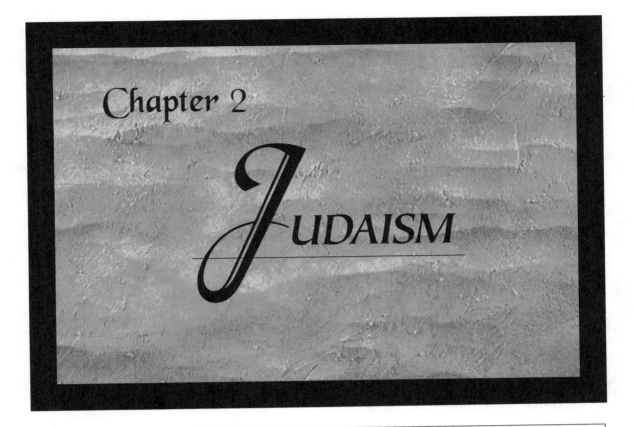

Judaism

ong ago, in the city of Safed in the land of Israel, there lived a great rabbi who was known as the Ari, which means "the Lion." The Ari prayed with all his heart and all his soul, and his prayers were dear to God. In fact, there was only one other whose prayers were more precious. And one Yom Kippur God decided to reveal this other one, so that the Ari might understand what is precious to God in prayer.

While the Ari was praying in the synagogue, an angel came to him and whispered in his ear the existence of this one whose prayers had reached the highest heavens. The angel told him the name of the man, and the city in which he lived, which was Tiberias. And when Yom Kippur was over, the Ari went to that city to seek out that man. For he wanted to learn the secret of his praying.

When the Ari reached the city, he first looked for the man in the House of Study. But he was not to be found among any of the men there. Then he sought him in the market. And there he was told that the only man by that name in Tiberias was a poor farmer who lived in the mountains.

So the Ari climbed into the mountains to find that man. When he reached his house, he was surprised to see that it was just a hut, for he was very poor. The poor farmer greeted him and invited the Ari to come in. And when they were together at last, the Ari did not waste any time. He asked the man to tell him the secret of his prayer. The man was very surprised by this, and said: "But, rabbi, I am afraid that I cannot pray. For I cannot read. All I know are the letters of the alphabet from Aleph to Yod."

The Ari was astonished to hear this, for had not the angel said that the prayers of this man were precious to God? Then the Ari said: "What did you do on Yom Kippur?" The man replied: "I went to the synagogue, of course. And when I saw how intently everyone around me was praying, my heart broke. And I began to recite all that I know of the alphabet. And I said in my heart: 'Dear God, take these letters and form them into prayers for me, that will rise up like the scent of honeysuckle. For that is the most beautiful scent that I know. 'And that is what I said with all my strength, over and over."

When the Ari heard this, he understood at once that God had sent him to learn that secret: that while man sees what is before his eyes, God looks into the heart. And that is why the prayers of the simple farmer were so precious.

Quoted from *Gabriel's Palace: Jewish Mystical Tales* by Howard Schwartz copyright ©1994 by Howard Schwartz. Used by permission of Oxford University Press, Inc.

The Ari learned from the poor man. What would you like to learn from Judaism? Initially the Ari prejudged the social status of the man who would be precious in God's eyes. What are some prejudgments you have of Judaism that you need to set aside to gain from the wisdom of this religious tradition?

Many Christians think of Judaism as the religion described in the Old Testament. Christians also understand Judaism as the religion practiced by Jesus when he was living on earth. Or, they may think of Judaism as the religion that is still waiting for God's chosen one after not accepting Jesus as the Messiah. Unfortunately, some Christians have held Jews or Jewish leaders as responsible for the crucifixion of Jesus. (The Catholic Church has recently condemned this mistaken view.) Christians are correct in defining Judaism as the religion of the Hebrew Bible, the religion of Jesus, and a religion still longing for God's chosen one. These understandings, though true, do not describe the essence of Judaism.

This chapter points out further elements which define Judaism as a living religion. You will look at ways in which Jews express their beliefs through personal and communal prayer, the study of the Torah, and lives lived in holiness before God. Judaism is not based on a set of abstract doctrines. Ideally what a Jew believes is reflected in how a Jew acts. The actions of a Jew reveal what it means to be part of a historical religion and what the operating values are in a Jew's life. The proclamation of one God, the reverence and study of the Torah, the recognition of Israel as both a nation and a people, and the setting aside of sacred places and times all combine to reveal the religious expression of Judaism.

Before attempting to define Judaism the religion, it is important to first look at what it means to be a Jewish person. To say Judaism is the *religion* of the Jews is not to say that all Jews practice Judaism. Being a Jew has both an ethnic and a religious connotation. Just who is a Jew is rather difficult for non-Jews to understand. Whereas a Christian is a follower of Christ and a Muslim is an adherent to Islam, a Jew

c. 1800	Abraham enters the Promised Land
c. 1250	Moses, the Exodus, and reception of the Law
c. 1200	Re-entry into Promised Land
c. 1050	Davidic Kingdom
c. 1000	Written Torah begins
c. 950	Construction of first Temple in Jerusalem
586	Babylonian exile and destruction of first Temple
537	Return from Babylonian exile
c. 500	Construction of second Temple begins
331	Jerusalem conquered by Alexander the Great
168	Antiochus IV demands that Jews cease with their rituals
165	Maccabean revolt
150	Septuagint compiled

CE

c. 10	Hillel and Shammai
70	Destruction of second Temple by Romans
c. 600	Completion of two Talmuds
1000	Golden Age of Judaism commences in Spain
1492	Jews first expelled from Iberian Peninsula
1897	Beginning of Zionist movement
1933	Beginning of Holocaust
1948	Establishment of the State of Israel
1967	The Six-Day War
1993	Peace accord between Israelis and Palestinians brokered

may or may not practice Judaism. Therein lies the confusion. There are *ethnic* Jews and *religious* Jews. A religious Jew practices Judaism. An ethnic Jew may or may not practice Judaism. A religious Jew may also be an ethnic Jew, but it is just as likely for a religious Jew to be from another ethnic group. Both ethnic Jews and religious Jews are found on virtually every continent. For the purposes of understanding Judaism, the rest of this chapter will focus on an understanding of religious Jews.

I. A BRIEF HISTORY OF JUDAISM

Judaism is the religion of the Jews. It is the religious expression of a people whose history spans thousands of years. Judaism can be dated from the time of Moses, though the seeds of Judaism can be traced to the time of Abraham. From its formation in the Sinai desert, triumphs and tragedies, ambiguities and misunderstandings, laughter and tears have written the history of Judaism and of the Jewish people. Though a minority group throughout much of its history, Jews have contributed substantially to the history of the world, particularly the western world.

Biblical Period

A history of Judaism finds the Jewish people on the move or controlled by foreign governments much of the time. The biblical period often begins with Abraham (c. 1800 BCE) and concludes with the death of Alexander the Great (323 BCE). Jews believe God called Abraham to leave his country and sojourn to a foreign land. With great faith and obedience to God's will, Abraham and his wife Sarah left Ur in Mesopotamia and moved to the land of Canaan along the Fertile Crescent. There, despite many obstacles, God's promise that Abraham and Sarah would have a son and that Abraham would be the "father of all nations" was fulfilled. In Canaan the *habiru*, or Hebrews, formed nomadic tribes. These nomadic tribes gradually settled into an agricultural system.

Generations later many Hebrew people moved to prosperous Egypt to avoid a major drought in Canaan. At first welcomed, they soon found themselves slaves under the powerful Egyptian government. As slaves, the Hebrew people were a small part of an immense army of people that helped build the majestic cities of Egypt. In approximately 1250 BCE Moses freed the Hebrew people from Egyptian bondage and led them back to Canaan, known to the Hebrew people as "the Promised Land." In the forty years they took to return to Canaan, the Hebrew people became a covenantal community, owing their allegiance to one God only. Moses died on the outskirts of Canaan, leaving Joshua to lead the Hebrew people back into the land "flowing with milk and honey." However, after living four hundred years in Egypt, the Hebrews found it necessary to conquer the present inhabitants of Canaan before they could resettle.

Once settled again in Canaan, the Hebrew people became a confederation of tribes and began to establish a powerful kingdom around 1050 BCE under the leadership of Kings Saul, David, and Solomon. A Temple was built in Jerusalem under the patronage of David's son, Solomon. As the Hebrew people became more powerful, they saw less need for the God who once freed them. Prophets such as Samuel and Nathan became more prominent, exhorting the Hebrew people to follow the ways of the one God rather than the ways of the neighboring Canaanite gods. During this time the oral tradition of the Hebrew people began to be transcribed into what became known as the *Torah*, a word meaning "law" or "instruction." After the death of Solomon the kingdom was divided into two, with the kingdom of Israel to the north with ten tribes and the kingdom of Judah to the south with two tribes. As the kingdoms weakened due to idolatry, Israel and Judah became more vulnerable to outside threats. Israel fell to the Assyrians around 722

BCE, exiling most of the northern kingdom. By 586 BCE the Babylonians conquered the Judeans, ravaging their land, destroying their Temple, and sending the majority of people to Babylon. As prophets had predicted the fall of Judah, so they predicted its rise. Approximately fifty years later the Persians conquered the Babylonians and allowed Judeans to return to their land. Some chose to stay in Babylon while others returned to a country that, though destroyed by war, was nevertheless holy because it had been given to them by God. The land would be restored and the Temple would be rebuilt.

Now living in the land of Judah, the Hebrew people became known as Jews. During this time the compilation of the Torah was completed. Prophets were becoming less numerous, but their writings kept their words alive for generations to come. In addition, wisdom literature was emerging. Writings such as Psalms, Proverbs, Job, Ruth, Esther, and Chronicles later came to be included in the Hebrew Scriptures.

What event marks a defining moment in the history of your family?

Rabbinic Period

A second major historical period of Judaic history is the *Rabbinic Period*. Also known as *Classical Judaism*, this historical period began in 323 BCE, the year Alexander the Great died. The closing of the period may be dated 625 CE, the year Jerusalem fell to the Islamic army coming out of the Arabian Peninsula. By the end of this era, many Jews found themselves living in a world that was both Christian and Muslim.

Through foreign occupation and conquest over a number of centuries, the Jews found themselves driven from their homeland. This growing number of Jews not living in Judea—as the area around southern Palestine came to be called— was known as the *Diaspora*, for they were dispersed from their land. Late in the fourth century BCE, Alexander the Great was victorious over much of the known world, including Judea. Soon after the Greek ruler Antiochus IV prohibited the practice of Judaism in Judea and took over the Temple. The Jewish family of the Maccabees led a revolt against the Greeks in 168 BCE, regaining possession of the Temple in 165 BCE.

The original conquests of Alexander the Great had lasting repercussions and resulted in the *Hellenization*[1] of much of the known world. Judea was no exception. Jews accepted the Hellenistic influences in varying degrees. In Egypt, the city of Alexandria became a thriving Jewish center. Philo of Alexandria was a very prominent Jewish philosopher living around the time of Jesus. Philo was comfortable in integrating Jewish theology with Greek philosophy. The rise of the synagogue and the establishment of centers for Jewish learning were features of this period. The Hebrew Bible was translated into Greek in the third century BCE. It became known as the *Septuagint*, a word meaning "seventy." According to tradition, seventy translators, working independently of one another, came up with exactly the same translated text from the Hebrew translation of the scriptures. It is very likely that some of the New Testament authors were familiar with this Greek translation of the Bible.

The Rabbinic Period saw tremendous Jewish sectarian development into a variety of competing groups. The three largest groups were the Sadducees, the Pharisees, and the Essenes. The Sadducees were Jews who defined themselves as biological descendants of Zadok, the last high priest before the Babylonian exile. The Sadducees held a strict position in the interpretation of the Torah. Oppositely, the Pharisees held a looser interpretation of the Torah, utilizing the oral tradition and popular customs in their interpretation of the law of Moses. The Pharisees also accepted the doctrine of resurrection while the Sadducees did not. While Sadducees and Pharisees are mentioned in the New Testament, the existence of the Essene community was unknown until 1948. In that year a young boy found clay jars filled with writing fragments from the Essene community in caves near Qumran. These writings, which became known as the "Dead Sea Scrolls," indicated the monastic nature of the Essenes and their scrupulosity for the Law.

Greek rule in Judea ended in 63 BCE when the Roman army conquered the region. Romans occupied Judea during much of the Rabbinic Period. In 70 CE, Roman soldiers stormed Jerusalem and destroyed the Temple. At that time, Jews had the choice of disappearing into history or reinterpreting their religious practice without the Temple. They chose the latter. The Sadducee and Pharisee sects disappeared, and rabbis[2] gained new prominence. To this day rabbis are the spiritual leaders of Judaism.

The rabbis began a process of systematically transforming the Temple rituals for practice outside of the Temple. Dozens of rabbinical schools sprang up, and with them dozens of different interpretations on how Jews should worship and live their lives. During the time of Jesus the schools of rabbis Shammai and Hillel were the most notable. A famous story is told about these two men:

> A heathen once came to Shammai and said, "I will become a proselyte on the condition that you teach me the entire Torah while I stand on one foot." Shammai chased him away with a builder's measuring stick. When he appeared before Hillel with the same request, Hillel said, "Whatever is hateful to you, do not do to your neighbor. That is the entire Torah. The rest is commentary; go and learn it." (*Mehilta Bahodesh* 1)

Over the next few centuries Torah commentaries were finally compiled, codified, and written into two works called the Babylonian Talmud and the Jerusalem Talmud. Along with the Torah, the *Talmud*[3] inspires and guides Jews in their religious life.

How can you apply Hillel's teaching of the Torah to your own life?

Medieval Period

During the Medieval Period (638-1783 CE) the Diaspora was moving further away from Palestine. Jews began to live in places they had never lived before: western, central, and eastern Europe, Asia, the Arabian Peninsula, and portions of North Africa. There was a resurgence in science, mathematics, philosophy, and commentaries on the Bible and Talmud. Rabbi Shlomo ben Itsak, a French Jew who became known as "Rashi", wrote commentaries on the Bible and Talmud that most Jews learned at a very young age. Through the development of Jewish philosophy there were attempts to harmonize reason with faith. The most famous Jewish philosopher was Moses Maimonides. He argued that there was no contradiction between the philosophy of Aristotle and the Jewish religion.

The Medieval Period was also marked by Jewish persecutions. French and German Christian Crusaders burned and destroyed almost all the Jewish communities along the Rhine River, murdering thousands of Jews. In 1391 *pogroms*—officially encouraged massacres—started against Jews on the Iberian Peninsula. In 1492 Jews were expelled from Spain. Three years later those Jews who had moved to Portugal were expelled from that country too.

Modern Period

The Age of Enlightenment[4] ushered in the Modern Period (1783 CE-present). Closely associated with this movement was a philosophy of Jewish enlightenment which was meant to emancipate Jews from their social and legal situation. No longer the chattel or property of prelates or feudal monarchs, Jews were achieving equality before the law alongside their Christian fellow citizens of Germany, France, the Netherlands, and Britain. Western Europe saw an explosion of sectarian groups in the Jewish tradition. In Germany and later in the United States, Reform Judaism emerged, advocating full integration into the culture where one lived. In the United States the rise of Conservative Judaism counteracted Reform Judaism, modifying Jewish tradition in a limited manner. This Orthodox Judaism was also a reactionary movement in response to Reform Judaism. Orthodox Judaism is the most traditional wing of Judaism, insisting its members strictly follow the Torah. In the 1930s Reconstructionist Judaism emerged from Conservative Judaism, advocating Judaism as a culture, not only a religion. Reconstructionist Jews do not believe in an all-powerful God. Nor do they accept the Torah as given by God.

The end of the nineteenth century saw the beginning of Jewish nationalism, known as Zionism. The Zionist movement sought a return by Jews to the Jewish homeland, Palestine. The worldwide community was more responsive to the goals of Zionism after the despicable murder of about six million Jews at the hands of the Nazi Germans in the Holocaust of the 1930s and 40s. In response to the Holocaust, the United Nations returned Palestine to the Jews in 1948. The new nation called itself the State of Israel. Yet the city of Jerusalem was still divided between the countries of Jordan and Israel. The holy places of Christians, Muslims, and Jews were under the jurisdiction of a Muslim country, Jordan. In 1967 the State of Israel recaptured all of Jerusalem in a war of

Jerusalem

© Galyn C. Hammond

23

self defense that became known as the Six-Day War. One of the results of the Six-Day War was that the ancient holy places in Jerusalem were opened to all visitors. Returning Palestine to the Jews has caused tremendous upset in much of the Middle East. Bringing peace to that part of the world requires a delicate balance that as yet has not been found.

How do you think the issue of the jurisdiction of Jerusalem should be decided?

SECTION 1 SUMMARY

✤ The Biblical Period found the Jews living in occupied Palestine or exiled to a foreign land.

✤ The Rabbinic Period was a time of emerging institutional structures in Judaism.

✤ During the Medieval Period Jews contributed much to the emerging western culture. This time was also marked by Jewish persecutions.

✤ The Modern Period reflects one of the most devastating times and one of the most triumphal times in the history of Judaism. The Holocaust resulted in the murder of about six million Jews. Following this, the United Nations approved the return of Palestine to the Jews.

SECTION 1 REVIEW QUESTIONS

1. What did the Hebrews become in the forty years it took to return to Canaan from Egypt?

2. According to the rabbi Hillel, what is the summation of the Torah?

3. Who was Moses Maimonides and what did he argue for?

4. Name and briefly differentiate the four types of Judaism that are present in the Modern Period.

Who Is My Neighbor?

JUDAISM IN AMERICA

Jews come in all shapes, sizes, and colors, so just by looking at a person you cannot tell whether or not he or she is Jewish. Jews do not form a single racial group or ethnic group. There are black Jews—Sammy Davis, Jr. and Whoopi Goldberg among the more popularly known—and black Jews generally find a welcome in synagogues. (The State of Israel recognized as authentic Jews the dark-skinned "house of Israel" of Ethiopia and undertook heroic efforts to save nearly the entire community from massacre during the wars there.) There are blond Jews and brown-haired Jews, rural Jews and urban Jews, rich Jews and poor Jews. American Jews live in most localities and are found in all social and economic groupings.

It is not easy to tell a Jew from a gentile, except in one important way: most Jews believe in one religion—Judaism. Of the nearly six million Jews in the United States, about three-quarters, or about 4.5 million, define being Jewish as a matter of religion. So while Judaism is not the religion of a single people, the Jews are a people with a single religion.

Quoted from "Judaism in the World and in America" by Jacob Neusner in *World Religions in America: An Introduction* (Louisville: Westminster/John Knox Press)

II. BELIEFS AND ACTIONS

If Judaism could be summed up in three words, those words would be *God*, *Torah*, and *Israel*. God gave the Torah to Israel. In this case Israel is not to be thought of as the political State of Israel with national boundaries, but as a people chosen by God with a specific purpose.

God

Who is this God who chose a small group of people to be a "light to the nations?" The opening words of the *Sh'ma*, a statement recited daily by devout Jews, offers an answer: "Hear, O Israel, the Lord our God, the Lord is One" (Deuteronomy 6:4). For Jews, God exists, God is one, God is creator, and God is good. Judaism is a monotheistic religion, that is, Jews believe in one, supreme God.

Unlike Christians, Jews do not have a set of formal doctrines of their beliefs. Yet, whatever branch of Judaism, all believe in one God. Not only does God exist, but also God is the creator of all things. The opening line of the Bible reads; "In the beginning, God created . . ." (Genesis 1:1). God created, and thus, God is good. Because God is good, God desires goodness from all creation. Scripture again is helpful in clarifying Jewish understanding of the responsibility of humankind:

> So now, O Israel, what does the LORD your God require of you? Only to fear the LORD your God, to walk in all his ways, to love him, to serve the LORD your God with all your heart and with all your soul, and to keep the commandments

of the LORD your God and his decrees that I am commanding you today, for your own well-being (Deuteronomy 10:12-13).

How have you personally experienced God as good? God as creator? God as one?

Torah

Torah

The basic source for how to live as a Jew is the Torah. The Torah is literally God's revelation to his people. Jews believe that God gave the Torah to Moses on Mount Sinai. Jews distinguish between two Torahs: the written Torah and the Talmud. Christians know the written Torah as the first five books in the Old Testament: Genesis, Exodus,

Talmud

Leviticus, Numbers, and Deuteronomy. Early rabbis wrote commentaries on the Torah known as *Midrash*. The summation of the Oral Law is known as *Mishnah*. It was not written down until the third century CE. Over the next couple of centuries commentaries were written on the Mishnah. One set of commentaries was compiled in the Palestinian area and was called the Jerusalem Talmud. A second collection of commentaries was compiled in the Babylonian area and called the Babylonian Talmud, which is seen as more authoritative than the Jerusalem Talmud.

Jewish Living

When Christians think of Jewish law, they imagine it as contained in the Ten Commandments. Actually, to Jews, the Torah contains 613 commandments that are particular ways in which the Torah is made real in the world. As the Jewish sages explain, there are 613 words in the *Decalogue*,[5] so implicit within the Ten Commandments are 613 commandments.

What has taken place in the history of Judaism is the interpretation and application of these commandments through a variety of new situations that Moses and the ancient Israelites could not have anticipated. For example, in reference to the third commandment to keep the *Shabbat*[6] holy, Jews desist from "forty minus one" categories of labor. From these categories rabbis interpret various kinds of bodies of knowledge in order to make a specific commandment or injunction for a specific situation applicable. This process of interpretation is known as *halakhah*, the total body of Jewish law. For example, according to Jewish law, kindling a fire is prohibited on Shabbat. A Jew may place tape over the light mechanism in a refrigerator, not because it is one of the 613 commandments, but because it is related to Torah law prohibiting the kindling a fire on the Sabbath.

Do you feel the application of Jewish law dealing with the refrigerator light is scrupulous or not? Explain.

Israel

Jews are often described as God's Chosen People. (Many religious traditions have the belief that their members are chosen or elected). Another word for "chosen" is "holy." When Jews talk about being God's Chosen People, they are really talking about being "holy" or "separate."

The Jews' call to holiness originated with the call of Abram (later named Abraham) in Genesis 12:1-3. In that biblical passage, Abraham was called by

God to leave Ur, the land of his father, and follow God. In return for his breaking with idolatry and his show of faith in the one God, Abraham was gifted with progeny and land. In addition, God blessed those who blessed Abraham and his descendants and cursed those who did not.

Being chosen by God brings with it both privilege and responsibility. Being "chosen" is not passive, but active. Jews are Jews only insofar as they act out "chosenness," that is, they are holy. The privilege of being a member of God's Chosen People is that God has made a special covenant with the Jewish people to be their God. The responsibility of being a member of the Chosen People is that Jews must "choose" to accept God's commandments and live lives that are holy and righteous, lives that are examples to the rest of humanity. This "chosenness" is passed from one generation to the next: "I have given you as a covenant to the people, a light to the nations" (Isaiah 42:6).

What are ways in which Jews act as Chosen People? A traditional Jew is an "observer of the commandments" and participates in the various *halakhic*[7] obligations. For Jews, all life is holy. Setting aside special times at special places is just part of ongoing religious expression for Jews.

What do you feel chosen or destined to do in your life?

SECTION 2 SUMMARY

✤ The essence of Judaism can be summed up in three words: God, Torah, and Israel.

✤ Judaism is a monotheistic religion, focusing on one God only.

✤ The Torah is taken in two parts: a written Torah and an oral Torah. The oral

Torah developed over centuries until it was finally transcribed in the third century CE.

✤ For Jews, being a "Chosen People" has both privilege and responsibility.

SECTION 2 REVIEW QUESTIONS

1. What do Jews believe about God?

2. What do Christians understand the Torah to be?

3. What does it mean to say that Jews are God's Chosen People?

III. SACRED PLACES

Judaism is unique in that most religious festivals and life cycle rituals are performed in the synagogue with a corresponding ritual in the home. Synagogue comes from a Greek word that means "place of assembly" outside of one's homeland. The sacredness of synagogue and home for Jews are featured in this section.

Synagogue

The Temple in Jerusalem was the center of Jewish worship for centuries. The Temple was where the ritual sacrifice of animals, the main expression of worshipping God, took place.

With the scattering of the Jews in the Diaspora and the eventual destruction of the Temple in 70 CE, a number of alternatives were established over the centuries to replace the institution of the Temple and its rituals. Some Jews maintained that the deeds of righteous people were equivalent to the sacrificial order of the Temple. Others equated personal prayer with Temple sacrifices. The three daily periods of prayer replaced the three daily animal sacrifices. Also, the synagogues became the place where Jews could worship God communally. Originally, when captives in Babylon, the exiles met in private homes for worship. These were the forerunners of synagogues. Over the centuries the functions of the synagogue and number of synagogues multiplied.

A synagogue became multidimensional. It was a House of Prayer (where Jews address God), a House of Study (where Jews study the Torah), and a House of Assembly (where Jews meet socially). These three names suggest the three separate yet interrelated functions of the synagogue.

Synagogues are now typically built to replicate Zion in the shape of a square with the bimah[8] in the center representing Mount Zion. There is a gathering space for men, women, and children, and a central chamber for the reading of the Torah and for prayer. The Torah is kept in an Ark on the eastern wall. The people face the east, not only facing the Ark, but also facing Jerusalem.

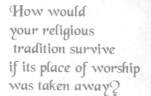

How would your religious tradition survive if its place of worship was taken away?

Home

The home of a Jew is distinguishable because it is transformed into sacred space. A traditional Jewish home attaches a *mezuzah*[9] on at least one doorpost of a house. In some Jewish homes one wall is designated the *mizrakh*, or eastern wall. This wall is sometimes marked with a special picture or embroidery, showing the direction one must face for prayer. A *kosher* home is one that has special dishes for eating and cooking that separate meat from dairy products. Since a traditional Jewish table is not only a place for building familial relationships but also a place for ritual, food must be kosher or "proper." Pork and shellfish are forbidden. Other meats

Interior of a Synagogue

must be slaughtered in a kosher manner. The combination of meat and dairy products is forbidden. On Shabbat, a "Sabbath-like" atmosphere prevails in the home. The house must be especially clean, and a Shabbat cloth must be on the table along with the Shabbat candlesticks.

What outward signs designate your house as holy?

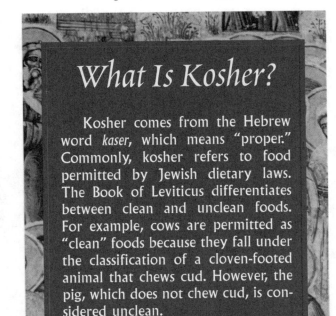

What Is Kosher?

Kosher comes from the Hebrew word *kaser*, which means "proper." Commonly, kosher refers to food permitted by Jewish dietary laws. The Book of Leviticus differentiates between clean and unclean foods. For example, cows are permitted as "clean" foods because they fall under the classification of a cloven-footed animal that chews cud. However, the pig, which does not chew cud, is considered unclean.

Originally, the reasons for differentiating between edible and inedible meats probably had something to do with health issues, but through their naming in the scriptures, the kosher laws for food took on a religious sense. A more accurate reason Jews observe kosher laws is to remind themselves that they are to be a holy and separate people.

Today, Orthodox and Conservative Jews observe kosher laws to varying degrees.

SECTION 3 SUMMARY

✤ After the destruction of the Temple in 70 CE the synagogue replaced the Temple as the central place of worship for Jews.

✤ The synagogue has three main functions: House of Prayer, House of Study, House of Assembly.

✤ A traditional Jewish home is a place where both fellowship and ritual take place.

SECTION 3 REVIEW QUESTIONS

1. What does the word "synagogue" mean?

2. What takes place in a synagogue?

3. What makes a home *kosher*?

IV. SACRED TIMES

For Jews, all life is holy. Further, sacred time is cyclical to the Jews. From the earliest waking hours of the day through the long hours of the night, from infancy to old age, all life is holy. Hence, all life is to be devoted to God, including a person's very thoughts, actions, memory, and talents. To mark the sacredness of life, Jews take special moments annually during the life of a person to remember and to celebrate. To understand sacred times, a better grasp of the Jewish calendar is needed.

Most people operate under several different kinds of calendars. There is the academic calendar that starts in the fall and ends in late spring. There is the civil calendar that begins on January 1. A personal income tax calendar follows the civil calendar, but many non-profit organizations have a fiscal year that begins July 1. Christians use a liturgical calendar that begins with the first Sunday of Advent, occurring in late November.

So, too, the Jews have a special, sacred calendar. While our civil calendar is a solar calendar in which a day begins and ends at midnight, the Jewish calendar is a lunar calendar with a day beginning and ending at sunset. Also, the Jewish calendar has 354 days and begins in the fall on *Rosh Hashanah*, the Jewish New Year. In addition, the Jewish calendar is eleven days shorter than the civil calendar. The Jews found it necessary to adjust this eleven-day discrepancy so that a holiday that is celebrated in the fall as commanded in the Bible will not eventually end up in the spring. The eleven-day discrepancy is reconciled in two ways. First, a month is added seven times in nineteen years. Second, one day is added or subtracted each year to two different months. This section names and describes the main festivals and holy days on the Jewish calendar.

Festivals and Holy Days

The major Jewish festivals are divided into two main cycles: the *Tishri* cycle in the fall and the *Nisan* cycle in the spring. Tishri is named for the first month of the cycle (occurring in September or October) and contains, besides Rosh Hashanah, the festivals of *Yom Kippur* and *Sukkot*. Nisan is the first month of the spring cycle. The name "Nisan" comes from the Sumerian word for "first fruits." The Nisan cycle contains two festivals, *Pesach* and *Shavuot*. Rosh Hashanah and Pesach are similar in that both are memorial festivals. Rosh Hashanah memorializes the creation of the world while Pesach memorializes the creation of the Jews as a people. Sukkot and Shavuot are both harvest festivals.

In comparison to the other feasts, two relatively minor festivals are celebrated during the Jewish year. Hanukkah and Purim are festivals that each celebrate freedom from the wrath of foreign rulers.

Rosh Hashanah and Yom Kippur

The period between Rosh Hashanah (Jewish New Year) and Yom Kippur—which means "Day of Atonement"—is known as the "days of awe." This ten-day penitential period is the high holy time for Jews during which the creation of the world is ritually commemorated.

Rosh Hashanah is celebrated on the first day of the Jewish month of *Tishri* (September or October). Besides marking the creation of humanity, Rosh Hashanah is also the day that Jews believe God judges each individual for his or her actions of the previous year. Yom Kippur, generally accepted as the holiest day of the year for Jews, is a day of prayer, fasting, and repentance. Jews ask forgiveness for both communal and personal sins. In asking for forgiveness, Jews go directly to the person they offended, if possible.

During the "days of awe" between Rosh Hashanah and Yom Kippur, Jews strive for repentance, or more accurately a turning back to the proper way of living. This is known as *tishuvah*.[10] God's judgment on whether tishuvah took place is sealed in a symbolic Book of Life at the end of Yom Kippur.

The central ritual in the celebrations of Rosh Hashanah and Yom Kippur is the blowing of the *shofar*, or ram's horn. A ram's horn is used rather than a calf's horn because the latter conjures up the image of the idolatrous golden calf from the Israelite's time in the desert. Also, the bent nature of the ram's horn signifies that Jews must bend their heart towards God.

What would be a first step if you were to seek repentance for the purposes of reorienting your life?

Sukkot

Sukkot is another festival during the Tishri cycle. It is also known as the Feast of Tabernacles or the Feast of Booths. (Sukkot means "booths.")

Pesach

Pesach retells the story of the Exodus. It is the first major feast of the Nisan cycle. Pesach is more commonly known as Passover, celebrating the Hebrews' freedom from Egyptian slavery when the angel of death "passed over" the houses of the Hebrews that were marked with blood from a lamb.

Blowing a shofar

Sukkot begins five days after Yom Kippur and lasts for eight days. Sukkot commemorates the time when the Jews were in the desert for forty years and later when in Israel they had to protect themselves from the elements during harvest. To do so they erected covered huts, or booths. With this protection from the weather Jews also came to understand that God alone was their great protector. Sukkot also marks the end of the fruit harvest season, especially the harvest for grapes used for making wine.

The story of the first Passover is told in the Book of Exodus:

Then Moses called for all the elders of Israel and said unto them: "Draw out, and take you lambs according to your families, and kill the passover lamb. And ye shall take a bunch of hyssop, and dip it in the blood that is in the basin, and strike the lintel and the two side-posts with the blood that is in the basin; and none of you shall go out of the door of his house until the morning. For the Lord will pass through to smite the Egyptians; and when He seeth the blood upon the lintel, and the two side-posts, the Lord will pass over the door, and will not suffer the destroyer to come in unto your houses to smite you. And ye shall observe this thing for an ordinance to thee and to thy sons for ever. And it shall come to pass, when ye be come to the land which the Lord will give you, according as He hath promised, that ye shall keep this service. And it shall come to pass, when your children shall say unto you: What mean ye by this service? that ye shall say: It is the sacrifice of the Lord's passover, for that He passed over the houses of the children of Israel in Egypt, when He smote the Egyptians, and delivered our houses." And the people bowed the head and worshipped (Exodus 12:21-27).

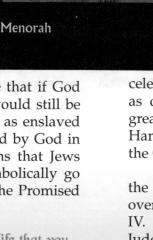

Menorah

Today each Jew celebrates being personally freed by God. They believe that if God had not freed them, they would still be slaves. Jews see themselves as enslaved in each generation and freed by God in each generation. This means that Jews from every generation symbolically go forth from Egypt towards the Promised Land.

What is something in your life that you are symbolically or literally a slave to?

Shavuot

Shavuot means "week" in Hebrew. Shavuot is celebrated fifty days after the first day of Pesach, so some see Shavuot as the conclusion of Passover. Shavuot was originally a harvest festival celebrating the first fruits of the wheat harvest. Centuries later Jews associated Shavuot with the giving of the Torah to Moses on Mount Sinai.

Today, Jews also combine the celebration of Shavuot and the reception of the Torah with Jewish confirmation. In a confirmation ceremony, Conservative and Reform Jewish teenagers publicly state their acceptance of Judaism.

Hanukkah

Hanukkah ("festival of lights") celebrates one of the great military victories in Jewish history. Nevertheless, Hanukkah is not a major Jewish holiday. In fact, Hanukkah was not celebrated much at all until Jewish parents felt it was important to counteract the strong influence of Christmas on non-Christian members of American society. Since Hanukkah is also a winter celebration and, like Christmas, has light as one of its symbols, Jews placing a greater emphasis on the celebration of Hanukkah was a natural counterpart to the Christmas season.

Hanukkah celebrates the victory of the Jews led by Judas the Maccabean over the Syrian Greeks led by Antiochus IV. Besides mandating Hellenism in Judea, Antiochus denied Jews the freedom to practice their religion. Worst of all, Antiochus captured the Temple and converted it into a pagan temple. In 165 BCE the Jews recaptured the Temple, cleansed it from pagan impurities, and rededicated it to God.

Hanukkah is an eight-day celebration. Its main ritual is the lighting of one additional candle of a Hanukkah *menorah*[11] each evening. This commemorates a tradition that after the Temple had been recaptured by the Maccabeans, there was enough oil for the relighting of the Temple menorah for just one day. However, the miracle was that the candle stayed lit for eight days. Hence, the lighting of one candle for each day of Hanukkah.

Purim

Purim translates to "feast of lots." Purim celebrates the victory of Jews living in Persia in the fifth century BCE over Haman, the prime minister of Persia. The feast of lots refers to the lots Haman randomly cast to determine which day he would slaughter the Jews. The Jewish Queen Esther heard about the plot and was able to convince King Ahasueros of Persia to desist with the plan. Instead, Haman and his family were executed on the gallows prepared for the Jews. This story is recounted in the Book of Esther.

Shabbat

While the festivals described in the previous section occur annually, Shabbat, the Jewish Sabbath, is a weekly event. Shabbat is celebrated from sunset Friday until sunset Saturday. Keeping holy the Sabbath is the fourth commandment (according to Jewish count) given by

Celebrating Shabbat

God to Moses on Mount Sinai. It is a reminder to the Jews that God rested from work on the seventh day, and so, too, must they. As the scripture text reads:

> Remember the sabbath day, to keep it holy. Six days shalt thou labor, and do all thy work; but the seventh day is a sabbath unto the Lord thy God, in it thou shalt not do any manner of work, thou, nor thy son, nor thy daughter, nor thy man-servant, nor thy maid-servant, nor thy cattle, nor thy stranger that is within thy gates; for in six days the Lord made heaven and earth, the sea, and all that in them is, and rested on the seventh day; wherefore the Lord blessed the sabbath day and hallowed it (Exodus 20:8-11).

Friday evening is the Shabbat dinner, a family ritual that ushers in the Sabbath. On this holiest day of the week observant Jews refrain from work, attend synagogue services, and study the Torah. A common greeting for the Sabbath is "Shabbat Shalom," that is, "Sabbath peace."

The Sabbath dinner table includes a white tablecloth, two candles, wine, and a braided loaf of bread called *challah*.

Sabbath begins eighteen minutes before with the lighting of the Sabbath candles. A prayer of blessing over the candles is generally recited by the woman of the house:

> Blessed are you, Lord our God, King of the Universe, who has blessed us with your commandments and commanded us to light the Sabbath candles.

The blessing over the wine and bread is:

> Blessed are you, Lord our God, King of the Universe, who creates the fruit of the vine.

Blessed are you, Lord our God, King of the Universe, who brings forth bread from the earth.

After these blessings, the meal

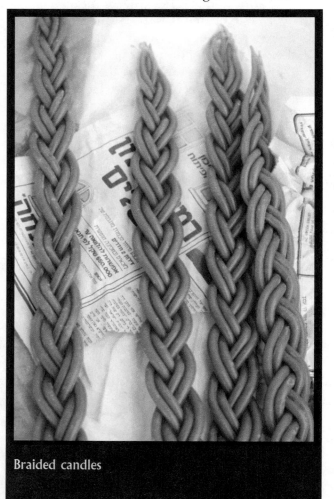

Braided candles

begins. The Sabbath candles are not extinguished. They are allowed to burn themselves out.

Sabbath ends at sunset Saturday. A brief ceremony called *Havdalah*[12] concludes this sacred time. A braided candle is lit and held in the hand so one can see its reflection of light on the fingertips. Again, wine accompanies this closing ceremony as a symbol of thanksgiving and joy. A box of aromatic spices is lit, carrying the aroma of the Sabbath into the week.

For you, what does it mean to keep a day "holy"?

Life Cycle Celebrations

For Jews, life cycle celebrations focus on transitional moments in their personal lives. Until recently, most of these ceremonies were male-oriented with no female counterpart. For example, *Bar Mitzvah* (literally "Son of the Commandment") is the coming of age ceremony for a thirteen-year-old boy, recognizing that the boy has become an adult and is responsible for his religious and moral training. The counterpart ceremony for girls, the *Bat Mitzvah*, was created just this century. Other ways Jews mark important times in life include:

Birth   Circumcision, the cutting away of the foreskin of the penis, usually takes place eight days after birth. This practice dates from the time of Abraham (see Genesis 17:10-11) when God commanded Abraham to circumcise all his male descendants as a sign of the covenant between God and his people. Circumcision gives a permanent mark to Jews as a way to differentiate them from other people.

Coming of Age   The ceremony for an infant girl involves the giving of her name. She is brought to the synagogue where she is welcomed into the congregation. The full Hebrew name of the child is revealed for the first time by the rabbi.

A Jewish child becomes a mature individual, responsible for keeping the Torah. Religious maturity is associated with the age of thirteen for boys and twelve for girls. When the individual is minimally competent in prayer and the Torah, he or she is called to read publicly from the Torah.

Marriage   The three major elements of the marriage ritual include the *hupah*, the blessings, and the breaking of the glass. The hupah is a canopy held up by four poles representing the future home of the bride and groom. There are usually vegetative symbols embroidered on the canopy, representing the notion that the bride and groom are in the Garden of Eden and are the first man and woman. The symbolism of the breaking of the glass is linked to the destruction of the Temple in Jerusalem in 70 CE.

Death   For Jews, funerals take place as soon as possible, often within twenty-four hours of the death. At the burial, blessings are made, prayers are said, and psalms are read aloud.

Reading the Torah

SECTION 4 SUMMARY

✤ For Jews, all life is holy. A person's every thought, action, memory, and talent is to be devoted to God.

✤ Two main cycles in the Jewish calendar are the creation cycles of *Tishri* and *Nisan*.

✤ Yom Kippur, the Day of Atonement, is the holiest day of the year for Jews.

✤ Sukkot and Shavuot were originally harvest festivals that eventually gained deeper religious significance in the Jewish people's relationship to God.

✤ Shabbat, the Jewish Sabbath, is a weekly event that is celebrated from sunset Friday until sunset Saturday. Keeping holy the Sabbath is the fourth commandment given by God to Moses on Mount Sinai.

SECTION 4 REVIEW QUESTIONS

1. How is the Jewish calendar different from the civil calendar?

2. Cite the similarities between Rosh Hashanah and Pesach.

3. What are the "days of awe" and what is their significance?

4. Explain what takes place on Shabbat.

Conclusion

From a sociologist's point of view, Jews should have disappeared off the face of the earth at the time of the Babylonian Exile. Sociologists point out that such a small group of people that are continually exiled, expelled, enslaved, and exterminated would not seem to be able to continue. Either assimilation or annihilation or both would have claimed this small community. A plausible answer to sociologists would be that they underestimate God, the Torah, and Israel as powerful resources for Jews. The single-minded belief of Jews in one God, the Torah as a living document, and Israel as both a Promised Land and a Chosen People have sustained Jews against incalculable odds. This three-fold essence is the heart of Judaism. As the opening story of this chapter pointed out, it is in the pure intent of the heart that the God of the Jews is most interested.

CHAPTER 2 IN BRIEF

✣ Jewish history spans more than three thousand years. Much of the time Jews were ruled by foreign governments.

✣ Judaism is the religious expression of the Jews.

✣ The essence of Judaism is God, the Torah, and Israel.

✣ Jewish beliefs are expressed through actions, not doctrines.

✣ Both the home and the synagogue are places for Jewish ritual worship.

✣ Jewish festivals and holy days memorialize and celebrate the religious history of Judaism.

CHAPTER 2 REVIEW QUESTIONS

1. How is a Jewish home made sacred?

2. What are the two meanings of the term "Israel" to Jews?

3. What is the *Diaspora*?

4. What is the *Talmud*?

5. What are major characteristics of Orthodox, Conservative, Reform, and Reconstructionist Judaism?

6. Briefly describe the significance of the time between Rosh Hashanah and Yom Kippur, including each of those holy days.

7. How do Jews mark major times in the life cycle: birth, coming of age, marriage, and death?

RESEARCH AND ACTIVITIES

1. The words *Hebrew, Jew,* and *Israelite* are commonly interchangeable with regard to the Jewish people. Write an essay on the difference between these terms.

2. Interview a Jewish teen or adult. Ask the person to offer his or her personal perspective on the main themes of Judaism offered in this chapter: history, belief, sacred time, and sacred place.

3. Research how various Jewish groups (Orthodox, Conservative, Reform, Reconstructionist) celebrate one of the following:

Rosh Hashanah   Shavuot

Yom Kippur   Hanukkah

Sukkot   Purim

Shabbat   birth

Bar/Bat Mitzvah   marriage

Include both the synagogue and the home observance when applicable. Note the similarities and differences.

4. Read and write a book report on one of the following novels by Chaim Potok: *The Chosen, The Promise,* or *My Name is Asher Lev.*

5. Research *Hasidism* and its presence in the United States.

SELECTED VOCABULARY

Bar Mitzvah	Purim
Bat Mitzvah	rabbi
circumcision	Rosh Hashanah
covenant	Sadducees
Essenes	Shabbat
habiru	Shammai
Hanukkah	Shavuot
Hillel	Sh'ma
Israel	shofar
kosher	Sukkot
Maimonides	synangogue
mezuzah	Talmud
Mishnah	tishuvah
Moses	Torah
Passover	Yom Kippur
Pesach	Zionism
Pharise	

Chapter 3

*C*HRISTIANITY

*T*aizé is a monastic community of about one hundred Protestant and Catholic brothers from more than twenty-five countries and every continent. The community welcomes thousands of visitors each year. Visitors are invited to join with the brothers in their prayer. The mission of the community is reconciliation among the diverse Christian communities. Reconciliation is not an end in itself. Rather, the community encourages those who visit to return home as leavens of reconciliation in their own communities.

Three times each day, everyone gathers in the "Church of Reconciliation" for prayer together. The church was built in 1962 and was enlarged in 1990. The "songs of Taizé" are easily recognizable. They are made up of a simple phrase taken up again and again, in many different languages, and they are a way of expressing a basic reality, quickly grasped by the mind and then gradually penetrating the entire person. In the evening, the sung prayer continues far into the night. Meanwhile, brothers remain in the church to listen to those who wish to talk about a personal problem or question.

The Saturday evening prayer is celebrated as a vigil of the Resurrection, a festival of light. On Friday evenings, the icon of the Cross is placed in the center of the Church and those who wish can come and pray around it in silence as a way of entrusting to God their own burdens and those of others, and so accompanying the Risen Christ who remains close to all who are undergoing trial.

Adapted from www.taize.fr

How many Christian denominations different from your own can you name? What is one way you have personally experienced the division that exists among Christians of different denominations?

The history of Christianity is rich and diverse. From its inception approximately two thousand years ago as a small Jewish sect[1] to the present as one of the world's largest religious traditions, Christian history is full of saints and sinners, expansion and division, music, art, and wars.

The diversity of Christian denominations can be dramatically witnessed on Sunday morning television. As you "surf" the channels, you cannot help but see the differences. There are evangelists exhorting people to "receive Jesus into your heart." There are gospel choirs singing in full voice. You may see a Christian preacher in a Jewish prayer shawl and *yarmulke,* or scull cap. Usually a Catholic Mass is televised, or in some places a Catholic nun in full habit is explaining a Catholic teaching. Don't forget the Dutch Reform preacher delivering the Word from a "crystal" cathedral or a Southern Baptist preacher exhorting the faithful in an athletic-sized arena.

What is the most unique Christian television program you have ever watched?

This chapter examines the various branches of Christianity, beginning with a brief overview of the history of Christianity from its beginnings as part of Judaism to its expansion and splintering into various denominations. For all Christians, Jesus of Nazareth is the central figure of their faith. As recorded in the Christian Bible, it is through his life, death, and resurrection Christians find both meaning in life and instruction in

how to live. Major Christian feasts commemorate important events in the life of Jesus and the lives of his followers. These holy days are celebrated at both church and home, though the physical church building is considered the more sacred place.

Church is defined as both a people and a location, and Christians define themselves by what they believe. Christianity has many doctrines[2]—traditions and beliefs vary widely from denomination to denomination. Yet, there is a core of beliefs that almost every Christian can accept. For example, Christians believe that Jesus is Lord of all and is risen from the dead. Christians also believe and follow the two great commandments of love, which translate to giving full love and commitment to God and neighbor.

BCE

4   Jesus of Nazareth is born

CE

30   Jesus is crucified

50s   Epistles written by Paul of Tarsus

90s   Last gospel written

c. 250   Rise of monasticism

313   Edict of Milan

325   Council of Nicea I

451   Council of Chalcedon

500s   Reform of monasticism

978   Vladamir I brings Christianity to Russia

1054   Great Schism

1204   Crusaders ravage Constantinople

1517   Luther's *Ninety-five Theses* posted on church door

1534   Act of Supremacy in England

1563   Council of Trent closes

1701   John Wesley and Methodist movement

1948   World Council of Churches

1965   Second Vatican Council closes

I. A BRIEF HISTORY OF CHRISTIANITY

What we know about the beginning of Christianity and its early years is largely through sources written by followers of Jesus of Nazareth. These writings include both faith statements and historical facts. Biblical scholarship in the last 150 years has helped to define the actual actions and words of Jesus and the developing traditions about Jesus, even as both are included in four books of the New Testament known as *gospels* ("good news").

Jesus of Nazareth

The history of Christianity begins with Jesus of Nazareth. Stories of the birth of Jesus are recorded in the gospels of Matthew and Luke. A point of agreement in the two accounts is that the birth of Jesus was in fulfillment of Jewish prophecy found in the Hebrew Bible. According to both gospels, Mary, the virgin mother of Jesus, conceived him by the power of the Holy Spirit. Jesus was born around 4 BCE [3] in Palestine, in the town of Bethlehem in the Roman-occupied province of Judea. There is little known about the childhood of Jesus other than that his family settled in Nazareth in the province of Galilee. Joseph, from the lineage of King David, was a carpenter, so it is likely Jesus took up the same trade.

The public ministry of Jesus was inaugurated by his baptism in the Jordan River by a Jewish baptizer named John. John's was a baptism of repentance and preparation for the coming of the long awaited Jewish *Messiah* ("Chosen One"). After a period of temptations, Jesus returned to the region of Galilee where he became known as a storyteller and miracle worker. His message included themes of repentance and reconciliation as well as love and justice. In particular, Jesus taught that the kingdom of God was at hand. The "kingdom" as Jesus described it was not to be an earthly, political kingdom. Rather, it was a kingdom of justice where the poor would not go empty-handed and the oppressed would be freed. Even more astonishing, prostitutes and tax collectors would enter the kingdom before the righteous. The kingdom was one that was both present with Jesus' words and yet still to come in the future. Jesus' unusual actions in the name of the kingdom included physical healing, casting out demons, taming nature, and raising the dead to life.

Eventually, as Jesus' followers multiplied, the Jewish leaders and Roman authorities became alarmed. Jesus was accused by the Jewish leaders of blasphemy, of making himself God. He was brought before the Roman procurator, Pontius Pilate, as an insurrectionist. Pilate condemned Jesus to death and he was crucified publicly on a cross.

Yet, Jesus' story did not end there. Three days later his followers found an empty tomb. Several of his followers, including Mary Magdalene and Jesus' apostles, were visited by the risen Jesus in the days and weeks that followed.

If Christians did not believe Jesus is risen from the dead, what significance do you believe the religion would have today?

The Early Church

After a period of forty days, some of Jesus' disciples witnessed his return to heaven. Subsequently they returned to Jerusalem for the Jewish spring harvest festival of Shavuot. As the disciples hid in an upper room for fear that the same people who arrested and crucified Jesus would come for them, they experienced a phenomenon that they determined to be the coming of the Holy Spirit. At this, the disciples lost all fear and went out into the streets of Jerusalem to preach to the Jews. In their native languages, Jews from the Diaspora heard about Jesus for the first time. A number of Jews became followers of Jesus on that day, known as Pentecost because it is fifty days after the resurrection of Jesus. Pentecost has become known as the "birthday of the Church."

For Christians, God made a new covenant through Jesus Christ. In that covenant, the Church became the New Israel. Jerusalem became the first center of Christianity. From there missionaries went to other places in Palestine, including the region of Samaria. They quickly moved beyond Palestine to other cities

The Colosseum in Rome

with Jewish populations such as Antioch, Alexandria, and Rome. In Antioch the followers of Jesus first became known as "Christians." In their minds they were not starting a new religion. Rather, the coming of Jesus was the fulfillment of God's promise to send to the Jews a Messiah.

What does it mean to say that "Jesus was not a Christian"?

The spread of Christianity drew opposition from both Jews and Romans. Preaching about a Jewish Messiah in a synagogue evoked a spectrum of responses—from acceptance, to polite disagreement, to outright hostility. Paul of Tarsus was originally a Pharisaic Jew who persecuted Christians. After a conversion experience, Paul helped found Christian communities in Asia Minor and Greece. He wrote letters called *epistles* to the fledgling communities to encourage their new life in Christ. Internal dissensions also were prevalent. Christians had to decide which Jewish laws Gentile[4] converts would need to follow.

Anti-semitism means discrimination against Jews. Anti-semitism involving Christians had its roots in the early Church. How so?

As Christianity was illegal in the first three centuries of the Common Era, many Christians of that era were persecuted. The city of Rome was the most notorious in its persecution of Christians. Many Christians welcomed their fate, for their persecution was an opportunity to suffer as Jesus did. Things changed for Christians when the Roman Emperor Constantine proclaimed official toleration of all religions in his Edict of Milan (313 CE), including Christianity. Not only did Constantine legalize Christianity, he made it the official religion of the Roman Empire. In addition, he became a Christian on his death bed.

Legalized Christianity

As the persecution ceased, Christians organized themselves with bishops—successors of the apostles—as leaders. Questions of Christian identity arose. Unlike Jews, who were defined as Jews at birth or by conversion, Christian self-definition was not as clear. A central issue was to express a unified understanding of Jesus, the God Jesus called Father, and the Holy Spirit he sent. Another issue involved Jesus' divinity and his humanity.

A number of church councils were convened (for the most part by the emperor of Constantinople) between 325 and 451 CE to address the questions of the nature of God and the nature of Jesus. With regard to Jesus' relationship with the Father and the Holy Spirit, the Nicene Creed was composed at the Council of Nicea (325) and at the Council of Constantinople (381). The Nicene Creed spells out what is believed about the nature of God. The doctrine of the Trinity states that God is three persons in one substance, Father, Son, and Holy Spirit. With regard to the nature of Jesus, the Council of Ephesus (431) declared that Mary was indeed the human mother of Jesus as well as the Mother of God while the Council of Chalcedon (451) declared Jesus to be fully human and fully divine. Belief in these doctrines came to define a person as a true Christian.

As Christianity became more accepted, some men and women withdrew into the Egyptian desert for an austere life of prayer and solitude. The word monk comes from the word *mono*, meaning "one." Athanasius, an important figure at the Council of Nicea, wrote a biography of St. Antony of Egypt (362). This book was widely read in both Greek and Latin. Antony later became known as the "father of monasticism." Less austere but no less dedicated, Benedict, the founder of Monte Cassino, a monastery in Italy, wrote a "rule" for his monks that became a foundation for monasticism throughout the centuries. Benedict's rule emphasizes a balanced life of prayer, work, and study.

Of prayer, work, and study, which has the most prominence in your life? Which has the least prominence?

Growing Divisions

Constantine's decision to move the capital of the Roman Empire to Constantinople in 330 resulted in two political centers. This decision exacerbated the already existing differences between the Greek-speaking east and the Latin-speaking west. Christianity was not immune to this division. The church became more easily separated into the Roman Church in the West and the Eastern Church in the Byzantine Empire. Differences in language, culture, music, art, architecture, government, and ritual became increasingly distinct between the eastern and western wings of the church.

The Council of Chalcedon established five major centers of Christianity. These patriarchates[5] were Constantinople, Antioch, Alexandria, and Jerusalem in the east and Rome in the west. Each center developed autonomously. The leaders of these Christian centers, called "patriarchs," made up a loose confederation of equals. As the Roman Empire decreased in

power, the patriarch or bishop of Rome increased in his esteem. Believing Rome to be the burial place of Peter, the person on whom Jesus would build his church, the bishop of Rome claimed primacy over the other patriarchates. The eastern

Jesus said to Peter, "I will give you the keys of the Kingdom of Heaven." (Mt 16:19)

© Galyn C. Hammond

patriarchs agreed *respect* should be given to Rome, but they disagreed that the bishop of Rome should have *primacy* over them. In fact, the patriarch of Constantinople believed his city was the

44

New Rome because it was the seat of the Emperor (though he did not believe he had more authority than the other patriarchs did).

As the Roman Empire collapsed in the fifth century, the Germanic tribes moved into Europe in great numbers. With no strong political leader, the bishop of Rome (called the "pope"[6]) took on some of the temporal leadership. A large number of conversions to Christianity took place within these tribes. Often the conversion of the tribal leader meant the conversion of the entire tribe, as with the Frank leader, Clovis. The more conversions, the stronger the western church became as an institution. On Christmas Day in the year 800, Pope Leo III crowned Charlemagne emperor of the newly-established Holy Roman Empire.

In the seventh and eighth centuries, Muslims, adherents of the new religion called Islam, began conquering the Byzantine Empire. Egypt, Syria, and Palestine were captured. Thus, three of the four eastern patriarchates—Alexandria, Antioch, and Jerusalem—were controlled by Muslims.

By the Middle Ages the tension between the eastern and western church reached its boiling point. While the claim of primacy by the bishop of Rome, the crowning of Charlemagne as Emperor in the west, and the missionary efforts of the east into Slavic lands were major issues, other differences compounded the problem: for example, the use of leavened bread for Eucharist in the east and unleavened bread for Eucharist in the west, the ordination of married men in the east, and differences in lenten observances. In addition, at the Council of Toledo western bishops added a line ("the Holy Spirit . . .who proceeded from the Father *and the Son* ") to the Nicene Creed without consulting eastern patriarchs. Not happy with the addition and excluded from the discussion, eastern patriarchs found the statement heretical. Known as the *filioque* ("and the son") controversy, this was the final straw. In 1054 a mutual excommunication between Rome and Constantinople took place. Even if that did not seal the split, the destruction of Constantinople by western Christian Crusaders in 1204 did.

Though the emperors at the Council of Lyons (1274) and the Council of Florence (1438-39) made attempts at reconciliation, Eastern Church authorities rejected the attempts. The patriarchs, who considered each other, including the pope, as equals, could not accept the claim of papal superiority. Eastern Christianity became known as Orthodox Christianity. The word *orthodox* means "straight." The Christians of the east believed their form of Christianity came *straight* from Jesus and the apostles.

Of all the causes leading to division between East and West, which to you seems most serious? Why?

Seeds of Reformation

In both the east and west, church-state relationships were not always amicable. In the west a controversy grew over who could appoint local bishops. Kings felt they had the power to do so, but church leaders disagreed. The controversy became so great that King Henry IV and Pope Gregory VII clashed. The pope excommunicated the king. Eventually, the king gave in to the sovereignty of the pope as long as the king had the right to approve of the pope's choices for bishops.

The church and state were more likely to cooperate when they had a common enemy. One example of this was when the Muslims captured Jerusalem. To counter the Muslim insurgence, the Crusades[7] were launched from Europe. However, after three centuries of Crusades Christians were unable to permanently restore Jerusalem to their possession.

The western Church—commonly called the Roman Catholic Church—of the twelfth and thirteenth centuries was becoming more temporal and less spiritual, exerting great political power, especially through its landholdings. Many bishops and abbots possessed as much power as the local princes did. Attempts were made to reform the church. Francis of Assisi (1182-1226) introduced a new religious order in which its members owned few, if any, possessions. Rather, he and his followers were *mendicants* ("beggars") who encouraged people to imitate Jesus by embracing poverty.

Not all efforts at internal reform worked. In 1309 the French king controlled the election of the pope and the French pope, Clement V, took up residence at Avignon, France, where the western church was ruled until 1377. Arguments over who was pope, where the pope should reign, and pockets of corruption within the institutional church all contributed to the growing dismay with the Roman Catholic Church. These and other factors compromised the integrity of the church and left the door open for further reform.

Though there were others before him, the German Augustinian priest Martin Luther is generally recognized as the catalyst of the Protestant Reformation. On October 31, 1517, the eve of All Saints, Martin Luther nailed his *Ninety-five Theses* to the door of the church at Wittenburg. His action set off a firestorm between him and Roman Catholic officials. Luther had come to believe that authority within the Catholic Church should lie solely within the Bible and not church tradition or church leaders. He believed salvation came not from a person's actions, but in a person's faith. He also believed in the priesthood of all believers, not just a few. With the Bible as his sole source of authority, Luther left the priesthood and a denomination of Christianity emerged that was eventually called Lutheran.

The Protestant movement spread throughout much of northern Europe, Scandinavia, and North America. Luther's reform had a dramatic effect on Christians in Germany. Southern Germans tended to stay with the Catholic Church while northern Germans tended to follow Luther. National churches following the Lutheran tradition soon sprang up in the Scandinavian countries of Norway, Finland, Sweden, and Denmark.

There were other reformers in the sixteenth century besides Luther. The French-born John Calvin and the Swiss-born Ulrich Zwingli began church reforms of their own in Zurich and Geneva, Switzerland, respectively. Along with Luther, however, Calvin and Zwingli retained a number of Catholic liturgical practices.

More radical Protestant groups believed that the reformers had not gone far enough. The Anabaptists and Mennonites abolished most liturgical practices, calling for still simpler forms of worship. They did not accept infant baptism, insisting baptism into Christ was an adult decision. They were also against the establishment of a state church. The Anabaptists, Mennonites, as well as the Puritans, escaped to America because of religious persecution by the more traditional Protestant groups like the Calvinists and Lutherans.

As the Protestant movement grew, King Henry VIII of England was having his own problems with the Catholic Church. Henry received a dispensation from the Pope to marry his dead brother's widow, the Spaniard, Catherine of Aragon. Henry insisted his heir to the throne be male, but Catherine did not bear a son who lived to maturity. So Henry petitioned Pope Clement VII to rescind his dispensation so Henry could marry the young Anne Boleyn. The pope would not grant the king his wish, so Henry countered by declaring himself head of the Catholic Church in England. Anyone who refused to accept his Act of Supremacy was considered a traitor to the throne. The Catholic Church in England declared its independence from papal authority and became a national church, known as the Church of England. Most inhabitants of England accepted this change because there was little difference in the doctrine or practice of the faith. The difference came in who was in charge.

The English Reformation spread to other parts of the British Empire, each becoming national churches, such as the Church of Scotland or the Church of South Africa. The growing confederation of national churches is known today as the Anglican Communion.

Though it is difficult to generalize about the more than two thousand Protestant denominations today, those Protestant groups that began in the sixteenth century do have some broadly held beliefs that were articulated by Martin Luther. For example, most Protestants hold that salvation is by faith alone, defer authority on matters of faith to what is written in the Bible, and accept just two sacraments, Baptism and Eucharist.

Name some occasions of reform you have witnessed in your own religious community.

Canterbury Cathedral in England is the symbol of the unity of the worldwide Anglican communion.

The Catholic Reformation

In 1545 the Catholic Church called a council to address the issues promulgated by the reformers. The decisions made at the Council of Trent (1545-1563) were to have lasting effects within the Roman Catholic Church and with its relationship to Protestantism and Anglicanism for the next four hundred years.

The Council of Trent reiterated Catholic teaching in several doctrinal areas. The council reaffirmed papal supremacy. It said that salvation is marked by faith plus good works. It named the Mass as a true sacrifice and defined transubstantiation[8] as the doctrine stating Jesus is truly present in the bread and wine. It named marriage as a sacrament and said that there are seven true sacraments.

An often-asked question is, "What is the difference between a priest and a minister?" Before the destruction of the Second Temple, Jewish priests offered sacrifices to God on behalf of the people or an individual. Those Christian denominations that have priests believe a sacrificial element is maintained in Eucharist. For them there is a relationship between the Last Supper and the sacrifice of Jesus on the cross. Priests are seen as representatives of Christ on earth. (Denominations without priests also recognize the relationship between the Last Supper and the crucifixion. However, the entire Church is seen as a representative of Christ, not just the priest.)

Ministers, on the other hand, are not mediators between God and the people. Rather, ministers, as the name implies, are at the service of the people. It is their role to "stir up" the faith of the people so individuals may have a personal relationship with Jesus.

Only men can be Catholic or Orthodox priests. Recently women were allowed to be ordained into the Anglican priesthood. It is an exception for Catholic priests to be married, whereas Anglican and Orthodox priests can marry. Most Protestant churches allow the ordination of women. All Protestant ministers can marry. Incidentally, the Society of Friends, or Quakers, have no ordained ministers.

The Modern Period

A revolution of ideas known as the Age of Enlightenment in the seventeenth century inaugurated the Modern Period. For example, rationalists stressed the power of human reason. Empiricists taught that reality is perceivable only in the five senses. Religion in this period was diminished by an increasing emphasis in the belief that people could determine their own destiny and had little need for God. There was a growing movement toward democracy and the separation of church and state.

More positively, the Modern Period witnessed successes in the missionary efforts in the New World from the three major branches of Christianity. French Catholics went to North America, Indochina, and Africa. Spanish Catholics went to North America and South America. Portuguese Catholics went to Brazil, Africa, China, and India. Dutch Reformers went to Africa and Indonesia. In the late eighteenth and early nineteenth centuries, various other Protestant groups made headway in Asia, Africa, and especially North America (except for the French Province of Quebec, Canada).

In the east, the czars[9] subordinated the Orthodox Church in Russia. In fact, Czar Peter the Great abolished the Russian patriarchate and had the church administered by the state. Though the patriarchate was reestablished during the Russian Revolution, Communism persecuted all forms of religious expression not only in Russia, but wherever Communism ruled. It was not until the breakup of the Soviet Union in 1991 that the Orthodox Church in eastern and central Europe and in Russia regained some life.

A bright light within the vast diversity of Christianity is the *ecumenical movement*. This movement attempts to bring about understanding among the various Christian groups. The World Council of Churches based in Geneva was founded in 1948 and presently has over 300 members from Orthodox, Anglican, and Protestant denominations. Also, the Second Vatican Council (1962-65) made major strides in recognizing the validity of the existence of the various religions in the world. Such openness was exhibited when members of the Eastern Orthodox churches, Anglican Communion, and some Protestant churches were invited to attend the Council.

Agree or disagree?
The division among Christian groups is a great scandal to Christianity.

Movements Within Protestantism

The words *fundamentalism*, *evangelicalism* and *pentecostalism* are often interchangable in popular culture. However, though related, they are distinct movements within Protestantism.

Christian fundamentalism is a movement begun at the beginning of the twentieth century in the United States. The distribution of a series of pamphlets called *The Fundamentals* advocated returning to what was understood as the basics or fundamentals of Christianity. Believing Protestantism was becoming too secularized, especially in the area of science, fundamentalists advocated the infallibility of the Bible on issues of historical and scientific matters. In other words, fundamentalists hold that what is written in the Bible is to be understood in its most literal sense. Hence, the world was created in six days of a seven-day week.

Though related to fundamentalism, evangelicalism is more moderate. It too is a movement within Protestantism, based mainly in North America and Northern Europe. The word "evangelical" comes from the Greek word for "good news." Evangelicalism emphasizes a personal faith in Jesus Christ and the Bible as an individual's sole religious authority. In addition, "witnessing" or sharing faith with others is important in this movement. The evangelical movement is manifested in such events as tent revivals and crusades like those initiated by Billy Graham.

Pentecostalism is one form of evangelicalism. It is a movement that emphasizes the "gifts of the Holy Spirit" as recorded at the first Pentecost in the Acts of the Apostles. These gifts may include speaking in tongues, healing, holy joy, and holy tears. Pentecostalism exhibits the widest spectrum of doctrinal beliefs and can be found in all branches of Christianity.

SECTION 1 SUMMARY

✤ Jesus of Nazareth is the central figure in Christianity.

✤ Christianity began as a small Jewish sect but later became distinct from Judaism.

✤ Early Christians were defined by what they believed.

✤ Many Christians were martyred for their faith; later, monasticism became the most austere life a Christian could choose.

✤ Eventually the Church was divided into East and West in what is known as the Great Schism.

✤ The Protestant Reformation was a multifaceted attempt to reform Christianity.

✤ The Council of Trent highlighted the Catholic reformation and restated Catholic teaching on several doctrinal issues.

✤ In the Modern Period Christianity encountered rationalism and empiricism.

✤ The ecumenical movement is an attempt to unify the Christian churches.

SECTION 1 REVIEW QUESTIONS

1. What do Christians believe about Jesus of Nazareth?

2. Why is Pentecost significant to Christians?

3. What was the role of Paul in the spread of Christianity?

4. Explain the significance of the Emperor Constantine in the history of Christianity.

5. Name two important Christian doctrines that were defined at the Church councils between the fourth and fifth centuries.

6. Who was Benedict?

7. Briefly trace the events that led to the division between the Church in the east and the Church in the west.

8. What major doctrines and beliefs do most Protestants share?

9. How did Anglicanism begin?

10. How did rationalism and empiricism effect Christianity during the modern period?

11. What is the ecumenical movement?

12. Define fundamentalism, evangelicalism, and pentecostalism.

II. BELIEFS AND ACTIONS

For all Christians, Jesus is the central figure. He is the Son of God. The importance of his life, death, and resurrection is not questioned. Christians articulate their beliefs in creeds. The Apostles' Creed, formulated about 150 CE, is the most widely used among Christians. The apostles did not write it, but it does articulate what the apostles passed on:

> I believe in God, the Father Almighty, creator of heaven and earth. And in Jesus Christ his Son, our Lord, who was conceived by the Holy Spirit, born of the Virgin Mary, suffered under Pontius Pilate, was crucified, died, and was buried. He descended into hell and on the third day he arose again from the dead. He ascended into heaven and sits at the right hand of God, the Father Almighty. From there he shall come to judge the living and the dead. I believe in the Holy Spirit, the holy catholic church, the communion of saints, the forgiveness of sins, the resurrection of the body, and life everlasting.

The Nicene Creed, formulated by church leaders who attended the Council of Nicea in 325, is often recited at a Sunday worship service. It is similar to the Apostles' Creed in that it begins with a statement of belief in God the Father, followed by beliefs about Jesus, the Holy Spirit, and the Church. An explanation of some of the most prominent Christian beliefs and actions follows.

Trinity

Like Jews, Christians believe in one and only one God. God is the creator of all things, both visible and invisible. In addition, Christians believe God is all-knowing, all-loving, and all-powerful. God is present everywhere and is unchanging. God desires only the best for all creation. However, Christians hold that there are three persons, Father, Son, and Holy Spirit, in one God. This doctrine of the Holy Trinity is central to Christian faith.

Jesus

Jesus is the second person of the Trinity, making him God. According to the doctrine of the Incarnation,[10] God became flesh in the person of Jesus. Christians state this in terms of the two natures of Jesus: Jesus is fully human and fully divine. God became human so that human beings could get closer to God. Jesus was like all humans in everything but sin.

Sin

An understanding of sin helps us understand why Christians need Jesus. Sin is an offense against God. For Christians, Adam and Eve were the first sinners. God commanded them not to eat from the tree of the knowledge of good and evil, but Adam and Eve disobeyed. Thus, the first sin of humankind was the sin of disobedience. Christians believe that the sin of Adam and Eve "closed the gates of heaven" and this sin—known as the original sin—became a part of the human condition. Original sin is washed away in Christian baptism, though the propensity of humans to commit actual sins remains.

Salvation

God chose to redeem humankind through Jesus. Though people sin, they can be reconciled to God. There is nothing more pleasing to God than one who turns away from wrongdoing and returns to God. There is no sin that God cannot forgive. Christians believe that those who truly follow Jesus and his way of living are saved. When they die, they will be fully united with Jesus in heaven.

Scriptures

The word scripture means "writings." The holy writings used by Christians are collectively called the Bible. The Bible is a book of books. The Christian Bible includes the Hebrew Scriptures used by Jews, more commonly known to Christians as the Old Testament. The New Testament includes the gospels which are the stories of the life of Jesus, as well as epistles or letters of the early Christian communities. All Christians agree on the twenty-seven books of the New Testament. There are some differences between accepted Old Testament books of the Protestant and Catholic Bibles.

Christians use the Bible in both public and private settings. Individuals may read the Bible as part of their prayer life. The Bible is often used as part of family devotions or study groups. All Christians use the Bible in their worship services. Catholics, Anglicans, and some Protestants have three readings on a Sunday. Generally the first reading is from the Old Testament, the second

reading is from one of the epistles, and the third reading is from one of the Gospels.

Christian Living

The Bible offers instruction on Christian living. Christians follow the Ten Commandments, contained in the Torah. Answering a

question by one of his followers on which is the greatest commandment, Jesus said, "You shall love the Lord your God with all your heart and all your soul and with all your mind. This is the greatest and the first commandment. The second is like it: You shall love your neighbor as yourself" (Matthew 22:38-39).

Known as the "Great Commandment," it is the foundation of a Christian life, though Christians have interpreted it in very different ways. For example, some Christians believe that to love God they must destroy what they perceive to be the enemies of God. Others have interpreted loving God as loving what God created, including imperfect human beings. Some have interpreted loving God as abstaining from alcohol, dancing, or card playing.

Nevertheless the Great Commandment and its resulting love (the way Christians practice) has attracted many converts to Christianity. "See how the Christians love one another" has been a familiar refrain.

> "There is something almost cruel about the Christian's being placed in a world which in every way wants to pressure him to do the opposite of what God bids him to do with fear and trembling in his innermost being. It would be something like the cruelty of parents if they were to threaten and sternly order their child to do thus and so—and then place the child together with the kind of children who would pressure him in every way to do just the opposite."
>
> — Søren Kierkegaard
> (1813-1855)

What is your reaction to Kierkegaard's statement?

The Church

With the myriad divisions of Christianity, it is difficult to speak about one homogeneous group. Christians are defined as those who believe in the divinity of Jesus. Further, Christians are those who accept the Bible without adding or subtracting writings. Church is a gathering of those who believe under the guidance of the Holy Spirit that Jesus is God. The word *church* means "the assembled." One can hear in some churches from time to time expressions like, "Isn't that right, church?" or "Let the church say 'Amen!'" As Jews are considered Israel in a spiritual sense, Christians would consider themselves the New Israel. As Jews are bound by a covenant between God and themselves established with Moses in the desert, Christians are bound by a new covenant established by Jesus. Christianity does not supersede Judaism. Rather, Christians believe the coming of Jesus is the fulfillment of God's promise to the Jews.

SECTION 2 SUMMARY

❖ The most important Christian doctrines are contained in creedal statements such as the Apostles' Creed.

❖ The scripture used by Christians is the Bible. Not all Christians recognize the same books of the Old Testament as authoritative. However, all Christians accept the same twenty-seven books in the New Testament as authoritative.

❖ The Great Commandment on love is foundational for Christian living.

❖ "Church" is defined as a gathering of people who proclaim Jesus as God.

SECTION 2 REVIEW QUESTIONS

1. According to the Apostles' Creed, what do Christians believe about God?

2. Define Trinity, Jesus, sin, and salvation.

3. Give examples of two different ways Christians have interpreted the Great Commandment.

4. Define scripture.

5. What are two ways in which Christians use the Bible in their lives?

III. SACRED PLACES

Air Force Academy Church

© Galyn C. Hammond

Protestant church

© Galyn C. Hammond

© Galyn C. Hammond

Chapel

National Shrine of the Immaculate Conception

Chartres Cathedral

The Church of Jesus Christ of Latter-day Saints

Rock Church Interior

Interior of Episcopal Church

A physical place called a church is the most sacred place for Christians. A church is where the community comes together for worship and fellowship. A church is the place where new members are initiated and rites of passage are marked. Besides churches, Christians also hold the place on earth where Jesus lived and walked to be sacred. This area in modern day Israel is known to Christians as the "Holy Land."

Church

Besides meaning "a gathering of people," church is also a building. A church is the most sacred place for Christians. The exterior architecture of a church does not always clearly tell the church denomination. For example, a Gothic style church may be, among others, Catholic, Anglican, or Presbyterian. An urban storefront church may be Lutheran, Assembly of God, or Catholic.

The inside of a church is more telling. A church with an altar in the middle and a pulpit on the side would tend to be Catholic, Anglican, Orthodox, and perhaps Lutheran. If, in addition,

there are statues of Jesus, Mary, and the saints, then the church is likely to be Catholic. If, instead of statues, there are icons,[11] it is most likely Orthodox. Protestant churches tend to be simpler in ornamentation, some with just a pulpit in the center of the sanctuary.

All Christian denominations would agree that how God is worshipped is more important than where God is worshipped. In times of war, persecution, or natural disasters Christians have worshipped in any type of building available, or outside in a meadow, forest, seashore, or desert.

Holy Land

Since Jesus is the central figure in Christianity, where Jesus lived, ministered, died, and rose from the dead is sacred to Christians. Many areas within the present state of Israel are known as the Holy Land to Christians. Bethlehem, where Jesus was born, Nazareth, where Jesus grew up, and the region of Galilee where Jesus did much of his preaching and healing are especially sacred. In addition, Jerusalem and areas surrounding it are holy spaces. Jesus preached

56

and healed the sick in that locale. Inside the walls of Jerusalem Jesus was tried as a criminal. Outside the walls of Jerusalem Jesus was crucified, died, buried, resurrected, and ascended to heaven.

Name a holy place that fills you with the presence of God.

SECTION 3 SUMMARY

✤ Exterior church architecture varies widely among Christian denominations.

✤ Church interiors provide insight to what is important to that worshipping community.

✤ Christians agree that how they worship is more important than where they worship.

✤ Places where Jesus carried out his ministry are sacred spaces to Christians. These places in modern Israel are known as the Holy Land.

SECTION 3 REVIEW QUESTIONS

1. Describe the various church architecture depicted in the photos on pages 55-56.

2. Why are Protestant churches often less formal interiorly than Catholic, Orthodox, or Anglican churches?

3. Name and explain the significance of several sacred places in the Holy Land.

IV. SACRED TIMES

Like Jews, Christians find that keeping sacred time is important. The Christian calendar is centered on the life, ministry, death, and resurrection of Jesus. These sacred times, whether they are celebrated daily, weekly, or annually, have the power to sanctify life. Christian festivals and holy days vary widely among the denominations. Generally the more formal the worship service of a denomination, the more festivals and holy days it celebrates.

For all Christians, Sunday is a holy day. As the first Christians were Jewish, they kept Saturday as their weekly day of rest, but also commemorated Sunday as the Lord's Day. Early Christians associated Sunday with the resurrection of Jesus, so they celebrated Sunday as a "little Easter." As the Christian population became less Jewish and more Gentile, Sunday became the official Christian Sabbath.

All Christians celebrate Christmas and Easter. Many Christians expand their celebration to the Christmas cycle and the Easter cycle. The Christmas cycle includes Advent, Christmas, and Epiphany while the Easter cycle contains Lent, Easter, and Pentecost. More information on these annual Christian cycles follows.

The Christmas Cycle

Advent

The annual Christian calendar begins with the first Sunday of Advent, which falls four Sundays before Christmas. It is a season of preparation for the *advent* or coming of Jesus. Not only does Advent celebrate the first coming of Jesus 2,000 years ago, but Advent is a preparation time for the coming of Jesus into the hearts of humankind today and a readying for Jesus' Second Coming at the end of time. The season of Advent is in the winter, a time when the light of day gets shorter and shorter until the winter solstice on December 21. In symbolizing that the coming of Jesus is a light in the darkness,

many Christians light candles on an Advent wreath. The wreath is decorated with a circle of evergreens and contains four candles. An additional candle is lit on each Sunday of the four weeks in Advent.

Christmas

The Advent season ends on Christmas Day. Christmas celebrates the birth of Jesus, when God became human. Christmas is the second holiest day in the Christian year. For most Christians, Christmas Day is December 25, but for some Orthodox churches, Christmas is celebrated January 7, the day after Epiphany. Actually, the date of the birth of Jesus is unknown. In the fourth century Christians began to celebrate the birth of Jesus (the Son of God) to contrast with the pagan winter solstice celebration of the Unconquered Sun, which was celebrated near December 25.

Epiphany

Twelve days after Christmas, using the western Gregorian calendar, is the feast of the Epiphany. The word *epiphany* means "manifestation" or "revelation." In the early days of Christianity, Epiphany was associated with three moments in the life of Jesus where he first revealed some aspect of himself to the world. Those three moments were his birth, his baptism, and his first miracle at the marriage feast of Cana. In the fourth century the birth of Jesus came to overshadow Jesus' baptism and first miracle as moments of initial revelation. Thus, in the west, Christmas and Epiphany became two separate feasts, while in most Orthodox churches the more ancient celebration of Epiphany was maintained.

The Easter Cycle

Lent

Easter, the greatest feast in the Christian year, is preceded by forty weekdays of preparation called Lent. The word *lent* comes from an old English word for "springtime." The forty days of Lent are in remembrance of Jesus spending forty days in the wilderness. Ash Wednesday begins the lenten season. It is called "Ash" Wednesday because a small cross of ashes is inscribed on the forehead of a person, reminding them that their physical bodies are transitory. During Lent, Christians prepare for the great feast of Easter by praying, doing penance, fasting, and abstaining from other pleasures.

The last week of Lent is called Holy Week. This most solemn of weeks begins with Palm Sunday, remembering the occasion when Jesus was welcomed into the city of Jerusalem with palm branches. Holy Thursday, or Maundy Thursday, commemorates the Last Supper Jesus had with his disciples. The word *maundy* comes from the Latin word meaning "commandment." At the Last Supper, according to the gospel of John, Jesus gave his disciples the commandment to "love one another as I have loved you." Good Friday commemorates the crucifixion and death of Jesus. Holy Saturday remembers the day when Jesus descended to the abode of the dead. It is observed by a quiet time of prayer until that evening.

Why do you think Christians call Good Friday "good"?

Easter

Easter is the holiest day for Christians. Easter celebrates Christ's resurrection from the dead. It is a movable feast related to the Jewish Passover. It is celebrated annually by most Christians on the first Sunday after the first full moon of spring.

Catholic, Orthodox, and Anglican churches have an Easter vigil service on Holy Saturday evening. These services recall the darkness of the tomb and Christ's breaking forth from that tomb, bringing light to the world. Many Protestant churches have an Easter sunrise service that begins in darkness and continues as the sun rises, symbolizing that Jesus is the Son that rises from the dead.

Pentecost

Pentecost means "fiftieth day." As described in the Acts of the Apostles, the Holy Spirit descended on the frightened disciples of Jesus like "tongues of fire." This extraordinary experience enabled the disciples to go out into the streets of Jerusalem and proclaim the good news of Jesus. Thousands of Jews were converted on the first Pentecost. For this reason, Pentecost is known as the "birthday of the Church."

Describe a time you were frightened or afraid to publicly admit to your faith.

Sacraments

Sacraments are defined as an "outward sign of an inward spiritual grace." Sacraments are more sacred times marked by Christians. Some Christians hold that sacraments are signs authorized by Christ that transmit God's grace to the participant, usually through something tangible like water, bread, wine, or oil. Baptism is the only sacrament recognized by all Christians. Most Christians also acknowledge Eucharist (under various names) as a sacrament.

Baptism is the sacrament that initiates the individual into the Christian community. Whether immersed in a river or pool or sprinkled with water, the priest or minister proclaims the words, "I baptize you in the name of the Father,

and of the Son, and of the Holy Spirit." Anglican, Catholic, Orthodox, and some more traditional Protestant groups such as Lutherans and Methodists have infant baptism. Other Protestant denominations have "believer's baptism" where a person is only baptized when old enough to proclaim a personal belief in Jesus.

Eucharist (also called the Lord's Supper or Holy Communion) fulfills Jesus' Last Supper command to break bread and share wine in his memory. This sacred meal not only brings the partakers into communion with Jesus, they also are in communion with one another as the "Body of Christ" on earth. Catholics and some Protestants (including Lutherans) believe that Jesus is truly present in the blessed bread and wine.

Other sacraments celebrated by Catholics and some Protestants are confirmation, penance, matrimony, holy orders, and the anointing of the sick.

How can the Eucharist bring Christians together? How can the Eucharist pull Christians apart?

Prayer

Prayer is another sacred time for Christians. Prayer is a two-way conversation between God and an individual or group. Prayer can be formal or informal, long or short, verbal or silent. Prayer can involve singing. Different postures and different gestures can be used at different times for prayer. A person can pray anytime and anywhere.

The Bible contains a number of prayers. The book of Psalms is a prayer book within the Bible. The Lord's Prayer, taught to the disciples by Jesus, is the prayer common to all Christians:

Our Father, who art in heaven,
hallowed be Thy name.
Thy kingdom come;
Thy will be done on earth
as it is in heaven.
Give us this day our daily
bread,
and forgive us our
trespasses
as we forgive those
who trespass against us.
And lead us not into
temptation,
but deliver us from evil.

For the kingdom, the
power and the glory are
yours now and forever.
Amen.

According to the Lord's Prayer, what do Christians believe?

SECTION 4 SUMMARY

❖ Christians commemorate the Sabbath on Sunday, the day of the Lord's resurrection.

❖ Easter is the holiest day for Christians.

❖ Most Christians observe the Christmas cycle and the Easter cycle of the Christian calendar.

❖ The Christmas cycle includes Advent, Christmas, and Epiphany. The Easter cycle includes Lent, Easter, and Pentecost.

❖ Sacraments are outward signs of inward spiritual grace. Baptism and Eucharist are two sacraments celebrated by most Christians.

❖ Prayer is a two-way conversation between an individual and God, or a community and God.

SECTION 4 REVIEW QUESTIONS

1. Why did the early Christians change their Sabbath from Saturday to Sunday?

2. How is the Christian calendar different from the civil calendar?

3. What are the special events in the Christmas cycle?

4. What are the special events in the Easter cycle?

5. What are two sacraments that most Christians celebrate?

6. Name some of the characteristics of prayer.

Who Is My Neighbor?

CHRISTIANITY IN AMERICA

In these terms, the history of Christianity in North America, as opposed to the history of North American Christianity, might not be so much about the gain or loss of cultural influence but stories about "signs of contradiction," moments when the faith offered something unexpected to a person, a problem, a situation, or a region. Such "signs of contradiction" existed, for example, when slave owners—perhaps against their better judgment—gave Bibles to their slaves. They were illustrated during the 1930s by the conversion of a few social radicals, such as Dorothy Day, from left-wing utopias to Christian faith. They are evident in documents such as Abraham Lincoln's Second Inaugural Address, in which he meditates on the secrets of divine providence rather than on the depths of Southern evil. They are illustrated supremely by the black acceptance of Christianity, offered as it was with a whip.

Whatever we conclude about the public fate of Christianity since World War II, we are able to see many "signs of contradiction" during this period. Among Roman Catholics, Hispanics were once largely neglected, yet from their midst came the Cursillo movement as a lively stimulus to renewal in communities far removed from Hispanic cultures. The relaxing of sexual standards has been a most visible feature of public life since the 1960s, but the same period has also witnessed the dramatic growth of family-strengthening movements such as Marriage Encounter among both Protestants and Catholics. The list could go on. It is an age of cynicism in politics and business but also of dramatic conversions of men and women who had risen to the top. It is an age of unbridled literary license and proliferating literary nonsense but an age in which more excellent writing of a distinctly Christian cast is being published than ever before in North American history. It is a day of death and devastation in inner cities but also a day in which committed churches, ministers, and philanthropists are organizing heroic efforts to hold back the urban night.

Quoted from *A History of Christianity in the United States and Canada* by Mark A. Noll (Grand Rapids: William B. Eerdmans Publishing Company, 1992)

What "signs of contradiction" about Christianity would you add to the list above?

Conclusion

A major symbol for Christianity is the cross. The cross without a body is a symbol of the risen Jesus, the Jesus that Christians believe is present in all creation. The cross has both a vertical and a horizontal beam. The place where the beams come together symbolizes the place where the God of heaven is made flesh on earth. In turn, because of the life of Jesus, humans can participate in the divine.

There is something very concrete about Christian beliefs. Christianity is about a God who participates fully in all that God creates. In turn, all creation is lifted up. Those Christian denominations that are sacramental in nature believe the use of ordinary things in their liturgies like bread, water, wine, and oil transform the ordinary into the extraordinary. (For those Christians in whom the word of God is emphasized, it is held in that word that has the power to transform lives.) In any case, it is Christians that state that belief in Jesus transforms lives.

It is ironic, then, that belief in Jesus can evoke so many different understandings. The chapter opened with a description of the Taizé community. Like so many other Christian communities and individuals, Taizé strives for reconciliation among Christians both institutionally and individually. It is the gift of diversity rather than the pain of division that most Christians believe Jesus Christ desires.

CHAPTER 3 IN BRIEF

✤ Jesus of Nazareth is the central figure in Christianity.

✤ Christianity began as a small Jewish sect and grew to be a predominantly Gentile world religion.

✤ The first Christians were persecuted by Roman authorities until the Roman emperor Constantine legalized Christianity.

✤ Monasticism was a response to the growing complacency of Christians.

✤ A number of church councils of the fourth and fifth centuries defined the major Christian doctrines.

✤ Growing divisions between east and west led to a split between the church centered in Rome and the church centered in Constantinople.

✤ The Protestant Reformation was initiated by Martin Luther, an Augustinian priest.

✤ The Catholic Reformation was punctuated by the teachings of the Council of Trent.

✤ The Age of Enlightenment posed a threat to many Christians because of its emphasis on rationalism and empiricism.

✤ The ecumenical movement attempts to emphasize the similarities rather than the differences between Christian denominations.

✤ The Bible is a "book of books." It is the sole source of authority for some Christians, while some denominations, including Catholics, recognize the authority of both scripture and tradition.

✤ The Christian Bible draws on its Jewish roots by including the Hebrew Scriptures.

✤ The doctrine of the Trinity is the central Christian doctrine. It states that

God, though one, is in three persons: Father, Son, and Holy Spirit.

✤ In Jesus, God became human. Jesus is both fully human and fully divine.

✤ The Great Commandment—loving God and loving neighbor—is foundational for Christian living.

✤ Church is generally defined as a gathering of those who under the guidance of the Holy Spirit believe Jesus is God.

✤ The physical church building is a sacred place for Christians.

✤ The Holy Land in the State of Israel is considered sacred by Christians.

✤ Easter, the day Jesus rose from the dead, is the preeminent Christian feast.

✤ Prayer—a two-way conversation with God—is essential to Christian life. The Lord's Prayer is the one common prayer among Christians.

CHAPTER 3 REVIEW QUESTIONS

1. Who was Jesus?

2. What are epistles?

3. How was Christian life different after the Edict of Milan?

4. What did the monastic rule of Benedict emphasize?

5. What doctrines were defined at the Council of Nicea and Council of Ephesus?

6. How did the eastern patriarchs regard the bishop of Rome?

7. Explain how Christian conversion of Germanic tribes often occurred.

8. What was the stated purpose of the Crusades?

9. What were some of the beliefs stated by Martin Luther in his *Ninety-five theses*?

10. What is the derivation of the word *lent*?

11. How did the Council of Trent respond to the reformers?

12. Why was religion in the modern period diminished?

13. What is the ecumenical movement? How is it manifested today?

14. What are some of the ways Christians use the Bible?

15. Name the Great Commandment that is the foundation of Christian living.

16. Define church.

17. How can the interior design of a church indicate which denomination worships there?

18. What two sacraments are accepted by most Christians?

19. What are some of the ways that Christians pray?

RESEARCH AND ACTIVITIES

1. Explain what the fallacy is in the statement, "I'm not Christian, I'm Catholic."

2. Research one Christian denomination. Include in your study its history, major beliefs, and forms of worship.

3. Interview a religious leader from a denomination other than your own. Ask questions to determine why the religious tradition is important to them, what are their main beliefs, and who are their role models.

4. Write a report on church-state relations in your country today.

Confessional booth

SELECTED VOCABULARY

Advent

Anglican

anti-Semitism

apostle

baptism

believer's baptism

Catholic

church

denomination

ecumenical movement

Epiphany

epistle

evangelicalism

filioque

fundamentalism

Good Friday

gospel

Great Schism

icon

Incarnation

Lent

Maundy Thursday

mendicant

minister

monk

Orthodox

Pentecost

pentecostalism

priest

resurrection

sacrament

sect

Trinity

© Galyn C. Hammond

Chapter 4

ISLAM

n the following conversation, Attallah, a college student, tells her parents she has recently converted to Islam.

"I know it must seem rushed to you," acknowledged Attallah. "And strange. But I've been going through a spiritual search for a long time and this year it really intensified. I didn't know what I was going to do with my life. I was struggling with how to think about myself. I felt lost, and without a sense of direction. And I felt there was something missing, a clear spiritual center missing in my life.

"You know, there is a concept in Islam about the importance of *jihad*, which means striving and struggling for God. My conversion is really about my experience of jihad, my effort to persevere toward what is right and good."

"Well, I've certainly read the word 'jihad' in the papers," said Attallah's father. "I thought it had to do with Islamic fundamentalism and militancy. Doesn't jihad mean going to war in the name of God? And doesn't it mean being so religiously committed to a political cause that violence and terrorism become acceptable?"

"The media has made people frightened of Islam. Yes, there have been terrorists who have called themselves Muslims. But there are also terrorists who call themselves Christians, or Jews, and no one implies that Christianity itself is suspect, or Judaism, just because some fringe group identifies with one of those religions.

"I've learned that there are two main kinds of jihad. The second or lesser jihad is striving 'in the path of Allah,' which means furthering the cause of Allah through words and deeds. This can mean telling others about our obligation to Allah, and furthering the spread of Islam. It can also mean standing up against injustice because injustice is not the path of God. Allah commands us to defend ourselves and to speak and stand up for ourselves and others in the face of evil and unfairness.

"The first and greater jihad is the struggle for God within the self, and that's what I've been experiencing and what my conversion is about. My first jihad has really been a struggle to find the truth and live by it. It's been a struggle against forgetfulness of Allah, a struggle to stay alert to his existence and greatness . . . It helps me remember my dependence on Allah and my obligations to him. Now my struggle to find myself is less confused, less painful, more clearly directed."

Quoted from *The Power of Religion: A Comparative Introduction,* by Amanda Porterfield copyright © 1997 by Oxford University Press, Inc. Used by permission of Oxford University Press.

What is a stereotype you have held about Islam?

Like Christianity and Judaism, Islam is a worldwide religion covering every continent and every race of people. While Christianity is the largest religion in the world, Islam is not far behind as the second largest. Islam is the fastest growing religion in the world with an estimated increase of approximately 135,000 members in the United States alone each year. Islam came on the world scene in the seventh century with the preaching of the Arab prophet Muhammad. Adherents of Islam are called *Muslims*, which means literally "one who submits to the will of God."

Islam is a monotheistic religion. In fact, Muslims are so adamant about the oneness of God that some are uncomfortable celebrating the birthday of Muhammad because that celebration may take focus away from God. Muslims use the Arabic word *Allah*, meaning "Supreme God," to address God. They believe all creation is Muslim. That is, all that Allah created naturally submits to divine will. While plants and animals instinctively submit to the will of God, human beings have free will to choose to submit or not. Allah does not force anyone to submit. Muslims insist that submitting to God is not a confining, negative command. Rather, it is a gracious surrendering to the all-compassionate, all-merciful Allah where true freedom lies.

Because all creation is Muslim at birth, adherents to Islam do not recognize Muhammad as the founder of Islam. According to Muslims, Islam has always been; it is a timeless religion. Muhammad did not found the religion—he restored it. Muhammad himself was both a political leader and a spiritual leader. It is incorrect to call Muslims Muhammadans for they are not followers of Muhammad. Muhammad is God's messenger to all humanity to return to their true calling, that is, to submit to the will of Allah.

This chapter offers a brief historical overview of Islam and of Islamic beliefs and how those beliefs are expressed in daily living. Islam is a universal community with members from all walks of life. Membership in the community carries with it certain obligations to God and others. As the opening story points out, Muslims worldwide have to overcome stereotypes proliferated by the media, especially that all terrorists are Muslims and all Muslims are terrorists. When the federal building in Oklahoma City was bombed on April 19, 1995, a media report first assumed that a Muslim committed the crime. This was proven untrue.

This chapter will report how Allah is at the center of Islamic life—physical, mental, economic, political, social, and spiritual and how this central belief affects Muslim life.

CE

570	Birth of Muhammad
610	First revelation from Allah
622	The emigration to Medina
632	Final revelation and death of Muhammad
640s	First of Caliphs
656	Uthman is murdered
1453	Muslims conquer Constantinople
1600s	Muslim dominance starts slow decline
1947	Pakistan breaks away from India to be a separate Muslim state
1979	Khomeni deposes Shah of Iran

I. A BRIEF HISTORY OF ISLAM

For Muslims Islam has always existed. Islam began with Adam, the first man. Muhammad is the "Seal of the Prophets," that is, the final messenger of God. He is the last of the prophets who received messages from God to pass on to humanity. He is not, therefore, the founder of Islam according to a Muslim definition.

Muhammad, the Messenger of God

Muhammad was born 570 CE in Mecca (Makkah), located in present day Saudi Arabia. His father died before he was born and his mother died when he was six years old. Orphaned, Muhammad was raised by his uncle, Abu Talib, who employed Muhammad as a camel driver. In his travels Muhammad often met with Jews and Christians and heard their stories. Then Muhammad met Khadija, a widowed businesswoman fifteen years his senior. She employed him and later, they married and had children.

Muhammad was accustomed to going to a cave about once a month for a time of prayer and reflection and to meditate on life's meaning. One evening, in the year 610 CE, he was in the cave and an angel appeared to him. The angel commanded, "Recite! In the name of your Lord and Cherisher, Who created—Created man, out of a sperm-cell" (Surah 96:1-2). Since Muhammad was illiterate, he memorized the words commanded of him. The messenger was revealed as *Jibril* or the Angel Gabriel.

According to Jibril, Muhammad was to be the messenger of Allah, the one God. Muhammad had a number of these revelations over a period of several years and shared these revelations with his wife and close friends. Few others believed Muhammad, for Mecca was a place of many gods. In the center of Mecca was a large, cube-like structure called the Ka'bah which housed over 360 idols. Asking the people to believe in only one God was too much for most of the people of Mecca. In addition, calling the various tribes of Mecca to be one people under one God was destructive of the diverse tribal social structures.

Eventually, Muhammad gained a small following. His wife Khadija always believed him and was very supportive of him. His two friends Abu Bakr and Uthman, his cousin Ali, son of his uncle Abu Talib, and a former slave, Zaid, were also among his first followers. Life became so unbearable for these Muslims at Mecca that they had to move. The move in 622 to present day Medina became known as the *hijrah* or "migration." The hijrah marks the beginning of the Islamic calendar. Hence, the Western calendar date of 622 CE is 1 AH (after hijrah) on the Islamic calendar.

Initially, things went well for the Muslims in Medina. Muhammad was not only a capable spiritual leader, but his gifts as a political leader were also recognized. As his following grew, so did his opposition. Muslims ended up battling Arabs and Jews in Medina, and took up the battle of various tribes in Mecca as well. After three battles, Muhammed captured Mecca. He then went immediately to the Ka'bah, the shrine for the worship of minor gods.

Muhammad ordered all the statues removed from the shrine except for a sacred Black Stone that sat in one corner. The Black Stone is said to be a meteorite given to Abraham by the angel Gabriel. To this day the Ka'bah contains only the Black Stone and is the central place of prayer for Muslims.

By the time Muhammad died in 632, many Arab tribes were calling themselves Muslim and submitting to the will of Allah.

What are some similarities between Christianity and Islam?

Classical Period of Islam

The successors of Muhammad were called *caliphs*.[1] The first to succeed Muhammad was Abu Bakr (632-34), one of Muhammad's original disciples. It was Abu Bakr who collected the revelations of Muhammad and compiled them in what is now known as the sacred scriptures of Islam, the Qur'an (Koran). Abu Bakr appointed Umar as his successor. At first an enemy of Islam, Umar oversaw the expansion of Islam to Persia, Damascus, and Jerusalem, often through military conquests. Before he died, Umar appointed a committee of six people to choose his successor. The committee chose Uthman (644-656). As caliph, Uthman was instrumental in the publication and distribution of the Qur'an. By now the Islamic empire or *caliphate* had spread throughout the entire Middle East. It included Egypt and Libya in North Africa, the Arabian Peninsula, Palestine, Syria, Mesopotamia, and Persia. Though Muslims were rulers of these regions, it took the majority of the people living in these countries a long time to become Muslim, for conversion to Islam was not accomplished on command or "by the sword" as it often was with Christians of various Germanic tribes.

Uthman could not handle the internal strife that overcame Islam. After six years as caliph he was murdered. Uthman's successor was Ali, the son-in-law of Muhammad. Ali attempted to avenge the death of Uthman, but was murdered himself. At the death of Ali, the Muslim community was split between the caliphs. The Shi'ite Muslims refused to accept the authority of the new caliph, who was not a direct descendent of Muhammad. The Sunni Muslims did accept Muawiya, the caliph who succeeded Ali after he was murdered. This division in Islam between Shi'ite and Sunni Muslims is a source of great tension to this day.

Medieval Period

Though rivalries among Muslims continued for centuries, during the Middle Ages Islamic civilization flowered. Islamic poetry, architecture, philosophy, and theology all became well established during this period.

All Muslims spoke Aramaic so they could recite the Qur`an and say their prayers in the same language. Muslims were the first to translate the Greek philosophers into Arabic. Like Christian and Jewish medieval philosophers, Islamic philosophers attempted to integrate Greek philosophy (especially Aristotle) with Muslim theology.

When the Ottomans came to power, Muslims conquered Constantinople in 1453. Not fond of the idea of a city being named after a Christian emperor, the Ottomans renamed the city Istanbul and set it up as the capital of the Ottoman Empire.

Modern Period

The Mongols stayed in power in India until the British took over in the nineteenth century. The caliphate was abolished at the time of World War I.

The Nation of Islam

In 1930, a man calling himself W. D. Fard Muhammad founded a temple (not a mosque[2]) in Detroit and called it Temple No. 1. His followers called him God, Allah, or the Great Mahdi. He taught that the white man and his white religion, (Christianity) were the "devil." Fard called for the establishment of a separate African-American homeland on American soil where his so-called Nation of Islam could be a nation within a nation.

After Fard's mysterious disappearance in 1934, Elijah Muhammad, head of the temple in Chicago, succeeded Fard as leader of the Nation of Islam. Elijah Muhammad was called the Messenger of Allah and the Holy Prophet by his followers. Elijah Muhammad expanded the Nation of Islam to other urban cities of the North as well as state and federal penitentiaries. He continued Fard's anti-Christian teachings regarding the nature of Allah as the "Supreme Black Man," African-Americans as the "Lost-Found Nation of Islam," black supremacy, the resurrection of the mind, and separation from the white race. In the 1960s, Malcolm X, leader of the Nation of Islam Temple in New York, went on a pilgrimage to Mecca where he met Muslims from all over the world and from every race and ethnic background. He began to challenge Elijah Muhammad's leadership in the teachings of Islam, but was assassinated by Nation of Islam rivals in 1965.

After the death of Elijah Muhammad in 1975, one of his sons, Wallace D. Muhammad, aligned the Nation of Islam with the more universal, orthodox Islam. The Five Pillars of Islam were enforced. The temples were renamed mosques and non-black people were admitted for worship. But a faction led by Louis Farrakhan disagreed with the younger Muhammad's reconciliation with orthodox Islam.

The British colonized many lands where the Muslims once dominated. Europeans also colonized parts of the Middle East.

Especially since Napoleon's invasion of Egypt, Muslims have been attempting to regain their place in the world as in the first six centuries of their history. The tide changed when Pakistan broke away from India in 1947 and became an Islamic republic with Islamic law in force. When the Ayatollah Khomeni deposed the Shah of Iran in 1979, it for the most part marked the end of westernized leaders ruling Islamic nations.

What do you think it would be like to be ruled by a government that espoused a religion different from your own?

Louis Farrakhan purchased the main temple of the Nation of Islam located in Chicago. Because this temple was the same location from which Elijah Muhammad led the Nation of Islam for forty-one years, this gave Farrakhan a power base. There were some members of the Nation of Islam who had felt betrayed by Wallace D. Muhammad and were pleased to have Farrakhan resume leadership in the organization. Wallace Muhammad had let white people into the mosques, had become patriotic, and relaxed the dress code. Some adherents to the Nation of Islam believed the changes made by Wallace Muhammad degenerated into a relaxed moral standard, and wanted to see the "old" Nation return. Others felt that Wallace Muhammad and his followers were becoming more middle class, abandoning the poorer African-Americans, and falling into the same trap as some African-American Christian churches had. Poorer African-Americans found the separatist ideology and strict moral codes of the Nation of Islam more appealing than the universal brotherhood of orthodox Islam.

In contrast to Elijah Muhammad, Farrakhan's rhetoric regarding European-Americans was toned down, but the separatist doctrine continued. He believed that race problems in the United States were detrimental to all American citizens. Farrakhan admired the civil rights leaders of the 1960s, but believed their integrationist ideas were misguided. According to Farrakhan, Americans did not want integration, and this was all the more reason for the United States government to finance the separation of an African-American nation.

Martin Luther King with Elijah Muhammad (l) and Malcom X (r).

SECTION 1 SUMMARY

✤ Muhammad is the final messenger of God. He lived in present day Saudi Arabia from 570 to 632 CE.

✤ The successors to Muhammad were known as caliphs.

✤ The hijrah or migration of Muhammad to Medina marks the beginning of the Islamic calendar.

✤ In the Classical Period, Islam spread from the Arabian Peninsula to the borders of China, India, France, and Persia.

✤ In modern times the colonizers of the west, particularly the British, eroded the Islamic caliphates and thus, Islamic influence. In the twentieth century, some Islamic nations are attempting to remove secular governments and unify their faith.

✤ The Nation of Islam is an African-American separatist movement emphasizing self-help and self-improvement. It is not recognized as orthodox by the universal Islamic community.

SECTION 1 REVIEW QUESTIONS

1. Explain how Muhammad received his first revelation.

2. What are the major contributions of the first three caliphs of Islam?

3. Why could the Shi'ite not accept the successor of Ali as caliph?

4. What were some of the major causes of the decline of Islamic political power in the early modern period?

5. Summarize the history of the Nation of Islam in the United States.

II. BELIEFS AND ACTIONS

The two main sources of Islamic beliefs are the Qur'an and the Hadith.[3] Beliefs of Muslims are clearly formulated in what may be called the Islamic creed, the *al-imanul-mufassal*. Muslim behavior is guided by the Five Pillars of Islam, religious duties that each person is to perform.

Islamic Creed

The Islamic creed names seven beliefs: in Allah, in Allah's books, in Allah's angels, in Allah's messengers, in the last day, in Allah's providence, and in life after death. These seven beliefs are contained in three categories:

✤ The first category is the oneness of God. Two of the seven beliefs are contained in this category: "I believe in Allah," and "I believe in the fact that everything, good or bad, is decided by Allah."

✤ The second category is prophethood; beliefs in things that come from Allah: his angels, his books, and his messengers.

✤ The third category involves judgment and eternity and is contained in the statements: "I believe in the last day. I believe in life after death."

Of these three categories, the first is the most important. Muslims express their belief in one and only one God in many ways. Muslims believe Allah is the creator and sustainer of the universe. Like Christians, Muslims believe Allah (God) is all-loving, all-powerful, all-knowing, all-merciful, and present everywhere. Not only does Allah give

Tracery on a mosque entrance

life, but Allah also takes life away. Allah is the judge of all. It is Allah who determines whether a person will spend eternity in heaven or hell.

In stating that "everything, good or bad, is decided by Allah," Muslims believe in Allah's providence. Allah knows what happened in the past, what is presently happening, and what will happen in the future. However, Allah does not predetermine what is going to happen. Rather, Allah knows what choices people will make before they make them. Free will is an integral part of Allah's creation. People are to be obedient to Allah but not coerced into submission. Surrendering to Allah's will brings freedom, not bondage.

The category of beliefs under prophethood mentions belief in angels. Allah created angels to be instruments of carrying out his will. Angels are incapable of disobeying Allah. Angels praise Allah in all things and fulfill the most holy will.

Belief in "his books" refers not only to the Qur'an, but to the Torah, psalms, and gospels. These books are to be read with reverence. However, Muslims believe the Qur'an is the final revelation of Allah to humanity. Muslims believe the Qur'an contains the exact, literal words of Allah revealed to Muhammad

in Arabic. The revelations are not secret; they are to be given to all humanity. As Muhammad is the "Seal of the Prophets," analogously the Qur'an is the "seal of the books." In the Qur'an, all Allah's revelations to humanity are complete.

Beginning with Adam and concluding with Muhammad, the Qur'an mentions twenty-five prophets. These are the messengers referred to in the category of prophethood. Included in the list are Adam, Abraham, and Jesus, though the Islamic understanding of these prophets differs from the Judeo-Christian understanding.

Adam

To Muslims, Adam was not only the first human created, he was the first prophet. Before Adam there were the angels, created from divine light, and *jinn*,[4] created from smokeless fire. While angels were incapable of doing wrong, jinn were capable of choosing right from wrong. The angels and jinn were to prostrate themselves before Allah. While the angels obeyed, a jinn named Iblis did not. Because of disobedience, Allah cast Iblis from Paradise. Angered, Iblis vowed to steer Adam and his descendants away from Allah. Adam and his wife Hawwa disobeyed Allah's command not to eat the forbidden fruit from the tree of the knowledge of good and evil. For their disobedience Allah cast Adam and Hawwa out of paradise.

Abraham

Upset with the idolatry in Ur, Abraham, his wife, Sarah, and nephew Lot all migrated to Canaan. A drought in Canaan forced them to move to Egypt where Abraham married a slave girl named Hagar. She bore him a son named Ishmael. Allah tested Abraham several times. On one occasion, Abraham was to leave Hagar and Ishmael in a hot, dry place called Bakka. Ishmael cried in thirst, but Hagar was unable to find water in such a wilderness. As Ishmael sat kicking at the ground in despair, water sprang up from the dirt under his feet. Today this desert place is called Mecca, and the location where water sprang up is the well of Zam Zam, an important site for Muslim pilgrims.

Allah commanded Abraham and Ishmael to rebuild the Ka'bah. There Abraham and Ishmael prayed to Allah for wisdom to understand the scriptures. Allah's answer to their prayer was to send Muhammad.

Jesus

Muslims accept Jesus as a prophet born of Mary. According to Islamic tradition, Jesus could talk even as a baby. When he was about thirty years old he went about preaching, healing the ill, and raising the dead. For Muslims, Jesus was a great prophet, but he was not the Messiah or God's Son.

Allah sent prophets throughout the ages to aid people in their Islamic living, knowing that they would need guidance in the direction of right and good. The prophets were that guidance. Muhammad is the final prophet Allah will send to humanity.

Judgment

Muslims believe that there is life after death and that how a person will spend eternal life depends on how he or she lived on earth. This belief is in the third category of the Islamic creed. If a person does the will of Allah, he or she will be rewarded with heaven, a place of eternal bliss. If a person does not submit to the will of Allah on earth and willfully does wrong or evil, transgressing all bounds, he or she will be eternally punished with hell, a place of suffering. At the Last Judgment all will be gathered, and each person will be questioned about his or her deeds. Not only individuals, but also nations will be judged for their deeds of good or evil. Dominance or destruction will result in judgment upon the evil nations by other nations. Practicing the Five Pillars of Islam is the most obvious way of submitting to the will of Allah, and thereby gaining the rewards of heaven.

How do you understand God's providence for your life?

The Five Pillars of Islam

As Islam is to be understood as a "way of life" and not a particular religion, the Five Pillars serve as the religious duties that each Muslim is to perform. Without practicing all of the pillars, a person's religious life is not fulfilled.

1. Profession of Faith

Reciting the Arabic words *La ilana illa Allah; Muhammadur Rasul Allah,* translated as, "There is no god but Allah; Muhammad is the Messenger of Allah," is the first and most important of the Five Pillars of Islam. The other four pillars are outward expressions of the first.

This pillar, known as the *Shahadah*[5], is akin to the Jewish Sh'ma. Muslims declare this belief several times a day. A "crier" called a *muezzin* proclaims this creed from the towers of every mosque. The father whispers these words into the ears of the newborn child so that they are the first words heard on earth. A dying person attempts to have the Shahadah be the last words on his or her lips. A convert to Islam recites these words as a statement of belief. This public declaration of faith defines a person as a member of the Islamic community.

2. Prayer

Submitting to Allah is at the heart of Islam. The Qur'an commands Muslims to pray at fixed times during the day. Muslims ritually pray five times per day.

Before Muslims pray, they must cleanse themselves physically and symbolically. In the ritual washing, called the *wudu*, the wrist, fingers, throat, arms, mouth, face, ears, nape of neck, and feet are washed. The ritual opens and closes with a prayer.

In addition to a clean body, the person must be wearing proper clothing. Men must be clothed from the navel to the knees. Women must be clothed from head to toe. Shoes are not worn. To ensure that the person does not get dirty during prayer, a prayer mat is used. Some prayer mats even have a compass so that wherever a Muslim prays, they are facing the Ka'bah in Mecca.

The five fixed times for prayer are 1) between dawn and sunrise, 2) after mid-day, 3) between late afternoon and sunset, 4) between sunset and the end of daylight, and 5) night, until dawn. In Islamic regions of the world, the muezzin calls from a special tower of the mosque five times a day. Five times a day Muslims chant:

> God is most Great.
> I bear witness that there is no god but God.
> I bear witness that Muhammad is the Messenger of Allah.
> Come to prayer.
> Come to success.
> (At the first prayer of the day the following line is added: "Prayer is better than sleep.")
> God is most Great.
> There is no god but God.

In countries where Muslims are a minority, it is more difficult for Muslims to stop and pray. But many Muslims in school and work settings do reserve times to fulfill this religious requirement.

Friday is the special day of prayer for Muslims, though Fridays are not understood to be the equivalent of a Sabbath. On Fridays the second prayer time is made in a mosque and called *Jum'ah* or "Assembly." Besides the regular midday prayer, the *imam*, or prayer leader, delivers a sermon. Since Islam has no clergy, anyone whom the community considers knowledgeable about Islam can be a prayer leader and deliver a sermon. As might be imagined, Muslims in non-Muslim countries find it difficult to attend Jum'ah in the middle of a Friday work or school day. In the United States efforts are being made to make schools and businesses aware of this difficulty and, at least in larger cities, small mosques are being built near business areas to accommodate Muslims working there.

3. Almsgiving

Muslims give alms to the needy as an act of worship. Almsgiving is not an option, but an obligation. Muslims believe that almsgiving, called *zakat*, is one way a person can be freed from those things that are obstacles to Allah. The Qur'an does not specify how much wealth one should share with others, but two and one half percent of one's savings is the norm. Rather, it states: "They ask you how much they are to spend. Say: 'What is beyond your needs'" (Surah 2:219).

4. Fasting

Muslims fast from food, drink, and sexual intercourse during the ninth month of the year, *Ramadan*, the month Muhammad first received his revelations from Allah. The fasting from food, water, or any liquids takes place from sunrise to sunset.

The fast reminds Muslims to fulfill their obligations to care for the poor and needy. After sundown, special prayers and passages from the Qur'an are read and shared. If a person violates the fast, the penalty is strict. He or she must do one of the following: feed meals to sixty people, give sixty people money enough to buy their own meals, or fast for an additional sixty days.

5. Pilgrimage

The *hajj* is the name of a pilgrimage to the Ka'bah in Mecca, Saudi Arabia where Abraham submitted to the will of Allah. The hajj is compulsory once in a lifetime, though finances or illness may keep one from this pilgrimage.

When pilgrims arrive in Mecca they wear plain white robes as a sign of their unity before God. The hajj is made in the twelfth month of the Islamic year and is generally held as part of a three-day observance. Pilgrims go to the mosque and make seven circuits around the Ka'bah before touching the Black Stone and asking for forgiveness and guidance. They also visit other sacred sites in the region. The last rite of the hajj is the

sacrifice of a sheep, goat, or camel to represent Abraham's sacrifice.

Compose three or more pillars that represent the essentials of your faith.

Scripture

Besides the Qur'an, Muslims acknowledge the revealed writings of Judaism and Christianity. However, Muslims hold that these books (the Torah, psalms, and gospels) are corrupted by human error. On the other hand, the Qur'an is Allah's word as revealed to Muhammad without any element of the prophet reflected in it. Thus, according to Muslim beliefs, it is infallible.

The Qur'an is divided into 114 *surahs*, or chapters. The surahs are further divided into verses. The organization of the chapters is neither by theme nor chronology. Rather, the surahs are arranged by length (except for the first surah), beginning with the longest and ending with the shortest. Each surah, except chapter 9, begins with the words, "In the Name of God, the Compassionate, the Merciful."

The sacredness of the Qur'an is such that one should ritually wash one's hands before touching the holy book. In addition, the Qur'an should be kept on a high shelf to indicate its superiority to any other book. The beauty of the Arabic language in the Qur'an renders the sacred scripture as words that should be heard, for in Arabic *qur'an* means "recitation."

Recite! In the Name of your
　　　Lord who created
Created man from a sperm-cell,
Recite! How all together gracious is
　　　your Lord,
Who taught by the pen, taught man
what he knows not. (Surah 96)

The style of writing is prose that rhymes, with lines unequal in length. There is no narrative as in most other scriptures. The Qur'an does not "tell" stories of Muslims as a people. The tone is more like prophetic utterances, dictates, prescriptions, and instructions. The Qur'an covers every aspect of Muslim life. The Qur'an may be translated into other languages, but Muslims consider any translation an interpretation and not literally the sacred word. Allah spoke in such beautiful Arabic that translations lose some of the divine element.

Muhammad received the revelations in the Qur'an in both Mecca and Medina over a period of twenty-two years (610-632 CE). It is common to classify the Surahs according to one of these two locations of revelation. The earlier Mecca revelations speak about the power, glory, and oneness of Allah, moral living, the end times, and Judgment Day. The later Medina revelations have some of these themes, but also cover the topic of Muslim living, including legal, social, and financial matters.

Traditionally, the Qur'an is memorized and recited. One who is skilled at reciting by memory the entire Qur'an earns the honorary title of *hafiz*.[6]

The Hadith

The Hadith are collections of the words and actions of Muhammad. Muslims use the Hadith to interpret the teachings found in the Qur'an. Unlike the Qur'an, the Hadith is not infallible. The two major Islamic groups, Sunni Muslims and Shi'ite Muslims, each have their own Hadith. The Sunni have a collection of six Hadith, while the Shi'ite have a collection of five Hadith.

What is a passage of sacred writing that you have memorized or that easily comes to mind when you pray?

Community

The Islamic community is known as the *ummah*, a collective term meaning "nation." There is no long process in *becoming* a Muslim. To be considered a member one merely has to submit to the will of Allah. One demonstrates this submission through practicing the duties of a Muslim, that is, the Five Pillars of Islam. A ritual cleansing and a proclamation of the Shahadah before two witnesses is sufficient. However, the practice of *being* a Muslim and submitting one's will to the will of Allah is a lifelong endeavor.

Islamic Living

Islam covers all aspects of life—spiritual, social, political, economic. Allah is not only ruler of the earth, but of every aspect of a Muslim's life. The Qur'an has much to say about what an Islamic society should look like overall, as well as in the day-to-day concerns of family, life, and the specific roles of women and men in family and society.

Islam calls upon each Muslim to care for those in need, as held in the third pillar. The *zakat*, or "poor tax," is a required contribution to charity. In some Muslim countries the zakat is enforced by law. According to the Qur'an, Muslims who spend time thinking about the small things in life are losing sight of Allah. In addition, thinking that charitable giving results in depriving the giver of basic needs is incorrect. Those who worry about money are not trusting that Allah will provide for the needs of all creation.

Islamic law (*shari'ah*) is more than a body of works that spells out what is legal and what is illegal in Islamic society. Shari'ah also spells out the expected moral behaviors of the community and the individual. There are four sources for Islamic law: 1) the Qur'an, 2) the Hadith, 3) responsible individual opinion, usually by an Islamic leader who uses analogous reasoning, and 4) consensus of the community. The shari'ah evolved over centuries. Some nations (e.g., Saudi Arabia, Iran, and Pakistan) draw all of their laws from the shari'ah.

Women in Islam

Muhammad raised the status of seventh-century women of Arabia. Women were no longer to be simply the possession of men. Muhammad also abolished female infanticide and gave women some financial independence as well as more rights with regard to marriage and divorce. Though these changes were significant at the time, they are no longer sufficient according to twentieth century western views. Though the Qur'an dictates only that both men and women must dress modestly, some Muslim countries interpret the qur'anic passages in a strict way.

Some countries do not require Muslim women to be covered from head to toe. In the United States, for example, women have a choice on what to wear. When American Muslim women do choose to wear more traditional Islamic clothing, they fight the stereotype that they are "oppressed."

Shi'ite Muslims

About ten percent of the Muslims in the world are Shi'ite Muslims. They emerged when Muhammad's son-in-law Ali was assassinated and another member of Muhammad's family did not succeed him. Shi'ites believe that, beginning with Ali, there were twelve infallible leaders of Islam. They await the return of the twelfth leader who disappeared in 878, believing he will bring justice to the world. In the meantime, to Shi'ites, any Islamic imam is considered only partially legitimate.

SECTION 2 SUMMARY

❖ The Islamic creed, the al-immanual-mufassal, has seven major beliefs in three categories: Allah, prophethood, and the last day.

❖ The major religious duties of every Muslim are the Five Pillars of Islam: profession of faith, prayer, fasting, almsgiving, and pilgrimage.

❖ The Qur'an is the literal word of Allah to humanity. It is the most perfect scripture for Muslims, though Muslims read and respect the Torah, psalms, and gospels. Hadith is the collection of words and actions of Muhammad.

❖ The Islamic community is known as the ummah. One becomes a Muslim by practicing the five pillars.

❖ The shari'ah is the sacred law of Islam that is both legal and moral guidance for Muslims.

❖ Shi'ite is a sectarian group making up about ten percent of the Islamic community worldwide.

SECTION 2 REVIEW QUESTIONS

1. Name the seven major beliefs of Islam by their three categories.

2. Name and explain each of the Five Pillars of Islam.

3. Why is the Qur'an the most sacred writing for Muslims?

4. Compare the Hadith to the Jewish Talmud. How are they alike?

5. How does one become a Muslim?

6. What is the main reason the western world views Muslim women as oppressed?

7. What are the four sources for Islamic law?

8. Why have the Shi'ite chosen to separate from the main body of universal Islam?

III. SACRED PLACES

Of all the sacred places in Islam, the mosque is the most common. There are mosques in almost every urban area and several rural areas in the world. In addition, the holy cities of Mecca, Medina, and Jerusalem have special significance to Muslims.

Mosque

Mosque literally translates to "a place of prostration." It is the building of public worship for Muslims. The main purpose of a mosque is prayer. Prayer at a mosque can be either communal or private.

Traditionally, mosques are built from stone or brick in the form of a square. The distinctive exterior feature is the *minaret*. Generally, the minaret is a tower where the muezzin proclaims *adan*, that is, the call for prayer. Some modern mosques use a recording to call Muslims to prayer (much in the same way that some Christian churches have replaced the ringing of bells with a recording of bell sounds). In some areas where Muslims are a minority group, the adan is confined to the area immediately near the mosque.

The mosque can also be used for other social occasions like weddings or meetings. In non-Muslim countries, the mosque is a place where Muslim children learn to recite the Qur'an in Arabic. In addition, the mosque can be the place where funeral arrangements are made and a body is prepared for burial.

It is important for Muslims to enter a mosque clean of outside dirt and grime. To prepare for entrance, there is a place for Muslims to leave their shoes. In addition, there is a separate washing area where the ritual washing before prayer (the wudu), is performed.

The most important area of a mosque is the prayer hall. It is a large open area without seats. A decorated plaque called a mihrab is placed on the wall or an alcove within the wall that is in the direction of Mecca. A minbar is a short flight of stairs to a platform where the imam or prayer leader preaches.

Mosque walls are beautifully decorated. Arabesque patterns, mosaics of geometric patterns, and Arabic calligraphy of verses from the Qur'an adorn the walls. Mosques have no paintings or statues of God or Muhammad, since Muslims believe this to be idolatrous.

In your opinion, how should a person prepare himself or herself before entering your church?

Mecca

The hajj,[7] or pilgrimage to Mecca, is the fifth of the Five Pillars of Islam. Every Muslim tries to make this sacred journey at least once in his or her lifetime during the twelfth month of the Islamic year. This is an obligatory pillar for Muslims as long as they are not limited by poor health or finances. When Muslims return from Mecca, they recount their pilgrimage to their family and friends. The person is then known as *Hajji*, "a person who has made the hajj." The city of Mecca is so holy to Muslims that non-Muslims are not allowed to enter the city.

Mecca is the site of the Ka'bah, a large, black, cube-shaped monolith. At the time of Muhammad the Ka'bah was a place for idols. Muhammad had the

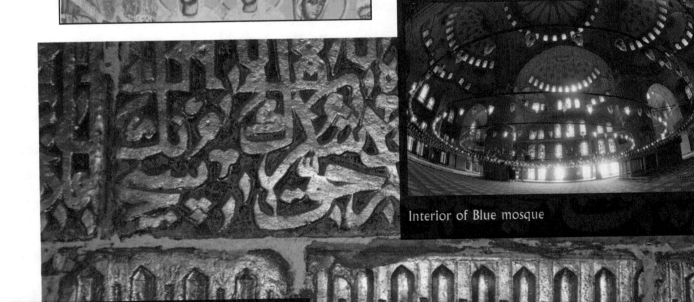

Interior of Blue mosque

Mosque interior wall detail

idols destroyed and proclaimed Mecca the center of Islam. Muslims believed that when Allah created the earth the first thing God created was the Ka'bah. The Ka'bah was rebuilt by Adam and his son and rebuilt again by Abraham and his son, Ishmael. It is toward the Ka'bah in Mecca that Muslims face five times daily to pray. According to the Qur'an, Abraham asked Ishmael to hand him a stone which Abraham placed to mark the exact spot where the ritual should begin. This Black Stone, as it is known, is there today. When Muslims begin the ritual of *Sa'y*, that is, circumambulating the Ka'bah, they begin at the Black Stone.

the site of the Dome of the Rock, Muhammed reportedly visited with Abraham, Moses, and Jesus, and ascend-

Dome of the Rock

© Galyn C. Hammond

ed to heaven to be greeted by Allah. When he returned to earth, Muhammad then began his preaching.

Also known as the Mosque of Umar, the Dome of the Rock was built forty years after Muhammad's death.

Medina

Medina is only some 300 miles from Mecca. This was the city Muhammad migrated to because of the strong opposition he faced to his preaching in Mecca. Muhammad's migration is known as the hijrah. During their time of pilgrimage to Mecca, many Muslims attempt to follow the migration of Muhammad to Medina. Muhammad is buried in Medina, and the first mosque was built there.

Jerusalem

The city of Jerusalem is holy not only for Jews and Christians. Muslims believe Muhammad made his "night visit" (also known as the *miraj*) to this holy city. The miraj refers to the night Muhammad was taken by the angel Gabriel from Mecca to the temple mount in Jerusalem. There, on what is presently

SECTION 3 SUMMARY

♣ The mosque is the place of public prayer for Muslims. Its primary use is communal prayer, but it also can be used for other social, educational, and business functions.

♣ Mecca is the holiest city for Muslims. It is the site of Muhammad's birth. In addition, Mecca is the location of the Ka'bah and is the place where pilgrims make their hajj, fulfilling the fifth of the Five Pillars of Islam.

♣ Medina is the second holiest city. It is the place where Muhammad and his first followers emigrated after it became intolerable to stay any longer in Mecca.

❖ Jerusalem is a holy site for Muslims as well as Christians and Jews. In Jerusalem, Muhammad's "night visit" with Abraham, Moses, and Jesus occurred.

SECTION 3 REVIEW QUESTIONS

1. Define mosque.

2. How did Mecca become a holy place for Muslims?

3. Why are Medina and Jerusalem also holy cities for Muslims?

IV. SACRED TIME

The Islamic calendar begins with the year of Muhammad's hijrah. Like the Jewish calendar, the Islamic calendar is based on lunar months. Whereas the solar calendar used by Christians and the western world is 365 days, the lunar calendar is 354 days. The Jewish calendar is adjusted for the difference so that the various Jewish festivals will always fall in the same season each year. For example, Jews adjust their lunar calendar so that Passover will always take place in the spring. The Islamic calendar does not adjust for the eleven-day difference. Hence, an Islamic festival is moved back eleven days each year and occasionally the celebration of the festival

changes seasons. Two Islamic festivals are *Eid al-Fitr*, the breaking of the fast at the end of Ramadan, and *Eid al-Adah*, which commemorates Abraham's obedience to Allah in his willingness to sacrifice his son.

Ramadan

Ramadan is the name for the twelfth Islamic month, the month in which Muhammad received the first revelation from God. During Ramadan all healthy Muslims are to fast during daylight hours. After eating a full meal, Muslims say evening prayer. Just before dawn, most Muslims also have a light meal. At the break of dawn the first prayers of the day are recited. Muslims are encouraged to read the entire Qur'an during this holy month.

The Night of Power occurs during one of the last ten nights of Ramadan. This night commemorates the actual time when the first revelation was given to Muhammad.

Eid al-Fitr marks the end of Ramadan, occurring on the first new moon twenty-nine or thirty days after the start of the month. Families come together for a festive meal in the homes

of relatives. Cards are sent out and children receive presents. Those who are less fortunate are also remembered through charitable giving.

Have you ever fasted from food for a day or more? What do you think are the spiritual benefits of a fast?

Other Festivals

Eid al-Adah is the second of the major festivals in Islam. This feast, commemorating the willingness of Abraham to sacrifice his son Ishmael in accordance with the will of Allah, is generally celebrated at the conclusion of the pilgrimage to Mecca. As the Angel Gabriel substituted a ram for Ishmael, so Muslims, whether on pilgrimage or not, slaughter an animal and share it with the family and those in need. Muslims not on pilgrimage celebrate this four-day feast of sacrifice from their homes in solidarity with those on pilgrimage.

Mawlid al-Nabi commemorates the birthday of Muhammad. Though the day of Muhammad's birth is unknown, Muslims believe the twelfth day of the Islamic month of Rabi' al-Awwal is both the day of the prophet's birth and death. Since Muhammad never celebrated his birthday, some Muslims do not celebrate on this day. (Some Muslims also believe that celebrating the birthday of Muhammad diverts attention from Allah.) Those who do celebrate Muhammad's birthday focus on his life and greatness as a prophet.

Muharram is the first month of the Islamic calendar. This is a time of renewal, when Muslims are exhorted to give up any sinful ways and begin afresh with the new year. Renewal is also reflected in a special way on the tenth of day of Muharram known as *Ashura*. On this date it is held that Allah created the heavens and the earth and Adam, the first man. Also on this date, according to

Muslim women praying

Muslims, Noah left the ark after the flood and Allah saved Moses from the Pharaoh. Muslims also believe that this is the date that Allah will judge the people.

Islamic Life Cycle

Muslims have no special ceremony to initiate children into the Muslim community because they believe that the newborn is already a Muslim. On the day of birth the father whispers the *adan,* or call to prayer, into the baby's ears so that the first thing the infant hears is "Allah is great." In some Islamic countries, seven days after the baby's birth he or she is taken to the mosque. A ceremony takes place in which the imam shaves the baby's head. The hair is weighed and a monetary amount equivalent to the weight of the hair is given to those in need. Parents bring their children up to be Muslims, but at adolescence they are expected to make their own decisions with regard to the Islamic faith.

An Islamic wedding generally takes place either in a mosque or a home. An imam is not required to officiate though at least two witnesses must be present. The wedding ceremony has no specific ritual. The family decides what the ceremony will entail. It is common to have readings from the Qur'an in which marriage and family are the themes. Part of the ceremony does entail responding to the question of whether the other is acceptable.

The groom is also required to give something of value to his bride. It is hers to keep no matter what the future of the marriage holds.

As all of life is Islam, at the point of death it is desirable for a Muslim to have the *Shahadah* be the last words on his or her lips. At death, the body is positioned in a coffin and taken to a mosque or cemetery where it is placed before an imam who faces Mecca. As the coffin passes those gathered, they stand out of respect. There are no gravesite monuments. As the body is lowered, prayers are shared in the hope that the deceased will live forever in eternity.

SECTION 4 SUMMARY

❖ Ramadan is a one-month observance of fasting for Muslims. It is also one of the Five Pillars of Islam.

❖ The two great feasts of Islam are Eid al-Adah and Eid al-Fitr. Eid al-Adah commemorates the end of Ramadan. Eid al-Fitr remembers Abraham's willingness to sacrifice his son.

❖ Mawlid al-Nabi observes the birthday of Muhammad, but not all Muslims celebrate this day out of deference to Allah.

❖ Ashura is a festival of renewal, held in Muharram, the first month of the Islamic calendar.

SECTION 4 REVIEW QUESTIONS

1. Explain the difference between the Jewish calendar, the Christian calendar, and the Islamic calendar.

2. What is Ramadan? How is it observed?

3. Why do some Muslims not celebrate Mawlid al-Nabi?

4. What happened on Ashura?

Who Is My Neighbor?

ISLAM IN AMERICA

In El Cerrito, California, Shahed Amanullah knows it's time to pray not by a muezzin's call from a mosque minaret, but because his PowerMac has chimed. A verse from the Qur'an hangs by his futon. Near the bookcases—lined with copies of *Wired* magazine and Jack Kerouac novels—lies a red Arabian prayer rug. There's a plastic compass sewn into the carpet, its needle pointing toward Mecca. At the programmed call, Amanullah begins his prayers, the same as those recited across the globe—from the Gaza Strip to Samarkand.

In his goatee and beret, 30-year-old Amanullah wouldn't remind anyone of Saddam Hussein or a member of Hizbullah, the sort of Muslims who make headlines. He has never built a biological weapon, issued a fatwa or burned Uncle Sam in effigy. "You think Muslim, you think Saddam Hussein, you think ayatollah," says one Muslim-American twenty something.

Not after meeting Amanullah. A native Californian, Amanullah grew up running track, listening to Nirvana, and reading the Qur'an. He is a member of a burgeoning subculture: young Islamic America. The children of the prosperous Muslim immigrants of the '60s and '70s are coming of age, and with them arrives a new culture that is a blend of Muslim and American institutions.

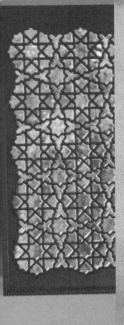

Online and on campus, in suburban mosques and summer camps, young American Muslims are challenging their neighbors' perceptions of Islam as a foreign faith and of Muslims as fiery fundamentalists or bomb-lobbing terrorists. That image problem may be this generation's biggest challenge in the New World. Within hours of the Oklahoma City bombing in 1995, Muslims were prime suspects. "You'll die," was one of the printable messages left on mosque answering machines around the country.

America's Muslims are not only taking on stereotypes, they're taking on the status quo. As it was for Christians and Jews before them, America is a laboratory for a re-examination of their faith. America's Muslim community is a quilt of cultures: about 25 percent are of South Asian descent, Arabs represent another 12 percent, and nearly half are converts, primarily African-Americans. U.S. society allows them to strip away the cultural influences and superstitions that have crept into Islam during the past 1,400 years. By going back to the basic texts they're rediscovering an Islam founded on tolerance, social justice, and human rights. Some six million strong, America's Muslim population will outnumber Jews by 2010, making it the nation's second-largest faith after Christianity. Richer than most Muslim communities, literate and natives of the world's sole superpower, America's Muslims are intent on exporting their modern Islam. From the Mideast to central Asia, they'd like to influence debate on everything from free trade to gender politics.

At home, it is a generation committed to maintaining its Islamic heritage while finding a niche in the New World. America's 1,500-odd mosques are spread from Alaska to Florida. Muslims pray daily in State Department hallways, in white shoe corporate law firms and in empty boardrooms at Silicon Valley companies like Oracle and Adapted. In 1997 Muslim organizations made life miserable for Nike when the company marketed a shoe with a design resembling the name of Allah in Arabic. After protests, Nike discontinued the style and started sensitivity training for employees. In Washington, the American Muslim Council lobbies on issues from school prayer to the Mideast peace process. "We're learning to use our clout," says Farhan Memon, a Muslim and 27-year-old partner in Yack!, a multimillion-dollar Internet publishing business.

Clout doesn't come without confidence, says Manal Omar, a Muslim woman raised in South Carolina. Tall and leather-jacketed, with a trace of Southern drawl, she explodes any stock image of the crushed and silent Muslim woman. In high school, she played basketball in hijab—the Muslim woman's head covering ("my coach nearly freaked"); at college, she won national public-speaking prizes. Friends thought she should become a stand-up comic. Instead Omar went into refugee relief. In her off hours, she's working on a series of books for Muslim-American teenagers—"a sort of Islamic 'Sweet Valley High,'" she says.

From *Newsweek* (March 16, 1998) © 1998, *Newsweek* Inc. Reprinted by permission.

What ways have you witnessed stereotyping of Muslims?

Conclusion

Though Muslims believe Islam was present from the beginning of time, it did not come to the fore until the seventh century CE at the time of Muhammad, making it in this sense one of the world's youngest religions. It is also now the second largest religion in the world. Islam is marked by zealousness for the will of Allah. Some of the attraction to Islam is its seeming clarity in what is expected. There are the duties of the Five Pillars of Islam as well as the Qur'an and Hadith as guides for fulfilling life's duties. However, placing Islam in specific cultural contexts makes performing the duties of a Muslim difficult. If one does not live in a predominantly Muslim country the structures that support Islamic life are not present and Muslims have to look elsewhere for support.

Muslims can find support in each other, in the ummah, a term that describes Muslim community. The egalitarianism of the ummah attracts a number of people to Islam. A person is a leader in the Islamic community through his or her knowledge of Islam, not because of an ordained leadership.

Through the centuries Muslims have made tremendous contributions to western civilization. In fact, some scholars claim that the European Renaissance would not have happened if it had not been for the contributions of Muslims, especially those of medieval Spain. Islam stands for the equality of all members. In fact, during the hajj at Mecca, the first thing a pilgrim is to do is to change the clothes he or she came with for a simple white robe. All Muslims are equal before Allah. And all honor is due to Allah and Allah alone.

CHAPTER 4 IN BRIEF

❖ The history of Islam begins with a rapid expansion in all directions from its beginnings in Mecca under the inspiration of Muhammad.

❖ Muhammad is the final messenger of God, the Seal of the Prophets.

❖ The Islamic creed has seven major beliefs in three categories. Belief in the oneness of God is central in Islam. Every other idea or action must center on this belief.

❖ Two other categories of Islamic belief center on prophethood and life after death.

❖ Muslims express their beliefs through the duties of the Five Pillars of Islam.

❖ The Qur'an is the infallible sacred scripture of Islam. While Hadith is extremely important to Muslims, it is not infallible. Muslims also read and respect the Torah, psalms, and gospels.

❖ Attention to Allah and caring for others are the most important duties of a Muslim.

❖ The ummah is the name of the universal Islamic community.

❖ The two major Islamic festivals are Eid al-Fitr and Eid al-Adah. Ramadan is a one-month period of fasting for Muslims.

❖ Mecca is the most important place for Muslims. Medina and Jerusalem are two other holy places.

CHAPTER 4 REVIEW QUESTIONS

1. Briefly outline the life of Muhammad.

2. Why is Muhammad not considered the "founder" of Islam?

3. Explain how the Qur'an is organized.

4. What types of writings can be found in the Qur'an?

5. Summarize the historical development of the Nation of Islam.

6. What are the seven beliefs found in the Islamic creed?

7. Name the Five Pillars of Islam and the duties associated with each.

8. Why is it really not proper to say that a person is a "convert" to Islam?

9. When did the Islamic calendar begin? Why do Islamic festivals fall on different dates each year?

10. What is required of a Muslim during Ramadan?

11. What are the prominent features of a mosque?

12. Explain why Mecca is the most sacred city for Muslims.

RESEARCH AND ACTIVITIES

1. Research what happens on a hajj.

2. Research and write an essay on one of the following topics:

The difficulties in being a practicing Muslim in the United States.

The similarities between Islam, Judaism, and Christianity.

The contributions of the Nation of Islam to the life of African-Americans.

Islam in Spain before 1492.

The Palestinian-Israeli conflict over the city of Jerusalem.

3. Give a class report about at least one of the following:
Islamic architecture
Islamic geometric art
Islamic calligraphy

4. Prepare an interview of a Muslim teenager, asking him or her to share the attractiveness of Islamic life as well as the difficulties of being a Muslim teen in western society.

SELECTED VOCABULARY

Abu Bakr	Mawlid al-Nabi
Abraham	Mecca
adan	Medina
Ali	minaret
Allah	mosque
Ashura	muezzin
Ayatollah Khomeni	Muhammad
caliph	Muslim
caliphate	Nation of Islam
Eid al-Adah	Ottomans
Eid al-Fitr	Qur'an
Elijah Muhammad	Ramadan
Hadith	Sa'y
hafiz	Shahadah
hajj	shari'ah
hijab	Shi'ite
hijrah	Sunni
imam	surah
Islamic creed	Umar
Istanbul	ummah
jinn	Uthman
Jum'ah	W. D. Fard
Ka'bah	wudu
Louis Farrakhan	
Malcolm X	

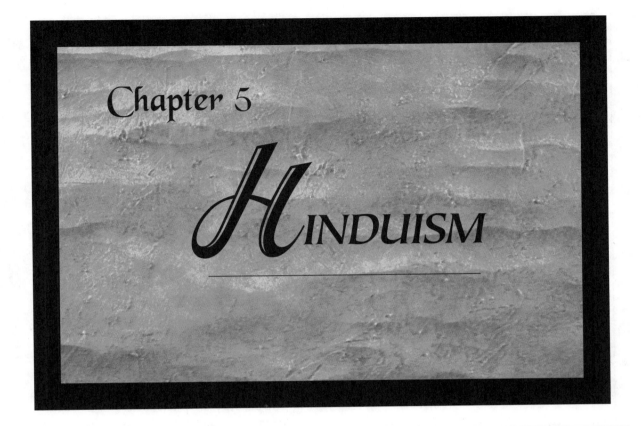

Chapter 5

HINDUISM

 vetaketu has just returned from twelve years of studying with the learned men of his religious tradition. Though he has "head knowledge," Svetaketu lacks knowledge of the heart. His father recognizes this and uses the lessons of a nyagrodha tree to show him that in the larger scheme of life, his personal importance is only equal to other things created.

The following is one of the most quoted passages of Hindu scripture:

> When Svetaketu was twelve years old he was sent to a teacher, with whom he studied until he was twenty-four. After learning all the Vedas,[1] he returned home full of conceit in the belief that he was consummately well educated, and very censorious.

His father said to him, "Svetaketu, my child, you who are so full of your learning and so censorious, have you asked for that knowledge by which we hear the unhearable, by which we perceive what cannot be perceived, and know what cannot be known?"

"What is that knowledge, sir?" asked Svetaketu.

His father replied, "As by knowing one lump of clay all that is made of clay is known, the difference being only in name, but the truth being that all is clay—so, my child, is that knowledge, knowing which we know all."

"But surely these venerable teachers of mine are ignorant of this knowledge; for if they possessed it they would have imparted it to me. Do you, sir, therefore, give me that knowledge, knowing which we know all."

"So be it," said the father. "Bring me a fruit of the nyagrodha tree."

"Here is one, sir."

"Break it."

"It is broken, sir."

"What do you see there?"

"Some seeds, sir, exceedingly small."

"Break one of these."

"It is broken, sir."

"What do you see there?"

"Nothing at all."

The father said, "My son, that subtle essence which you do not perceive there—in that very essence stands the being of the huge nyagrodha tree. In that which is the subtle essence all that exists has its self. That is the True, that is the Self, and thou, Svetaketu, art That."

(*Chandogya Upanishad*)

Svetaketu's father taught him that there is no distinction between him and all other creation. All share in the same essence. Though Svetaketu could not perceive the tree from nothing, it is possible to intuit such knowledge. Svetaketu's father hoped his son could understand his oneness in the nothing from which all things flow. This is a major lesson gleaned from Hinduism, one of the oldest of the major world religions.

Give an example of when you thought you knew everything until intuition and experience taught you otherwise. How did you respond to your new insight?

The origins of Hinduism are from around 1500 BCE and the Indus Valley region of the subcontinent of India. The word *Hindu* comes from the Sanskrit word "sindhu" meaning "river" (specifically the Indus River in northwest India). Hindu originally referred to people living in the Indus Valley region. Later it referred to all the religious beliefs and practices of the people of India. Though Hinduism moved beyond the Indian subcontinent in the nineteenth century, over 95 percent of the world's Hindus still live in India.

Hinduism did not begin with a founder nor a particular event that marked its beginning. Rather, Hinduism is a synthesis of many factors including the Vedic religion of the Indo-Aryans, the brahminical sacrificial rituals called *bhakti* (from a Sanskrit word meaning "devotion"), and the asceticism and meditation of, among others, the Jains and Buddhists.

Hindus accept the premises or parts of several religions. Yet Hindus hold that no one religion can possibly claim knowledge of the absolute truth. To Hindus, the ultimate reality that other religions may name as God is unknowable. In fact Hinduism encourages its believers to imagine a god that is best for them, even if that god comes from another religion. Though Hinduism is mostly confined to India, its many practices and loosely held beliefs merit study because of Hinduism's long history, the focus of Section I.

BCE

| 1500 | Aryans invade India |
| 550 | Foundations of Buddhism and Jainism |

CE

300	Classical Period of Hinduism begins
1175	Muslims begin rule of northern part of India
1446	Hindu poet Kabir born
1459	Nanak, founder of Sikhism, born
1818	Beginning of British rule in India
1860	Mohandas Gandhi born
1920	Self Realization Movement
1947	Indian independence from Britain; Pakistan established as Muslim country
1960s	Transcendental Meditation Movement
1965	Krishna Consciousness Movement

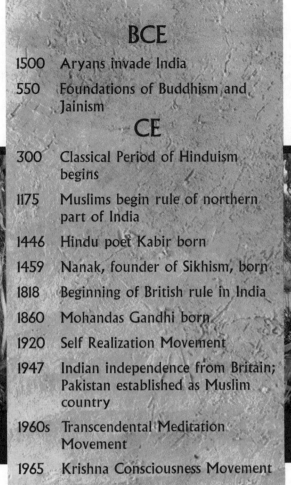

ground, become roots, and sprout new trunks alongside the old. In an old banyan tree it becomes difficult to distinguish what is the original trunk. So too, religions in India have expanded and changed so much that what we now call Hinduism does not have a linear line to a beginning.

Banyan tree

I. A BRIEF HISTORY OF HINDUISM

Besides sharing no doctrinal statements, Hinduism has no founder and no set date for its beginnings. Rather than speak about how Hinduism *began*, it is more correct to speak about how Hinduism *emerged* as a religion. What is now called "Hinduism" has continually grown and expanded over hundreds of centuries. The banyan tree is often used as an analogy to explain Hinduism to non-Hindus. A banyan tree does not only have branches that grow up. Some of its branches grow down into the

How might the banyan tree be symbolic of some aspect of your own life?

The Indus Valley Period
(3000-1500 BCE)

Before the Aryans[2] invaded northwest India in about 1500 BCE there was a thriving civilization in the Indus Valley and the area of the Punjab. It is likely that later Hinduism contains elements of this ancient civilization. Those who settled in India came to be known as Indo-Aryans. They brought with them what scholars tend to call Vedic[3] religion because of their Vedic hymns. Eventually Vedic hymns were compiled into a written text and became sacred scripture for

Hindus. Some Vedic gods seem to be precursors to Hindu gods. Vedic priests known as *brahmins*[4] performed ritual sacrifices to Vedic deities that were later absorbed into Hinduism.

The Brahmanical Period

(1500-300 BCE)

Indo-Aryans intermarried with the indigenous population and migrated south to the Ganges River area where they created an even more elaborate civilization by 900 BCE. During this period the ritual sacrifices of the brahmins were so elaborate and expensive that only the rich could afford them. Various "schools" of Brahmins began to specialize in certain types of sacrifices. Home ritual sacrifices also emerged. As the rituals became more complex, brahmins found it important to compose commentaries on the school rituals which became known as the *Brahmanas*. Eventually many of these commentaries, other reflections of the brahmins, and the Vedas were included in the *shruti*, the oldest of the Hindu scriptures.

Reaction to Brahminism

(550 BCE-300 CE)

From about 550 BCE to 300 CE the mediating role of the brahmin decreased as *gurus*[5] emerged, training disciples in *bhakti*, personal devotion to the gods. Two Hindu gods, Shiva and Vishnu, gained great prominence during this time. In addition, there was a rise in ascetical practices.

Classical Period

(300—1200 CE)

The Classical Period is called such because it is the period in which Hinduism becomes recognized as a religion. Ritual forms changed dramatically

Jainism

Mahavira founded Jainism in the sixth century BCE. Born a Hindu, Mahavira ("the Great Hero") reacted against some of the practices of Hinduism including the elaborate sacrificial rituals. Jainism contains some elements from both Hinduism and Buddhism.

Jains are most noted for the establishment of *ahimsa*, or non-violence, an attitude that influenced many other Hindus, including Mahatma Gandhi in the twentieth century. Jains practice non-violence or non-injury to the point that they will eat only those things that will not kill plants or animals. Thus, they are vegetarians whose diet consists mostly of milk, fruit, and nuts.

Worldwide, Jains number less than ten million members. Most Jains reside in India with others scattered in the United States and Canada, Europe, Africa, and East Asia.

during this period. There was the establishment of Hindu temples and the continual growth of home-based rituals. Sanskrit, the liturgical and scriptural language of Hinduism that only a few understood, gave way to the vernacular. Though the shruti scripture which contained the Vedas became the authoritative scripture believed to be written by the divine, another body of literature that the populace found more appealing emerged. Known as *smriti*[6] it includes two great epics, the *Mahabharata* (which includes the "Bhagavad Gita") and the *Ramayana*, which deals with the struggle between good and evil.

The Hindu-Muslim Period (1200-Present)

Muslim traders reached the borders of India at the end of the seventh century. By 1021 Muslims had conquered the northwest section of India. Throughout the twelfth and thirteenth centuries Muslims had moved into the northern and central sections of India, administrating the region from Delhi. Some Muslim rulers were tolerant of Hinduism, while others took to destroying Hindu temples and statues. The Hindu poet Kabir (1440-1518) was influenced by Islamic mysticism, while his disciple Nanak (1459-1539) began the new religion *Sikhism*, a synthesis of Hinduism and Islam. The ruler Akbar (1556-1605) attempted to syncretize the religions of India, even holding high level discussions on the topic, but was unsuccessful. After Akbar, Muslim toleration for Hinduism deteriorated. In fact, compromise on either side was negligible. For the most part, Hindus during this period established practices that clearly distinguished them from Muslims. In 1947 Muslims broke away from India and established Pakistan as a separate Muslim country. In the time since there have been many armed conflicts between Muslims of Pakistan and Hindus of India.

What do you see as a primary hindrance to interreligious dialogue?

Though Christians were on Indian soil from the first century CE on, it was not until the sixteenth century that a steady flow of Christian missionaries came to India. The influence of Christianity on Hinduism can be seen in the rise of Hindu reformers of the nineteenth century. Sri Ramakrishna (1836-1886) began the *Ramakrishna* movement with the belief that all religions are paths to God. Mohandas Gandhi (1869-1948), more popularly known as Mahatma ("Great Soul") Gandhi, advocated the equality of all religions, *ahimsa* (non-violence), and *satyagraha* (passive resistance) to British rule.

SATYAGRAHA

Satyagraha is an Indian term that means "the force of truth." Mahatma Gandhi employed the term and made it famous as the rationale for his various strikes, demonstrations, and efforts to arbitrate grievances between the British and Indian communities. Coupled with Gandhi's dedication to nonviolence and his conviction that God was the ultimate foundation of all truth, satyagraha undergirded the remarkable discipline of Gandhi's followers. Those who practiced satyagraha often met with brutal violence themselves, but Gandhi consoled them that the truth of their cause one day would bring them justice. "So satyagraha stands in the modern world as a challenging proposition: If one nonviolently demonstrates the truth of one's situation, the justice of one's cause, one will preserve one's own integrity and will shame or encourage one's adversaries into hearing their own better voices of conscience."

Quoted from *Eastern Ways to the Center: An Introduction to the Religions of Asia*, second edition, by Denise Lardner Carmody and John Tully Carmody (Belmont, CA: Wadsworth Publishing Company, 1992)

Is there a cause in which you would be willing to nonviolently demonstrate the truth of your situation, the justice of the cause?

Also occurring in the twentieth century has been the exportation of Hinduism outside of India. For example, the British rock group the Beatles brought Maharishi Mahesh Yogi and his advocation of Transcendental Meditation to the world's attention. In Transcendental Meditation, a person is given a mantra[7] on which to meditate daily. A. C. Bhaktivedanta Prabhupada (1896-1977) founded the International Society of Krishna Consciousness in 1965. More popularly known as the *Hare Krishnas* because of their continual "Hare Krishna" chant, devotees could be commonly seen wearing saffron robes in airports, on street corners, and on college campuses in the 1960s and 70s.

SECTION 1 SUMMARY

✤ Hinduism is a major world religion that has no clear beginning or founder. Rather, it has expanded from various religions on the subcontinent of India.

✤ The Vedic religion of the Aryans who invaded northwest India around 1500 BCE left a lasting legacy of scriptures and gods, the forerunners of Hinduism.

✤ Home sacrificial rituals increased as the rituals of the brahmins grew in elaboration and expense.

✤ The Classical Period (300-1200 CE) was the first time Hinduism was recognized as a religion.

✤ Muslim rule influenced Hinduism, but not to the point of compromise. In 1947 a Muslim nation, Pakistan, was formed from India.

✤ During the Modern Period Hinduism has expanded due to various unique movements.

SECTION 1 REVIEW QUESTIONS

1. What was the Aryan influence on the origins of Hinduism?

2. Who were brahmins and what was their main function?

3. What makes up the shruti?

4. Describe Jainism.

5. Why are the years 300 to 1200 CE known as the Classical Period of Hinduism?

6. What happened when the Muslims came to India?

7. What are some of the beliefs major Hindu figures of the nineteenth and twentieth centuries advocated?

8. What is one movement of Hinduism that contributed to its expansion outside of India?

II. BELIEFS AND ACTIONS

Hindus have no set statements of doctrine that they must believe. Yet there are some things that almost all Hindus accept as true. Included in these are beliefs about gods and goddesses, the cycle of rebirth, and the sacredness of all life. These areas are explained in more detail in this section.

Deities

Ask a Hindu how many gods there are in Hinduism and the answer is likely to be 330 million. This answer is meant to say that there are so many gods and goddesses in Hinduism that they cannot be counted. Yet most Hindus also hold that all the gods and goddesses are the myriad images of the one Ultimate Reality or Absolute Reality,[8] also called

Shiva, with Vishnu and Brahma

Hindu deity

Brahman.[9] While the gods and goddesses have attributes (for the most part human attributes) Brahman has no attributes. Brahman is transcendent,[10] beyond reach. The five senses combined cannot grasp Brahman. The mind, even that of a genius, falls short of fathoming Brahman. Brahman is the life-force of the universe, permeating it with an all-pervading presence. All things in the material and immaterial world are of one essence and that essence is Brahman.

Brahman is manifested in creation as the many Hindu gods and goddesses. Three primary forms of Brahman symbolize the cycle of life: Brahma is the Creator god, Vishnu is the Preserving god, and Shiva is the Destroying god. These and other gods and goddesses are worshipped as forms of Ultimate Reality or Absolute Reality, Brahman. So too, *avatars* are forms of Ultimate Reality. An avatar is the incarnation of a god or goddess who

has descended from the heavenly world to earth to rid the world of evil.

The two most popular avatars are those of the god Vishnu named Krishna and Rama. Interestingly, Krishna himself is considered a god. Also, Gautama the Buddha, the founder of Buddhism, is also considered an avatar of Vishnu.

Name three symbols you imagine representing the cycle of life.

Hindus also believe that the Ultimate Reality or Absolute Reality is identical to the innermost soul, the real self, of each person. The name for this "real self" is *atman*. The body, mind, and emotions of a person are not considered a person's real self. These are only illusions or *maya*. Hindus strive for release from maya in order to achieve union with Brahman, that is, atman. Brahman and atman are interchangeable.

Female Goddesses

Ultimate Reality also assumes female forms.

Saraswati is the goddess of learning, literature, and music and is often linked with Brahma.

Lakshmi is goddess of prosperity, good fortune, and beauty, and is often associated with Vishnu.

Parvati, the Divine Mother, often represents the goddess Devi, the Great Goddess, when she is presented in one of her milder forms. She is often connected with Shiva. However, she can be represented with a wilder side as Durga, riding on the back of a tiger, or as Kali, the black figure who is deliverer of justice.

Hindu goddess

Female goddess painted on watertower in Banaras, India

Cycle of Rebirth

For Hindus, life is cyclical, not linear. Bodies in the heavens are round. Every person is on a cycle determined by *karma*,[11] the moral law of cause and effect. Under karma, who one is and how one now acts is determined by deeds in the person's previous lives. In addition, how one acts now determines one's fate for the future. Death and rebirth are part of the cycle known as *samsara*,[12] or the transmigration of souls. In this cycle a soul passes from one body to another, for example, from a human body to an animal or to an insect. Though the physical body dies, the eternal atman lives on in another body. Good actions merit migration to a better situation in the next life, while bad actions merit migration to a worse situation. Hindus believe that there is liberation, *moksha*,[13] from this endless cycle of rebirth. Moksha is achieved by removing the karmic residue that has accumulated throughout countless deaths and rebirths. The three practices or "disciplines" that a person can choose to erode the negative karmic effects and move toward liberation are knowledge, good deeds, and devotion. These disciplines are called *yoga*.[14]

What questions do you have about the transmigration of souls?

Three Paths to Liberation

Yoga is a type of training designed to discipline the entire human person—body, mind, and spirit. The goal of yoga for Hindus is to make the identity between the atman and Brahman a reality, for there moksha or liberation is complete. The three paths to moksha are the Path of Action, the Path of Knowledge, and the Path of Devotion.

The Path of Action is *karma yoga* where selfless service to others brings liberation from the endless cycle of rebirth. In this path the devotee resolves that his or her right actions and deeds will be performed not for personal gain, but for the sake of Brahman. Even the person's desire for liberation must be purged, for Brahman is more powerful than the noblest desire.

The Path of Knowledge is known as the *jnana yoga*. There are three steps involved in this path: learning, thinking, and viewing oneself in the third person. Learning is the information the person receives from outside oneself. Thinking is the internal reflection on what one learned. Viewing oneself in the third person is like seeing from God's point of view. Meditation is the most common instrument in jnana yoga. Through meditation a person can see the truth in how he or she is attached to this world.

The Path of Devotion, known as *bhakti yoga*, is the Path followed by most Hindus. A pure, long devotion to Brahman can bring liberation. Devotees of bhakti yoga perceive that Brahman is more immanent than transcendent.

Of the paths to liberation mentioned above, which is most appealing to you? What areas of your life or societal life do you see a need for liberation?

The Sacredness of Life

Hindus believe Brahman is in all things—humans, plants, animals, and insects. With Ultimate Reality present in all things, all things are sacred. *Ahimsa* is the name that describes the desire not to harm any form of life. Ahimsa is the basis for the Hindu's belief in nonviolent means as a solution to problems. It is because of ahimsa that most Hindus are vegetarians and that the cow is considered sacred. Mohandas Gandhi had his own form of ahimsa he called *satyagraha*, where he and his followers practiced passive resistance toward British attacks when trying to free India from British rule.

Community

Though Hindus have very diverse views of what they believe, the typical actions of Hindus are more uniform. There are four stages of life laid out for typical Hindu males. Hindus also believe there are four major purposes for living, with the fourth being moksha. Of course, all discussions on Hindu community, stages of life, and purposes for living must be understood in light of the caste system.

Caste System

While Hindus are very tolerant of individual beliefs, they are less tolerant of straying from one's social group in Hindu society. These groups are commonly known as *castes*. The Aryans first introduced a three-fold caste system into India, and later a fourth caste was added. The castes are related to karma and samsara in that caste is dependent upon actions in a previous life. The castes are ranked from highest to lowest:

Brahmins are priests who make up the highest caste. They are from families who are considered the purest, wisest, and most learned.

Kshatriyas are warriors. They help protect and rule society.

Women carrying sacred cow dung on their heads

© Galyn C. Hammond

The cow is known as the god Matha and is a symbol of motherhood, life and abundance. There are over two million cows in India and each is to be treated with reverence.

© Galyn C. Hammond

Vaishya, the third level, are made up of those families who are farmers and merchants.

Shudra are servants, the lowest in the caste system. Shudra serve those in other levels of castes. Unlike the other three castes, Shudra are not permitted to study scripture.

Besides these four levels of caste, there is a fifth group that is deemed so low it is not even part of the caste system. These are the *asprishya* or "untouchables." They are the families that are considered defiled because they have the degrading jobs in society, such as cleaning up human waste. In addition, to be an untouchable means that actions in one's previous lives were, in some way, vile. As part of his nationalistic movement in the twentieth century, Mohandas Gandhi worked to uplift the untouchables from their degrading status in society.

Even though discrimination against the lowest castes is illegal in India today, the caste system still has a strong hold on Hindu society. A person is bound to the caste he or she was born into until death. The person must dutifully submit to all requirements (clothing, habits, religious practices) defined for that caste.

Though how one lives differs widely depending on the caste, the reasons for living are the same. Hindus subscribed to three major purposes for living until the time of the Buddha, when moksha was added as a fourth purpose. The purposes are:

1. *Dharma*—a person's duties in life, especially those related to social obligations within one's caste;

2. *Artha*—the pursuit of both material and political wealth;

3. *Kama*—the pursuit of artistic, recreational, and sensual pleasure;

4. *Moksha*—the pursuit of liberation from the cycle of rebirth through actions, thoughts, and devotions.

What group stratifications similar to the Hindu caste system can you find in American society or other institutions? How do the "castes" affect how a person practices his or her religion?

The Stages of Life

The four stages of life (called *ashramas*) are general patterns for Hindu males to follow, though most progress through only the first two stages. Men are to fulfill their obligations to family and society before pursuing these ascetic disciplines. Traditionally, women are to be daughters, wives, and mothers and live under the protection of a man. The stages for males are:

Brahmancarin—the student learns about the Hindu tradition, usually at the feet of a guru.

Grihastha—the stage of the householder, when he marries, raises a family, and contributes to society.

Vanaprastha—literally, the "forest dweller." This is the stage when a man begins to move away from ordinary life to life as a hermit in order to pursue more other-worldly desires.

Sannyasin—a spiritual pilgrim who renounces absolutely everything in this world for the purpose of pursuing moksha. In this stage the man abandons family and even family name, and lives as if with no memory of his previous life.

What would it be like to process through these four stages from your own religious tradition?

Women from India

© Anthony Dalton

© Anthony Dalton

Women in Modern Hinduism

In the nineteenth and twentieth centuries English-style education prepared the ground for women's participation in India's national movement. Women from various backgrounds (urban and village) responded enthusiastically to Gandhi's call to participate in the national struggle for freedom. They organized marches and political demonstrations, boycotted foreign goods, and gave generously of their time and energy.

Hindu woman

Although Gandhi was using traditional categories to encourage women to take part in the national movement, it had important implications. It called for the redefinition of roles within the family. Men and women became equal partners in a common cause. Women were able to come out in the open and thus break the barriers of caste and sex.

Since then women have played a significant role in Gandhi's *ashrams*[15] and in the secular sphere. Women availed themselves of educational opportunities and qualified for professions such as law, medicine, teaching, social work, and the like. There are colleges exclusively for women in Indian towns and cities, with a mostly female teaching staff. Men hardly figure in women's institutions except in non-professional roles, such as laboratory technicians, porters, or caretakers.

Adapted from *Women in Religion*, edited by Jean Holm with John Bowker (New York: Pinter Press, 1994)

Scripture

Of the two categories of sacred scriptures introduced earlier, shruti are the more sacred. They have been revealed to ancient seers by the gods and not one syllable is to be changed. Shruti means "that which has been heard." Smriti, the second category of scriptures, is a word that means "that which is to be remembered." Though less authoritative, the smriti texts contain Hindu traditions originally passed down orally through the ages and are more popularly read. Examples from each category follow.

Shruti Scriptures

The earliest scriptures—the *Vedas*—are from the Aryan era. The main form of worship for Aryans was a fire sacrifice to the gods where the priests chanted hymns known as Vedas. Only the priests knew and chanted these hymns from memory. The Vedas were considered "sacred knowledge" that was not to be passed on to anyone but other priests. There are four Vedas. The *Rig Veda* is the oldest and most sacred. The Rig Veda is a collection of more than one thousand hymns to various gods composed in Sanskrit about 1300 BCE.

Brahmanas are a second type of shruti scriptures. The Brahmanas are a collection of commentaries where myths are used to explain the meaning and purpose of the rituals.

The *Upanishads* are writings concerned with the nature of human awareness and the mystical relationship between Brahman and atman. Upanishad means "to sit down beside;" these stories were often shared in a dialogue between guru and student. The opening story about Svetaketu is from the *Chandogya Upanishad*. Svetaketu's father is instructing his son on matters that cannot be seen, heard, or thought. It continues in this way with his father saying:

"Place this salt in water, and in the morning come to me." He did exactly so, and he said to him, "The salt that you put in the water last night, bring it hither." But while he grasped for it he could not find it, since it had completely dissolved.

"Take a sip from the edge of it. What is there?"

"Salt."

"Take a sip from the middle. What is there?"

"Salt."

"Take a sip from the far edge. What is there?"

"Salt."

"Set it aside and come to me." And [the boy] did exactly that, [saying] "It is always the same."

He said to him, "Being is indeed truly here, dear boy, but you do not perceive it here.

"That which is the finest essence, the whole universe has that as its soul. That is Reality, that is the Self, that thou art, Svetaketu." (*Chandogya Upanishad* 6.13:1-3)

What does this passage teach about Brahman?

Smriti Scriptures

The *Mahabharata* is a Hindu epic poem with over 200,000 verses. The Mahabharata is the story of the war between two families over inheritance. Krishna, an avatar of Vishnu, supports the righteous family. Within the Mahabharata is the *Bhagavad Gita*, the most popular of Hindu scriptures and the best known Hindu scripture outside Hinduism. The *Bhagavad Gita* is the story of Arjuna, one of the brothers in the righteous family, who is caught between his obligation to protect his family from the wicked one and his dedication to nonviolence. He debates this dilemma with his charioteer, who turns out to be Krishna, that is, Brahman. The message of this epic is that for one who desires full union with Brahman, this union can happen without escaping the world:

> But if a man will worship me, and meditate upon me with an undistracted mind, devoting every moment to me, I shall supply all his needs, and protect his possessions from loss. Even those who worship other deities, and sacrifice to them with faith in their hearts, are really worshipping me, though with a mistaken approach. For I am the only enjoyer and the only God of all sacrifices. Nevertheless, such men must return to life on earth, because they do not recognize me in my true nature. (*Bhagavad-Gita* 30-32)

The second of the great Hindu epics is the *Ramayana*. This epic is about Prince Rama who is forced into exile with his wife and brother. The evil Ravana kidnaps his wife and Rama goes on a long journey to find her and bring her home. After he rescues her, the three return to their kingdom where Prince Rama becomes king.

The *Puranas* are a collection of stories about the three great gods of Hinduism—Brahma, Vishnu, and Shiva. Further, the Puranas contain stories and myths about the universe.

SECTION 2 SUMMARY

✤ Hindus believe in literally millions of gods and goddesses. These gods are merely images of the one Ultimate Reality known as Brahman.

✤ The Ultimate Reality is interchangeable with atman, a person's innermost self.

✤ Every human person is on a cyclical life pattern determined by karma.

Liberation from the life cycle is known as moksha. The three paths to liberation from rebirth are action, knowledge, and devotion.

✤ Hindus are born into one of four caste systems, each of which have hundreds of subcastes.

✤ Ideally, male Hindus in the first three castes progress through four stages of life, but in reality, most progress through only two. In the third and fourth stages Hindu males move from the ordinary life to the ascetic life. Traditionally Hindu women are called to be daughters, wives, and mothers.

✤ Hindus are called upon to pursue four goals in life, with the fourth being moksha.

✤ Hindu scriptures are divided into two main categories, shruti and smriti. Shruti texts are the authoritative, revealed texts of Hindus, though most Hindus are more familiar with the popular smriti texts.

SECTION 2 REVIEW QUESTIONS

1. What is meant by Brahman? How is Brahman linked to atman?

2. What are the three primary forms of Brahman?

3. Describe the Hindu cycle of rebirth related to the three paths of liberation.

4. Name and describe each of the four Hindu castes. Also define the "untouchables."

5. Name and describe the four stages of life for a Hindu male.

6. What are the four life goals for a Hindu male in the first three castes?

7. Explain the differences between shruti scripture and smriti scripture.

III. SACRED PLACES

Temples, public shrines, and shrines set up in individual homes are among the sacred places for Hindus. Also, as Brahman is present in all of creation, natural sites like mountains and rivers are also counted as sacred. The Ganges River is considered the most sacred place of all.

Temples

Some villages may be too small to have a temple where a brahmin can perform worship services, but most towns and all major cities of India do have temples. Temples have images of many gods and goddesses, but are dedicated to one god in particular. That special deity is often the god for a caste in that regional area.

Hindus seldom have congregational services at a temple. Though a group may be in attendance, there is still a sense of individuality on the part of the attendees. A brahmin often performs *puja*, the practice of honoring a god or goddess in a worship service with minimum participation by the people. The deity is awakened by bells, bathed, dressed, and offered incense, food, and flowers. There are sometimes special days for the deity when the statue, picture, or other image of the god (called a *murti*) are decorated and processed along the nearby streets.

Dhaka Durga Temple

© Anthony Dalton

Hindu Temple

© Anthony Dalton

An old Hindu temple on the banks of the Sitilakhya River

© Anthony Dalton

Whatever size or however complex, the underlying structure of Hindu temples is simple. There is the outer hall, the temple proper, and the "womb chamber" where the main deity of that particular temple, usually Vishnu, Shiva, or the goddess, resides. In fact, a Hindu temple is the temporary residence of a deity on earth. Each of these three areas have ambulatories so that devotees can circle in a clockwise direction as a sign of veneration.

Home Shrines

Most Hindu families have a shrine or special place in their home in which they perform puja. This place may be as large as a room unto itself or as small as a little table. Whatever the case, the household contains a murti of a god that has special meaning for that family. Flowers or fruit may also be part of the shrine surrounding the murti. The actual puja can be performed individually or collectively. Usually women conduct the home puja.

The home puja involves the welcoming of the god or goddess into the house by calling upon it to dwell within the murti.[16] The murti is also washed and dressed in fine clothes so that it is ready to receive guests. Fruits, flowers, and incense are offered to the murti. There may be prayers recited, hymns sung, and sacred texts read. In return for the offering, it is held that the individual or family receives a blessing from the deity. At the end of puja, those present eat the food that was offered to the deity.

Catholics often place flowers or other tokens around the shrines or statues of Jesus, Mary, and the saints. What do you think is the significance of these offerings?

Honoring Is Called Puja

By Sre Sri Ravi Shankar

Honoring is a sign of divine love. That honoring is called puja. The ceremony of puja imitates what nature is already doing for you. The Divine worships you in so many forms. In puja, you offer everything back to the Divine.

Flowers are offered in puja. The flower is a symbol of love. The Divine has come to you in love through so many forms: mother, father, wife, husband, children, friends. The same love comes to you in the form of the Master to elevate you to the level of divine love, which is also your own nature. Recognizing this flower of love from all sides of life, we offer flowers.

Fruits are offered, because the Divine offers you fruits in due season. You offer grain, because nature provides you food. A candle light and a cool camphor light are offered; in the same way nature continually revolves the sun and moon around you. Incense is offered for fragrance. All the five senses are used in puja, and it is performed with deep feeling. Through puja, we say to God, "Oh whatever you give to me, I give back to you." Puja is honor and gratefulness.

Have you seen children? They have small little pots and dishes.

They sometimes pretend that they make toast or tea. They come to the mom and say, "Now, please have some tea." They serve you. There will be nothing in the cup; it is all in their imagination. They play with you. Whatever you do to them, they also do. They put the doll to sleep. They feed it and bathe it. In the same way, puja is an expression of what the Divine is doing for you. Puja is a mixture of imitation, honor, playfulness and love. It is all these things together, made into a soup.

(Sre Sri Shankar is founder of the WorldWide Art of Living Foundation, Healing Breath Workshops, and Sahaj Samadhi meditation programs.)

Ganges River

Though Hindus are able to frequent shrines and temples more often, the Ganges River is considered the most sacred of all places for Hindus. It is the symbol for life without end. Every twelve years a festival called *Kubach* attracts millions to the Ganges.

The Ganges is considered the premiere place for spiritual healing. Hindus perform ritual bathing in the river, believing the Ganges has the power to wash away the karma that destines one for another life on earth. Many Hindus will request that upon their death their ashes will be sprinkled into the Ganges River, especially near the holy city of Varanasi, also known as Benares. Hundreds of temples line the banks of the Ganges at Varanasi.

Bathing in the Ganges river

SECTION 3 SUMMARY

❖ Mountains, forests, and rivers are sacred spaces for Hindus.

❖ Most homes have a special place or shrine for honoring the deity through a worship service called puja.

❖ Brahmins perform pujas at temples with minimal participation by other worshippers.

❖ The Ganges River is considered the most sacred place for Hindus.

SECTION 3 REVIEW QUESTIONS

1. Why is everything sacred to Hindus?

2. Describe a home puja and its purposes.

3. How does a temple puja differ from a home puja?

4. Why is the Ganges River the most sacred place for Hindus?

IV. SACRED TIME

Hindus use a lunar calendar, but it is one that is more complicated than the Islamic or Jewish lunar calendar. To compensate for the eleven-day difference between the lunar and solar calendars, Hindus make an adjustment of one month, but do not give the additional month its own name. Rather, the added month bears the name of either the previous month or next month. Cumulatively, about seven months are added approximately every nineteen years.

Also, rather than four seasons, the Hindu calendar has six. A simplified look at the Hindu calendar is as follows:

SPRING	
Claitra	(March-April)
Vaishakh	(April-May)
SUMMER	
Jyeshta	(May-June)
Aashaadh	(June-July)
Monsoon Sharaavan	(July-August)
Bhadrapad	(August- September)
AUTUMN	
Ashwin	(September-October)
Kaartik	(October-November)
WINTER	
Margasheersh	(November-December)
Paush	(December-January)
Dewey Maagh	(January-February)
Phalgun	(February-March)

Within the calendar year, Hindus celebrate several festivals. Also, Hindus mark various life cycle events and rites of passages with various celebrations and ceremonies.

Festivals

As Hinduism is a religion of many gods, there are also several Hindu festivals. However, there are few festivals that all Hindus celebrate in common. Descriptions of two of the largest annual festivals follow.

Divali

Divali is the autumn festival of Hindus that celebrates the return of Rama, the seventh avatar of Vishnu, from a fourteen-year exile. Rama's story is told in the epic poem, *Ramayana*. Rama is forced into exile with his wife Sita by his stepmother. While in exile, Sita is abducted. With the help of his brother, Rama rescues Sita and returns to take over the kingdom. Divali is a festival of lights where Hindus decorate their homes with colorful lights and candles, similar to Christmas for many

Christians. Bonfires are lit and images of the demon Ravana are burnt. Lights are symbolic for piercing the darkness of life's miseries. Divali is also known as the "festival of lights."

Holi

Holi is a spring festival of a rather riotous nature that commemorates the love between Krishna and Radha. Often the division between castes is suspended during this time of celebration. Fun-loving pranks are part of this day as a reminder of the fun Krishna had as a boy. Hindus squirt each other with colored liquid or throw red powder on each other during the Holi festival. Another story associated with Holi is that of the demon Holika attempting to kill the infant Krishna. Appearing as a lovely woman, Holika tried to feed Krishna poisoned milk from her breast, but Krishna sucked the blood out of her, exposing the dead Holika as the hideous demon that she was. Hence, the reason for the red colored power or liquid.

Hindu wedding

© Ramanand Mandayam

Life Cycle

Besides the various festivals, Hindus celebrate numerous occasions and rites of passage in the life cycle. These celebrations are called *samskaras*. There are sixteen samskaras. Hindus believe if they are properly observed the person can ward off bad karma and a better rebirth will be gained. The sixteen stages in life are listed below.

Birth

1. *Womb-placing*—This is the rite of conception where the physical union between the husband and wife is consecrated with the intention of bringing into the world a child with an advanced soul.

2. *Male rite*—This is a rite during the third month of pregnancy in which there are prayers for a male child and for good health to mother and child.

3. *Hair parting*—Between the fourth and seventh months of pregnancy the husband combs the wife's hair as a sign of love and support.

4. *Rite of birth*—At birth the father welcomes and blesses the infant and gives the newborn a taste of *ghee* (a clarified butter used in temple lamps) and honey.

Childhood

5. *Name-giving*—This rite welcomes the infant into the Hindu community of the family. It takes place anywhere between three and six weeks after birth. The given name is usually the name of a god or goddess. A person who converts to Hinduism also goes through the name-giving ceremony.

6. *Feeding*—The first time the child eats solid food (usually rice) is marked.

7. *Ear-piercing*—Boys and girls have both ears pierced and gold earrings inserted.

8. *First hair cutting*—This is a rite of passage for boys.

9. *Formal education*—The child marks his or her entry into formal education by writing the first letter of the alphabet in uncooked rice.

Adulthood

10. *Fit or proper season*—For girls, this is a purification after the first menstrual period. There is a home blessing marking their coming-of-age into adulthood.

11. *Beard-shaving*—This home blessing ceremony marks the boy's first beard shaving and maturation into adulthood.

12. *Settlement of aim or word-giving*—This is a betrothal ceremony where the man and woman pledge themselves to each other for marriage. A ring is given and presents are exchanged.

13. *Marriage*—Marriage is an elaborate ceremony that lasts for days. A ceremonial fire is present throughout, the gods are called upon, and vows are exchanged.

Funeral Rite

14. *Preparation of body*—The eldest son usually washes, dresses, and adorns the body with flowers.

15. *Cremation*—The body is laid on a funeral pyre, usually located near a holy river. The fire is set and ghee is poured on the fire. Prayers are recited and people usually stay until the fire is out.

16. *Scattering the ashes*—The ashes are usually scattered over a sacred river near the funeral pyre. The Ganges is the most popular for this ceremony

Name as many life cycle rituals from your culture that you can.

Sikhism

Sikhism is a blending of Hinduism and Islam. There are elements in each of these two religions that can be found in Sikhism. Sikhs would disagree, believing their religion to be unique of itself. Sikhs (a term meaning "learners") believe that God was revealed in a very special way to Guru Nanak in 1459 CE in the Punjab area that is now Pakistan. Nine other gurus believed to be the reincarnation of Nanak succeeded him. The last one, Guru Gobind Singh, died in 1708. The Sikh community and sacred scripture, the *Siri Guru Granth Sahib*, together are considered to be the eleventh and final Guru. When Indian Muslims formed their own homeland of Pakistan in 1947, many Sikhs moved out of the newly formed nation as Muslims moved in. Many Sikhs also have the desire to found and establish their own homeland.

Sikhism is like Islam in that it is a monotheistic religion. As in Hindu belief, God is transcendent but can be realized through nature and through the experience of each person. God is Ultimate Reality, immanent, and eternally real. God is formless, eternal, having no beginning and no end. The *Mool Mantra* is the statement of the Sikh's belief in God:

There is One God.
He Is the Supreme Truth
Is without fear
Is not vindictive
Is Timeless, Eternal
Is not born, so
He does not die to be reborn.
Self-illumined,
By Guru's grace
He is revealed to the human soul.
Truth was in the beginning,
and throughout the ages.
Truth is now and ever will be.

Sikhs also believe in karma, samsara and moksha, similar to Hindus. However, Sikhs reject the belief in the caste system, and hold that God created all people equal, both men and women. They also reject ahimsa and any kind of idol worship.

According to Sikh scriptures, Sikhs are to perform several ascetic practices and to wear or carry with them the following as signs of devotion:

Kesh—unshorn hair, a symbol of dedication to God (men wear a turban)

Kanga—comb, a symbol of cleanliness and purity

Kacha—short pants usually worn under the outer garments, a symbol of chastity and moral living

Kara—a steel bracelet worn on the right hand as a symbol of allegiance to the guru

Kirpan—a short sword, the symbol of an unconquerable spirit

Formal worship takes place in a temple. The service is generally led by a *granthu*,[17] though if one is not available anyone knowledgeable in religious affairs may conduct the service. The service, called *gurdwara*, consists of singing and reading sacred scripture passages.

Most Sikhs in the United States are immigrants from the Punjab area of India. They generally continue their language, customs, and dress from their place of origin. Sikhs born in the United States generally dress in white, and both sexes wear a turban. American Sikhs refer to themselves as the "3HO," the Healthy, Happy, Holy Organization. There are approximately 20 million Sikhs worldwide, with over 500,000 living in the United States.

Hindu Statuary

What is a visible sign of your religion that you would proudly wear in public?

SECTION 4 SUMMARY

❖ Most Hindus use a lunar calendar that marks six seasons of the year rather than four.

❖ The diversity of Hinduism is so great that few festivals are celebrated by all Hindus. Most Hindus do celebrate the festivals of Divali and Holi.

❖ The vast majority of Hindus celebrate life cycle rituals called samskaras, believing that a person can ward off bad karma and assure a better afterlife.

❖ Sikhism is a monotheistic religion that contains elements of both Hinduism and Islam.

SECTION 4 REVIEW QUESTIONS

1. How do Hindus compensate for the different number of days between the solar and lunar calendars?

2. What do the festivals of Divali and Holi celebrate? How are they celebrated?

3. Name and explain at least two of the sixteen stages of the Hindu life cycle.

Who Is My Neighbor?

HINDUISM IN AMERICA

Gopal Khanna laughed at that suggestion that local Minnesotans did not know that the autumn season was time for Divali, a great Hindu celebration.

"We've done a lousy job in reaching out," Khannna said.

More than 10,000 immigrants from India live in Minnesota.

Although many Americans "have mental pictures of people walking on hot coals, which does happen in India," Khanna said, the more typical Indian immigrant here is a University of Minnesota graduate student or—to cite the occupations of some leading Twin Cities Hindus—a heart surgeon, an artist, an engineer, or a banker.

At this time of year, many are homesick. Divali means "garland of lights" and that is what goes up in front of houses in India, much like Christmas lights in the United States. It is a time when "the darkness of misery is replaced by the radiance of innumerable lights."

Hinduism is finding appeal in America, Khanna said.

"Our philosophy represents a very different approach: meditation, yoga, realizing and recognizing an inner self, with an ultimate goal being that of all faiths—communion with the Lord. It seems to have appeal for those who are patient and willing to explore."

Adapted from "Hindus Preparing for 'Fabulous Fun' of the Holiday Divali" by David Peterson (*Minneapolis Star Tribune*, October 22, 1995)

Conclusion

Hinduism is a difficult religion to define because it has no founder, no universal creed, and no widely accepted scriptures. Hindus also name and honor millions of gods. Important concepts of Hinduism are Brahman (the Ultimate Reality), atman (equal with Brahman as the unification with one's real self), and karma (the actions a person does that will have a direct effect on the present life and also on what type of life he or she will have after rebirth).

Hinduism has proved itself to be a religion that has gone through many ups and downs and still lands upright. Though the caste system still has a great influence on Hindu life, the individual *person* remains more important than individual *beliefs*. For this reason, life cycle rituals play a very important role in Hinduism. Most Hindus are not interested in converting other people to Hinduism. Because Brahman has many faces, Hindus believe that other paths people take to attain unity with Brahman are valid.

CHAPTER 5 IN BRIEF

❖ The history of Hinduism shows its continual expansion and absorption from other religious traditions on the subcontinent of India.

❖ Hindus believe in millions of gods, yet each god helps to image the Ultimate Reality known as Brahman.

❖ Karma, samsara, and moksha are mostly universal beliefs within Hinduism.

❖ Hindus are born into four caste systems, each with hundreds of subcastes.

❖ Hindus progress through four stages and are called to pursue four goals.

❖ There are two categories of Hindu scripture, shruti and smriti.

* Besides nature, Hindu sacred spaces include temples, home shrines, and the Ganges River.

* Hindu life cycle rituals are more universal than festival celebrations.

* Most Hindus do celebrate the festivals of Divali and Holi along with life cycle rituals called samskaras.

* Jainism, Buddhism, and Sikhism all derived from Hinduism in some way.

CHAPTER 5 REVIEW QUESTIONS

1. Briefly summarize the main characteristics of each of the five main Hindu historical periods.

2. What do Hindus mean by the Ultimate Reality?

3. Explain the Hindu cycle of rebirth.

4. What are the three main paths to liberation for Hindus? Which of the three paths is the most prevalent among Hindus?

5. How are the caste system and the cycle of rebirth related?

6. Name and explain the four stages of life for Hindu males in the first three castes.

7. Why is the Ganges River so sacred to Hindus?

8. What elements of Hinduism can be found in Sikhism?

RESEARCH AND ACTIVITIES

1. Research and give an oral presentation on one of the following topics:

   The practice of *sati*

   The caste system in India today

   The "untouchables" in India today

   The former Indian prime minister Indira Gandhi

   The role of the Himalayas in Hinduism

   The Self-Realization Fellowship

   The Ramakrishna Missions

   Transcendental Meditation

   The International Society of Krishna Consciousness

   A typical Hindu wedding

   Sacred cows in India

   Sikhism or Jainism in India today

SELECTED VOCABULARY

ahimsa	maya
Akbar	moksha
Aryans	murti
ashramas	puja
atman	Rama
avatars	samsara
Brahma	samskaras
brahmin	Sanskrit
caste	satyagraha
dharma	Shiva
Divali	shruti
Mohandas Gandhi	Sikhism
Ganges River	smriti
ghee	transmigration
gurdwara	Ultimate Reality
Holi	untouchables
Jainism	Varanasi
karma	Vedas
Krishna	Vishnu yoga

© Anthony Dalton

Chapter 6

BUDDHISM

ccording to Buddhist thought, one of the main goals of each person is to gain wisdom and new insight through meditation. In meditation, the mind is cleared of all worldly concerns so that the person can concentrate on God, or in Buddhism the absolute in himself or herself that might allow a higher stage of spiritual awareness. The following news account describes an unusual setting for Buddhist meditation:

It's a shocking image—even to the accustomed eye.

Fourteen children, the oldest of whom is eleven, are lined up, marching with hands clasped behind their backs at Central Juvenile Hall in East Los Angeles. The youngest child, eight years old, is outfitted in bright orange prison garb, signifying he is a high-risk violent offender, a category that includes murder, assault and armed robbery. . . .

It's the spiritual realm these young offenders are being helped with today, as a team of Buddhist monks and teachers spends an hour teaching the children how to meditate and how meditation might help those who will need to survive extended time in the California prison system. . . .

Benzamin-Masuda rings a bell and asks the children to focus now on the center of the room.

The children settle down and begin to practice meditating.

"Part of the trouble is that these kids' defense systems are very high to begin with," says Kusala, who is with the International Buddhist Meditation Center in Los Angeles, which has been instrumental in bringing Buddhist spiritual practices into the juvenile halls. "Remember, people often had deceptive motives when they paid any attention to them. Some classes are more chaotic than others, and some are smooth as silk."

He says it's generally the older boys—15 and up—"who realize a little better what their reality is and know they need help and seem to catch on very quickly."

A visit to the meditation class of the "KL" group (boys 16 to 18 who are standing trial for murder) finds students who are attentive, intelligent and polite.

"When I stress about my case, and my situation, and the things that have happened, I can focus on my breathing and get a respite," says a 17-year-old boy who has been in the KL unit for a year. "Sometimes not having any word is better."

Javier Stauring, Central's Catholic chaplain, thinks the silence and meditative practices have a more profound result for troubled youngsters "rather than just having supportive people who show up to listen to their problems. The discoveries these kids are making about themselves is amazing. Our hope is that these discoveries will remain, and I think the silence has helped a lot. They don't get a lot of silence in this institution."

Quoted from "Soul Searching," by Janet Kinosian (*Los Angeles Times*, June 2, 1998)

How do you imagine a Buddhist monk?

The word "Buddhism" comes from the Sanskrit word *budhi*, meaning "to wake up." A purpose of Buddhism is to be awakened or enlightened about that which is real. Unlike Hinduism, Buddhism can be traced to a founder. He is Siddhartha Gautama, a Hindu who was born into the warrior caste in Nepal. Called simply the "Buddha" meaning "Enlightened One," Siddhartha Gautama taught that if people followed his teachings they too could be enlightened and reach nirvana.[1]

Buddhism is a human-centered religion, not a god-centered one. The responsibility for spiritual development rests totally upon the individual. Siddhartha Gautama was neither a god nor a messenger of a god. He was a human being who pointed to his teachings and not himself. Though some Buddhists believe Siddhartha Gautama had some divine element to him, what appears to be their worship of him is rather a symbol of deep respect for the most compassionate person in history. For some, bowing to the image of the Buddha is bowing to the Buddha nature that is within each individual.

Buddhism is over 2,500 years old and numbers over 300 million followers. Though most Buddhists live in Asia, a steadily growing number of Buddhists can be found on the continents of Europe, Australia, and North America.

What is one thing you know about Buddhism besides what you've read for this class?

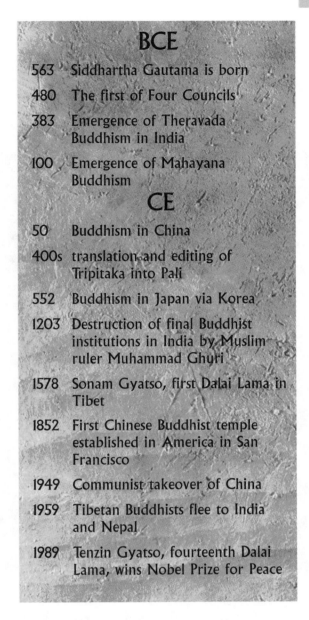

BCE

563 Siddhartha Gautama is born

480 The first of Four Councils

383 Emergence of Theravada Buddhism in India

100 Emergence of Mahayana Buddhism

CE

50 Buddhism in China

400s translation and editing of Tripitaka into Pali

552 Buddhism in Japan via Korea

1203 Destruction of final Buddhist institutions in India by Muslim ruler Muhammad Ghuri

1578 Sonam Gyatso, first Dalai Lama in Tibet

1852 First Chinese Buddhist temple established in America in San Francisco

1949 Communist takeover of China

1959 Tibetan Buddhists flee to India and Nepal

1989 Tenzin Gyatso, fourteenth Dalai Lama, wins Nobel Prize for Peace

I. A BRIEF HISTORY OF BUDDHISM

The origin of Buddhism begins with the birth of the founder of Buddhism, Siddhartha Gautama. The history continues with the preservation of the Buddha's teachings through four succeeding "councils" of his followers. Today there are Buddhists worldwide, including the western world where many are attracted to Buddhism's focus on meditation, spirituality, and wisdom.

Siddhartha Gautama

There are a number of stories about the life of Siddhartha Gautama, called Shakyamuni.[2] Born a Hindu of the warrior caste, his father was king of a small village located in present day Nepal. His mother, Queen Maya, dreamed that an elephant touched her right side and she conceived. Brahmins, the priestly Hindu caste, interpreted the dream for her: she would bear a son that would either be a great king or a great holy man.

Queen Maya traveled to her father's house around 563 BCE to prepare for the birth. In her travels she stopped in Lumbini Gardens. There she stepped off her chariot and held the branch of a tree for support and to rest. Immediately her child emerged from her right side without any help and took seven steps. He stopped and said, "No more births for me." He was named Siddhartha.

Seven days later Queen Maya died. Siddhartha's father took pains to shield him from all the world's pain and suffering. At age sixteen Siddhartha married Yasodhara and they had a son named Rahula. At age nineteen Siddhartha had his charioteer take him beyond where his father permitted. On these travels Siddhartha saw things that his father had tried to shield from him. These were later known as the "four sights," and they would change the course of the prince's life. Siddhartha saw an old man, a very sick man, a corpse, and a wandering holy man without possessions. Each of these sights made a dramatic impression on Siddhartha. One night, at age twenty-nine, Siddhartha quietly kissed his sleeping wife and son and had his charioteer take him to the edge of the forest. There Siddhartha donned the simple robes of a holy man and had his charioteer take all his princely clothes and jeweled possessions back to his father.

For the next six years Siddhartha took up the life of a wandering ascetic, meditating and eating only enough to stay alive. In fact, he had become so emaciated that he said he could put his finger in his belly button and feel his back bone. At one point, Siddhartha sat under a bodhi tree and sought answers to questions about life, especially suffering. In his meditations Siddhartha was tempted by Mara, the stealer of Wisdom, leaving one with ignorance and delusion. Mara tempted Siddhartha with thirst, lust, discontent, and sensuality, but to no avail. Going even deeper into meditation about suffering and the cycle of rebirth, Siddhartha finally reached the enlightenment he sought. He struggled with the thought of whether to share his new insights with others or not.

Returning to the Deer Park near where he lived, Siddhartha delivered his first sermon to five ascetics who had first traveled with him, but later abandoned him. He told them that neither indulgence nor asceticism could release people from samsara (the cycle of birth, death, and rebirth). Rather, it was the Middle Way, life in the middle of the spectrum between indulgence and asceticism, that led to moksha, that is,

freedom from the cycle. The Middle Way consists of following the Four Noble Truths, the fourth of which is the Noble Eightfold Path, eight practices dealing with wisdom, morality, and meditation.

Those first five wandering ascetics Siddhartha preached to in the Deer Park

Golden Buddha shrine

decided to be disciples of the Buddha. They formed a community of monks called the sangha.[3]

Siddhartha continued his travels and preaching and gained a number of followers. He returned to his homeland where he converted many fellow countrymen to his Middle Way, including his wife, son, and cousin.

At age 80, Shakyamuni died of food poisoning. As he lay on his right side dying, he asked the gathering crowd whether anyone had any questions.

There was no response. He told the people that nothing in the world was permanent and that they had to work out their own salvation with diligence. Then Shakyamuni died and entered nirvana. The year was about 483 BCE. He was cremated and his relics[4] were divided and distributed to places where he had traveled. *Stupas*, dome-shaped monuments, were erected over his relics and their presence became places of Buddhist pilgrimages.

Life lived to the extreme or life based on the Middle Way—which is more appealing to you?

The Four Councils

Siddhartha left no writings or documents of any kind to his followers. His legacy was the *dharma* ("Buddha's teachings"), which he shared with all who would listen. His teachings were shared orally, but his initial followers felt it necessary to maintain a unity in Buddhist teachings and practices. According to tradition, a number of Shakyamuni's long-time followers gathered a council about a year after his death to preserve his teachings through recitation of their memories. They recited to each other, revised the recitations, and tried to come to some agreement on Siddhartha's teachings.

About one hundred years later a second council was called. This council was called to deal with questionable practices of some "liberal" monks who sought a relaxation of monastic discipline, including permission to store salt, to eat after noon, to drink palm wine, and to accept silver and gold. The council found these practices unlawful, but the decision was the seed for a major split between the more dogmatic *Sthaviras* and the more liberal *Mahasanghikas* that was finalized almost forty years later. These two groups continued to subdivide over the next few decades until there were eighteen sects, ten belonging to the Sthaviras and eight belonging to the Mahasanghikas. Only the Theravada[5] sect from the Sthavira group survives to this day. However, the Mahasanghikas are a forerunner of *Mahayana*[6] Buddhism, which is in existence today.

The Third Council came about when King Ashoka of the Mauryan Dynasty of India became disenchanted with war and the military. He converted to Buddhism and ruled his country by the Buddhist ideals of pacifism. He built thousands of monasteries and stupas and sent missionaries as far south as Ceylon (present day Sri Lanka). The growth of Buddhism was so swift under Ashoka that a number of questionable teachings flourished. King Ashoka called for the Third Council, to purify the sangha of its various irregularities. A scripture text, the *Tipitaka* ("Three Baskets") was compiled. Ashoka's efforts extended and preserved Buddhism, for by the time Muslims invaded India and Buddhism was extinguished there, it had been established in many other areas.

By around 100 CE Mahayana Buddhism, with its emphasis on lay participation, had emerged as a distinct branch of Buddhism. Increased lay participation also brought a variety of interpretations of Buddhist scriptures. King Kaniska of Ceylon called an assembly, known as the Fourth Council, to rectify the problem. Monks were assigned to edit the *Tipitaka*, making references and remarks for clarification. This task took twelve years to complete; the final document is known today as the *Pali Canon* and is used by the Theravada branch of Buddhism.

Buddhist Expansion

By the beginning of the Common Era Mahayana Buddhism was moving into China. There it met resistance with traditional Chinese religions, including Confucianism. Chinese contributions to Buddhism included the *Ch'an* school with its emphasis on sitting meditation[7] and *Pure Land* Buddhism emphasizing faith and confidence in a buddha who, after attaining enlightenment, used this merit along with the powers of the Buddha to create his Pure Land. The Chinese communist revolution of 1949 effected Buddhism dramatically, forcing the sangha to leave China altogether. Today, there are remnants of Buddhism in China, but under strict government regulations.

Buddhism also reached other Asian countries, including Vietnam, Korea, and Japan. In the ninth century CE two Japanese Buddhist monks traveled to China and returned to Japan with the *Tendai* and *Shingon* sects of Buddhism. Zen Buddhism became popular in Japan as Japanese in the military were attracted to its emphasis on overcoming the fear of death. In Tibet, *Vajrayana*[8] Buddhism, a branch of Mahayana Buddhism, emerged in the seventh century CE. Vajrayana Buddhism puts a great emphasis on the person doing mantras, rituals, and meditations as a way to strive for enlightenment. In the fourteenth century Tibetan Buddhists came to believe that the leaders of their monasteries were reincarnations of great *bodhisatvas* who literally paused in the door before nirvana to muse over the suffering of those left behind. The head of Tibetan Buddhist monastic leaders is known as the *Dalai Lama*. The Dalai Lamas ruled over Tibet until the Communist Chinese forced the present Dalai Lama and thousands of his followers to leave Tibet in 1959. They fled to Northern India and Nepal where they set up an exiled Tibetan government in Dharamsala, India.

If you were able to look back at life in this world as you pass to the next world, what would be in your thoughts?

Thean Hou temple in Kuala Lumpur, Malaysia

Modern Buddhism

Ironically, Buddhism is flourishing today in India, the place of its founding. Since the 1950s about three and one half million "untouchables" have converted to Buddhism. Also, the exiled Tibetan Buddhists live in northern India.

Buddhism has also attracted interest in western nations, inspiring writers and thinkers of other religions, including Christianity, with Buddhist approaches to meditation, wisdom, and spirituality.

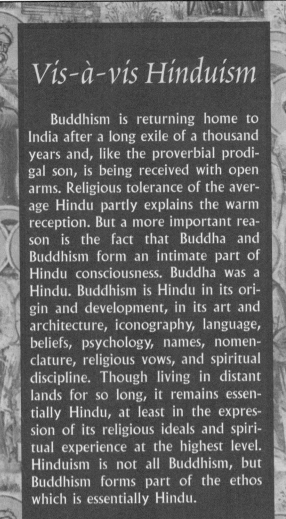

Vis-à-vis Hinduism

Buddhism is returning home to India after a long exile of a thousand years and, like the proverbial prodigal son, is being received with open arms. Religious tolerance of the average Hindu partly explains the warm reception. But a more important reason is the fact that Buddha and Buddhism form an intimate part of Hindu consciousness. Buddha was a Hindu. Buddhism is Hindu in its origin and development, in its art and architecture, iconography, language, beliefs, psychology, names, nomenclature, religious vows, and spiritual discipline. Though living in distant lands for so long, it remains essentially Hindu, at least in the expression of its religious ideals and spiritual experience at the highest level. Hinduism is not all Buddhism, but Buddhism forms part of the ethos which is essentially Hindu.

Quoted from an article by Ram Swarup (http://hindu.org/publications/ramswarup/buddhism.html)

SECTION 1 SUMMARY

❖ Siddhartha Gautama, called Shakyamuni by his followers, was the founder of Buddhism.

❖ As Gautama was a Hindu, Buddhism has its roots in Hinduism.

❖ The Four Councils of early Buddhism were assembled to codify monastic discipline and unify Buddhist scriptures.

❖ Buddhism received imperial patronage from King Ashoka.

❖ Three major schools of Buddhism are Theravada, Mahayana, and Vajrayana.

❖ The invasion of the Muslims into India eventually drove Buddhism from India, though Buddhism is reemerging there today.

SECTION 1 REVIEW QUESTIONS

1. Briefly summarize the main events in the life of Siddhartha Gautama.

2. What were the main issues addressed by each of the four councils?

3. What attracted King Ashoka to Buddhism?

4. Why were the Japanese attracted to Zen Buddhism?

5. Who is the Dalai Lama? Briefly recount the history of Tibetan Buddhism.

II. BELIEFS AND ACTIONS

The center of all Buddhist beliefs is the *Four Noble Truths*, from Siddhartha Gautama's earliest sermons. If one is ignorant of the Four Noble Truths, she or he will remain on the endless cycle of samsara. Oppositely, understanding of the Four Noble Truths leads to the *Noble Eightfold Path*, the Middle Way which reminds a person to avoid extremes, to take everything in moderation. These beliefs and subsequent practices are at the heart of Buddhism.

Four Noble Truths

The Four Noble Truths are named and described as follows:

1. *Life is filled with suffering.* Suffering refers to not only physical suffering, but also mental suffering that comes with facing the various traumas of life. We begin this life with the birth trauma. Then there is physical, mental and emotional pain, illness, injury, old age, and fear of death. Samsara is the endless cycle of suffering through death and rebirth, and karma is the cause of samsara. Suffering even goes beyond life's physical and mental pains. The reason for suffering includes concepts of impermanence, incompleteness, imperfections, and discontent.

All life is impermanent. Physical beings, both earthly and heavenly, are constantly changing. Human beings age, wood begins to rot, and stars are constantly being formed. Our thoughts, feelings, and attitudes are also impermanent. This is the Buddhist doctrine of anatma.[9] While Hindus taught that self or soul was God (atman), Gautama taught that if the soul was purely God then it is not a soul at all. Therefore it is "no-soul" or "not self."

2. *The cause of suffering is desire.* Because people believe the individual self is real, they have cravings. People constantly want things. When they do not get them, they are frustrated or disappointed. Even if a person gets what he or she wants, the resulting happiness is impermanent. Ignorance of the nature of the not-self and thus,

Buddhist monks

© Anthony Dalton

believing the self to be real (that is, permanent and unchanging) is the fundamental cause of suffering.

3. *To cease suffering one must cease desiring.* To end suffering is to end samsara and achieve nirvana. That is what is real in Buddhism. Everything is suffering, impermanent, and incomplete. The only thing permanent, and thus, real, is the end of suffering. Suffering ceases when we free ourselves of the bondage of desires

and cravings and stop believing that our individual self is real. This freedom brings people happiness and contentment. Nirvana is the "extinction" of that suffering through the endless cycles of rebirth.

4. *The path to the end of suffering is the Noble Eightfold Path.* This is the Middle Path between indulgence and self-denial. The Noble Eightfold Path is the moral standard of Buddhism.

Do you think that the ceasing of all desires is possible? Is even the desire to cease all desires itself a desire?

The Noble Eightfold Path

The Noble Eightfold Path is the path to end suffering and thus achieve nirvana, the fourth of the Four Noble Truths. A description of the eight standards follows:

1. *Right Understanding*—The first step of the Noble Eightfold Path requires that one see things as they really are. Right understanding is the understanding of the causes of suffering, the end of suffering, and the way one endures suffering. In short, this step is summation of the Four Noble Truths.

2. *Right Thought*—The mind must be purified of all that moves it away from enlightenment. Right thought is not just getting rid of wrong thoughts. It is replacing wrong thoughts, like hatred and desire, with right thoughts, like loving kindness and renunciation. Right thought is equated with the Christian beatitude of single-heartedness.

3. *Right Speech*—All forms of lying, slandering, gossiping, and using harsh words must be eliminated. Instead, a person must speak truthfully and kindly about others.

4. *Right Conduct*—Right conduct calls on people not to cheat, steal, murder, or engage in any kind of sexual misconduct.

5. *Right Livelihood*—This path calls upon people not to earn a living through actions that would harm other living things. For example, one's livelihood is not to be earned by slaughtering animals, doing anything involving weapons, or manufacturing or selling any kind of intoxicants such as drugs and alcohol.

6. *Right Effort*—This path has to do with a person's thoughts. He or she is to be diligent in getting rid of bad or delusional thoughts, while cultivating good, wholesome thoughts.

7. *Right Mindfulness*—A person is to be aware of everything he or she is thinking and doing. Right mindfulness is being aware of thinking, feelings, and actions at all times. Right mindfulness means knowing oneself.

8. *Right Concentration*—This final path is a form of meditation in which a person concentrates on one object, like a flickering candle, in order to give full attention to the object and dispel other distractions. This is the type of concentration that enables a person to see things as they really are, and thus, gain enlightenment.

The Noble Eightfold Path is categorized by three main practices—morality, meditation, and wisdom. Moral actions bring about meditation, meditation brings about wisdom, and, completing the circle, wisdom gives rise to good actions. Buddhism is meditative. It calls for each person to engage in self-awareness and self-understanding.

On a scale of 1 to 10, how well do you know yourself?

Community

Traditionally, *sangha* referred to a Buddhist community of monks. During his lifetime, it was monks who were the most devoted followers of Siddhartha Gautama. Recent developments have expanded sangha to mean the community of all Buddhist practitioners: monks, nuns, and lay people. Sangha is one of the Three Jewels of Buddhism. The two other jewels are the Buddha and dharma. The Three Jewels are considered the core of Buddhism. In becoming a Buddhist one proclaims refuge in these Three Jewels:

**I take refuge in the Buddha.
I take refuge in the Dharma.
I take refuge in the Sangha.**

Though the monastic and lay lifestyles are very different, each is dependent upon the other. Theravada monks are celibate and provide spiritual nourishment to the laity. The laity provide physical nourishment to monks who seek their daily food through begging at the households of Buddhist devotees.

To be enlightened and reach nirvana is an important goal of a Buddhist. For Theravada Buddhists, *arhat* ("worthy one") is the name that describes such a person. However, only those who have heard the teachings of Buddha can become arhats. Mahayana Buddhists likewise accept the status of arhat as an ultimate goal. However, the exemplar person in Mahayana Buddhism is a bodhisatva who has chosen to defer full enlightenment until all other humans have first reached nirvana. Because of their great compassion for all persons, bodhisatvas, who are not necessarily monks or nuns, will transfer merit they have gained to others so others can reach nirvana. The bodhisatva will enter nirvana last.

Mahayana monks abide by the same rules as Theravada monks. However, they add to the rules by witnessing about Siddhartha Gautama, his way of life, and emulating his attitudes of peace and compassion to others. The Japanese Mahayana Buddhist sect of Zen does not beg for alms. Rather, they earn their own livelihood. Another Japanese Mahayana sect known as Shin permits their monks to marry and raise a family.

What is your reaction to the bodhisatva notion of "waiting until last" to enter nirvana? How is this comparable to Christian teaching?

Scripture

The early Buddhist scriptures known as Tipitaka were passed down orally before they were written in Sanskrit around the first century BCE. The complete document of the Theravadans that is extant today was written in Pali. Hence, besides being called the Tipitaka, it is also called the Pali Canon. The "Three Baskets" Tipitaka refers to are the following three major collections that make up the Tipitaka:

Vinaya Pitaka

The Vinaya Pitaka is the code of monastic discipline for monks and nuns. There are 227 rules for monks and 311 rules for nuns. The rules highlight offenses in descending order of seriousness. Each rule is accompanied by a story that explains the reason for the rule. This basket also records the life and ministry of the Buddha.

Sutra Pitaka

The Sutra Pitaka is primarily made up of discourses of Siddhartha Gautama. Many of the topics of the discourse such as morality later became part of Buddhist doctrine. The story of the Buddha's birth and enlightenment can be found in this Pitaka.

Abidharma Pitaka

The Abidharma Pitaka examines the Buddha's psychological teachings. It spends a great deal of time analyzing Buddhist doctrine in detail. The Abidharma Pitaka is of more interest for monks or serious students than the average lay Buddhist.

The Tipitaka is the sacred scripture of Theravada Buddhism. Mahayanas also use the Tipitaka, but their main authoritative scriptures are sutras, a word meaning "sacred teaching." One of the most popular sutras is the Saddharmapundarika Sutra, more popularly known as the Lotus Sutra. Mahayana Buddhists believe the Lotus Sutra contains the final teachings of the Buddha. The other very popular Mahayana sutra is the Prajnaparamita Sutra, which is a treatise on achieving the perfection of wisdom of a bodhisatva.

Vajrayanas use Mahayana scriptures but add to them their own *tantric*[10] texts from India and China. The more popular scripture, however, is the *Tibetan Book of the Dead*. It contains various writings on death, dying, and rebirth.

Christians have a closed canon, meaning they are not able to add books to the sacred scriptures. Buddhists do not have a closed canon. What are the advantages of each practice?

SECTION 2 REVIEW QUESTIONS

1. Name and explain the Four Noble Truths.

2. Name and explain the Noble Eightfold Path.

3. What are the Three Jewels of Buddhism?

4. What is the *Pali Canon*?

5. What is the difference between the Theravada and Mahayana monastic order?

6. Explain the variations of the sacred scriptures for each of the three branches of Buddhism.

III. SACRED PLACES

Buddhist monasteries are often connected with temples. In Theravada Buddhism, men especially must spend part of their lives in a monastery. They may leave the monastery when it is time to marry, but often return again when their children have been raised. Also, lay people share in the merit of the monks by providing food to feed them and by maintaining the monasteries. The monastery is one sacred place for Buddhists, but there are some others.

Temple

The temple is especially sacred for Theravada Buddhists. Monks live at the temple and perform certain religious rites there. Lay people come to the temple for religious devotions, meditation, and instruction on Buddhist teachings. At a temple there are usually images of the Buddha and stories about the life of the Buddha depicted in paintings or statues. A stupa is usually present with relics from the Buddha or his followers.

SECTION 2 SUMMARY

❖ The foundations for Buddhist teachings are the Four Noble Truths and the Noble Eightfold Path.

❖ Sangha is the Buddhist community of monks and lay people.

❖ Each of the three branches of Buddhism has their own set of sacred scripture. The sacred Tipitaka is included in all three branches of Buddhism, but its authority differs in each of the respective branches.

Mahayana temples are likely to have a number of enshrined images of many people from the past who have become enlightened and thus are also called buddhas, but with a lower case "b." Mahayana and Vajrayana temples tend to have a number of shrines venerating bodhisatvas as well. A temple usually has a place for a monk to deliver a sermon on a special occasion.

Stupas

Originally stupas were small mounds made of stone or brick that housed the relics of the historical Buddha and were usually located near a temple. As Buddhism expanded, relics of the Buddha gave way to relics of other important Buddhist figures as well as other religious objects. Stupas are still places of pilgrimage for Buddhists. In Vajrayana Buddhism, people walk around a stupa several times out of

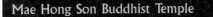

Mae Hong Son Buddhist Temple

Cox's Bazar Buddhist Stupa

© Anthony Dalton

Thean Hou temple in Kuala Lumpur, Malaysia

© Galyn C. Hammond

reverence. Larger stupas are called pagodas. Rather than a simple, small mound, pagodas are large, elaborately decorated domes.

What are symbolic "relics" in your life that you revere?

Places of Pilgrimage

Other sacred spaces for Buddhists are places that are, in some way, connected with the life and ministry of the historical Buddha. They are located in present day India or Nepal.

Lumbini Gardens

Lumbini Gardens is the traditional site of the birth of Siddhartha Gautama. It is located in Nepal. It became a place of pilgrimage shortly after the death of Siddhartha Gautama. In the third century CE King Ashoka had a twenty-two foot pillar erected there as a memorial to the Buddha.

Bodh Gaya

The bodhi tree under which the Buddha meditated and gained his enlightenment was located at Bodh Gaya. The tree now located there is said to be a descendent of the original bodhi tree. Near the tree is a sandstone slab marking the place where Gautama became enlightened. A stone under the present tree has a footprint which tradition says is the footprint of the Buddha. Buddhist pilgrims often bring things to decorate the area. People make offerings of flowers. Saplings from the original bodhi tree are planted throughout India. These also are places of pilgrimage.

Sarnath

It was the Deer Park near Varanasi where Siddhartha Gautama preached his first sermon about the Four Noble Truths. This was also the place where he gained his first disciples. A stupa there was constructed by King Ashoka. Deer still roam the park today.

Kushinara

Kushinara is the traditional place of the death of Gautama. The Kushinara Nirvana Temple was built in 1956 to commemorate the 2,500th year of the Buddha's entrance into

Bodhi Tree

© Galyn C. Hammond

nirvana. There is also a 1,500-year old red stone statue of a reclining Buddha located at Kushinara.

Name a holy place or shrine that you have visited. What is one impression you had of this place?

SECTION 3 SUMMARY

Monasteries are often connected to Buddhist temples. Mahayana temples include images of other buddhas and bodhisatvas besides images of Shakyamuni.

✤ A stupa contains a relic or other sacred objects of Buddhism.

✤ The most popular places for Buddhist pilgrims are those connected with events in the life of the Buddha. These sacred places are located in India or Nepal.

SECTION 3 REVIEW QUESTIONS

1. Name a difference between a Theravada temple and a Mahayana temple.

2. How does a pagoda differ from an ordinary stupa?

3. Name the four major sites of pilgrimage related to the life of Siddhartha Gautama. Why are these significant?

IV. SACRED TIME

Buddhists do not have a special day of the week for congregational worship. Theravada Buddhists can make offerings to images of the Buddha at any time. Mahayana Buddhists can do the same and also make offerings to images of other buddhas and bodhisatvas. In areas where there are no temples, Buddhists make offerings at home. For

both home and temple, the items offered might be flowers, candles, or incense. A recitation of the Three Jewels is usually part of the offering. The scent of incense reminds Buddhists of the influence of good virtue. Flowers, which soon wither, remind people of the impermanence of everything. Because Buddha is not a god, bowing to an image of the Buddha is a sign of profound respect rather than submission to a deity.

Three young monks

© Galyn C. Hammond

131

Meditation

Meditation is central to every branch of Buddhism. The last three paths of the Noble Eightfold Path are categorized as meditation. By following the paths of right effort, right mindfulness, and right concentration, Buddhists believe they are well on their way to enlightenment. For Buddhists, medita-

persists in practicing this form of meditation over a long period of time finds that the power of concentration becomes stronger, and that inner calm enters not only the mind, but also the whole person.

Most Buddhist meditations, including the Meditation of Loving-Kindness, begin with Mindfulness of Breathing. When the mind has been calmed, a person then focuses on the self and says

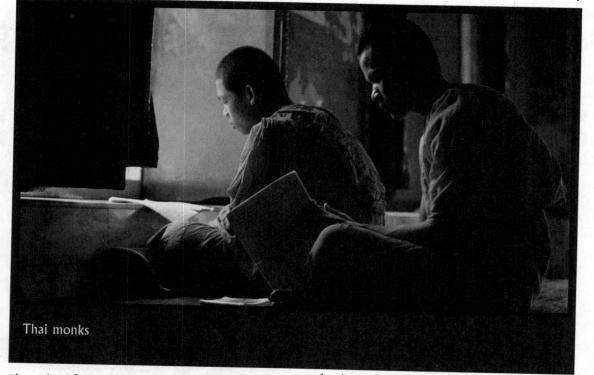

Thai monks

tion is also a means of heightened awareness. Meditation helps people cultivate the awareness of their dreams, goals, and self-identities and the means to engage in good karma. Siddhartha Gautama taught his disciples a number of types of meditation. Two of the most common are *Mindfulness of Breath* and *Meditation of Loving-Kindness*.

Mindfulness of Breath is one of the first forms of meditation Buddhists learn. As might be imagined, Mindfulness of Breath focuses on breathing as the person learns to pay close attention to the ebb and flow of breath. As one focuses on breathing, other thoughts and distractions try to intrude. The person who

loving things about himself or herself. For example,

"May I be a loving person."

"May I have a heart filled with love."

"May I be a peace-filled person."

"May I be a fulfilled person."

After focusing on self, attention is then turned to others: first to one the person loves, then to one whom the person is neutral about, and finally to one whom the person dislikes. In the Meditation of Loving Kindness, each of these three people is wished well over a long period of time.

Festivals

There are two categories of Buddhist festivals. One is centered around the life of the Buddha, while the other major category is centered around the sangha. Minor festivals mark the seasons, particularly spring and autumn. However, these are not specifically religious categories and they are connected more with countries and regions than that with which is specifically Buddhist. An examination of one festival from each of the two major categories follows.

Celebrating the Buddha

Visakha, or "Buddha Day," is the most holy day of the year for Theravada Buddhists. It is celebrated on the full moon day of May. For Theravadans, Siddhartha Gautama was born, became enlightened, and died all on the same date. The emphasis for this festival is literally on en*light*enment. Theravada Buddhists light colorful lanterns and candles around the monasteries where the celebrations occur. An image of the Buddha is decorated and a monk gives a sermon on some aspect of the life of the Buddha.

Many Mahayana Buddhists celebrate these significant events in the life of the Buddha on three separate days throughout the year. For Mahayanans, the celebration of the life of the Buddha may entail a bathing of the sacred image followed by a procession. The bathing not only signifies great reverence for the Buddha, it is also a reminder that there are faults in everyone's life that need to be washed away.

Celebrating Sangha

The sangha began as a mendicant ("begging") order of monks. They wandered, preaching the dharma during all but the three months of the monsoon season. The three month period became known as the Rains Retreat. Though a monastic retreat, lay Buddhists also consider the Rains Retreat to be a time of great holiness. The end of the retreat is celebrated with the great festival put on

Monk begging

by the lay people. At a special ceremony monks are presented with new robes. Lay people believe that the monks gain great spiritual power during the Rains Retreat and hope that some of that holiness will radiate onto them and shorten samsara.

Who is someone in your life whose holiness you wish would rub off on you?

Life Cycle

There are no specific Buddhist initiation ceremonies for infants. Initiation of a newborn into a community is based on local customs. However, Buddhists do

from sacred scripture and perhaps even a sermon on married life.

Buddhists do have funeral ceremonies in which monks play a significant role. The *Tibetan Book of the Dead* characterizes dying as a sacred act. Death rituals are important in Buddhism

Row of golden buddhas

connect birth with suffering and samsara. Buddhists believe that a newborn had previous existences and that the karma of previous lives could influence the character of the person in this life.

Like birth, marriage ceremonies are performed according to local customs. A marriage ceremony for a Buddhist couple may have no element of Buddhism. Very often a Buddhist couple is married in a civil ceremony and a monk or the local sangha is asked to bless the marriage afterwards. The marriage blessing may take place at a temple, a shrine, or a home. The blessing may include chanting

because of the Buddhists' great interest in life after death and the rebirth of the person. The most important interest is moving a person from samsara to nirvana.

SECTION 4 SUMMARY

❖ Meditation is a common observance in every branch of Buddhism; the two most common forms are Mindfulness of Breath and Meditation of Loving-Kindness.

❖ There are a number of Buddhist festivals, but few are celebrated by all Buddhists. All Buddhists do celebrate the birth of Siddhartha Gautama in one form or another.

❖ Lay people hope to receive spiritual benefits from monks who participate in the Rains Retreat.

❖ Buddhists have no specific life cycle ceremonies for birth and marriage, but they do have special funeral rituals.

SECTION 4 REVIEW QUESTIONS

1. Why is meditation important for Buddhists?

2. Briefly describe Mindfulness of Breathing meditation.

3. How do Theravada and Mahayana Buddhists celebrate the birth of the Buddha?

4. What is the origin of the Rains Retreat?

What do you think attracts Americans to Buddhism? What aspects of Buddhism do you find appealing?

Who Is My Neighbor?
BUDDHISM IN AMERICA

Have we all been here before? Yes, and in this lifetime too. America flirted with Buddhism in the 1950s and again in the '70s; vestiges of those dalliances still waft, pleasant yet amorphous, through the pop atmosphere. Phil Jackson (former Chicago Bulls coach) applied Zen to the art of Michael maintenance, and Tina Turner and Herbie Hancock chant Buddhist mantras. Terms such as Nirvana and koan are in common usage, if seldom understood. . .

But in fact intrigued Americans need not remain perplexed: they can investigate a vibrant, if small, U.S. community of believers. This does not mean the hundreds of thousands of Buddhist immigrants, who have yet to have an impact on mainstream culture. Rather, it refers to some thousands of American-born Buddhists, many of who have been practicing for decades and have, as sociologist Don Morreale puts it, "gone mainstream." While the Dalai Lama bestrides the globe, Zen Buddhists in San Francisco run two of the better-respected AIDS hospices, and their philosophy infuses the entire "good death" movement. In New York City and elsewhere, fans flock to talks by Thich Nhat Hanh, a French-based, socially engaged Vietnamese monk whose book *Living Buddha, Living Christ* sold 100,000 hardcover copies. In cyberspace the Manhattan-based Asian Classics Institute has transferred 100,000 deteriorating pages of scripture from Tibetan block prints onto the Internet. Mirabai Bush, a devotee of the non-Tibetan Vipassana school, teaches Monsanto executives nonreligious meditation, the number of English-language Buddhist teaching centers has jumped from 429 to more than 1,000. . . .

Some think meditation will constitute Buddhism's distinct contribution to American religious life. Different branches practice different varieties, but each begins with a simple awareness of breath drawn in and let out. Fields notes that a near mechanical process that allows each individual to look inside himself or herself for the divine fits in particularly well with the democratic tendency of the faith here: "Americans have always been a do-it-yourself culture, and this is a do-it-yourself philosophy."

Quoted from "Buddhism in America," by David Van Biema (*Time*, October 13, 1997)

Conclusion

Buddhism is unique among the world's religions. Though it does not deny the existence of gods, divine beings

Rock painting of Buddha in Tibet

are not central to Buddhists. And whereas the human person is at the center of Buddhism, Buddhists deny the existence of a human soul. Siddhartha Gautama, the founder of Buddhism, came to the realization that suffering was part of life and that it can be extinguished through the practice of the Nobel Eightfold Path.

Meditation is the method through which an individual gains the two most important virtues in Buddhism, wisdom and compassion. Through meditation one realizes that there is no permanence in life. Paradoxically, realizing that all is impermanent, unsatisfactory, and not-self brings one to that which is permanent bliss, nirvana.

CHAPTER 6 IN BRIEF

❖ Siddhartha Gautama, called Shakyamuni, founded Buddhism in the sixth century BCE. Gautama was a Hindu raised in the warrior caste.

❖ The Four Councils, after the death of Shakyamuni, aided in the development and expansion of Buddhism as well as its separation into Theravada and Mahayana Buddhism.

❖ As it spread, Buddhism broke up into a number of sects.

❖ Buddhism was expelled from India when Muslims gained control there.

❖ The Four Noble Truths and the Noble Eightfold Path are the foundations of the Buddha's teachings.

❖ The sangha comprises the Buddhist community of lay people, monks, and nuns.

❖ The Tipitaka is the Pali Canon or sacred scripture for Theravada Buddhists. Mahayana and Vajrayana Buddhists have other sacred scriptures in addition to the Pali Canon.

❖ Temples are places for Buddhists to make offerings for the purpose of merit-making.

❖ Stupas contain relics of the Buddha or other renowned Buddhists.

❖ Four sites in Nepal and India connected with Gautama's life are important sacred spaces of Buddhist pilgrims.

❖ Meditation is the most important observance for all Buddhists.

❖ Most Buddhist festivals are local or regional celebrations. The Buddha's birthday is the most common festival among all Buddhists.

❖ Buddhists do not have specific life cycle rites for birth and marriage, but they do for death.

CHAPTER 6 REVIEW QUESTIONS

1. Briefly summarize the life of Siddhartha Gautama.

2. Define dharma.

3. What is the Middle Way?

4. Highlight the accomplishments of the Four Councils.

5. Outline the expansion of Buddhism beyond India.

6. Compare the role of monks to lay people in Buddhism.

7. Briefly compare and contrast Theravada, Mahayana, and Vajrayana Buddhism.

8. What are the Three Jewels of Buddhism? When are they recited?

9. What is the meaning of atman to Buddhists?

10. Name some of the benefits of meditation.

11. Define stupa.

12. What is Zen Buddhism?

RESEARCH AND ACTIVITIES

1. View one of the following motion pictures and write an essay on how Buddhism is portrayed: *Little Buddha, Seven Years in Tibet,* or *Kundun.*

2. Read Herman Hesse's *Siddhartha* and write a book report summarizing its main plot and themes.

3. Write an essay comparing and contrasting Theravada, Mahayana, and Vajrayana Buddhism.

4. Research and report to the class on one of the following topics:

Buddhism and Communism in China (or Tibet, or Vietnam, or Cambodia)

Zen Buddhism's influence on art

The Dalai Lama and Hollywood

Asian Buddhism and American Buddhism in the United States

The attraction of Buddhism to Americans

The physical and mental benefits of Buddhist meditation

Christian Zen Buddhism or Jewish Zen Buddhism

Buddhist nuns

Buddhism and suffering

Buddhism as a religion, as a philosophy, and as a way of life

SELECTED VOCABULARY

anatma	Noble Eightfold Path
arhat	Pali Canon
bodhisatva	Pure Land
buddha	sangha
Ch'an	Shakyamuni
Dalai Lama	stupa
dharma	sutra
enlightenment	tantric
Four Councils	Theravada
Four Noble Truths	Three Baskets
King Ashoka	Three Jewels
Mahayana	Tipitaka
Middle Way	Vajrayana
nirvana	

Chapter 7

CHINESE RELIGIONS

The Four Dragons

A Chinese Tale

Once upon a time, there were no rivers and lakes on earth, but only the Eastern Sea, in which lived four dragons: the Long Dragon, the Yellow Dragon, the Black Dragon, and the Pearl Dragon.

One day the four dragons flew from the sea into the sky. They soared and dived, playing at hide-and-seek in the clouds.

"Come over here quickly!" the Pearl Dragon cried out suddenly.

"What's up?" asked the other three, looking down in the direction where the Pearl Dragon pointed. On the earth they saw many people putting out fruits and cakes, and burning incense sticks. They were praying! A white-haired woman, kneeling on the ground with a thin boy on her back, murmured:

"Please send rain quickly, God of Heaven, to give our children rice to eat."

For there had been no rain for a long time. The crops withered, the grass turned yellow and fields cracked under the scorching sun.

"How poor the people are!" said the Yellow Dragon. "And they will die if it doesn't rain soon."

The Long Dragon nodded. Then he suggested, "Let's go and beg the Jade Emperor[1] for rain."

So saying, he leapt into the clouds. The others followed closely and flew towards the Heavenly Palace.

Being in charge of all the affairs in heaven, on earth and in the sea, the Jade Emperor was very powerful. He was not pleased to see the dragons rushing in. "Why do you come here instead of staying in the sea and behaving yourselves?"

The Long Dragon stepped forward and said, "The crops on earth are withering and dying, your Majesty. I beg you to send rain down quickly!"

"All right. You go back first, I'll send some rain down tomorrow." The Jade Emperor pretended to agree while listening to the songs of the fairies.

"Thanks, Your Majesty!" The four dragons went happily back.

But ten days passed, and not a drop of rain came down.

The people suffered more, some eating bark, some grass roots, some forced to eat white clay when they ran out of bark and grass roots.

Seeing all this, the four dragons felt very sorry, for they knew the Jade Emperor only cared about pleasure, and never took the people to heart. They could only rely on themselves to relieve the people of their miseries. But how to do it?

Seeing the vast sea, the Long Dragon said that he had an idea.

"What is it? Out with it, quickly!" the other three demanded.

"Look, is there not plenty of water in the sea where we live? We should scoop it up and spray it towards the sky. The water will be like rain drops and come down to save the people and their crops."

"Good idea!" The others clapped their hands.

"But," said the Long Dragon after thinking a bit, "we will be blamed if the Jade Emperor learns of this."

"I will do anything to save the people," the Yellow Dragon said resolutely.

"Let's begin. We will never regret it." The Black Dragon and the Pearl Dragon were not to be outdone.

They flew to the sea, scooped up water in their mouths, and then flew back into the sky, where they sprayed the water out over the earth. The four dragons flew back and forth, making the sky dark all around. Before long the sea water became rain pouring down from the sky.

"It's raining! It's raining!"

"The crops will be saved!"

The people cried and leaped with joy. On the ground the wheat stalks raised their heads and the sorghum stalks straightened up.

The god of the sea discovered these events and reported to the Jade Emperor.

"How dare the four dragons bring rain without my permission!" The Jade Emperor was enraged, and ordered the heavenly generals and their troops to arrest the four dragons. Being far outnumbered, the four dragons could not defend themselves, and they were soon arrested and brought back to the heavenly palace.

"Go and get four mountains to lay upon them so that they can never escape!" The Jade Emperor ordered the Mountain God.

The Mountain God used his magic power to make four mountains fly there, whistling in the wind from afar, and pressed them down upon the four dragons.

Imprisoned as they were, they never regretted their actions.

Determined to do good for the people forever, they turned themselves into four rivers, which flowed past high mountains and deep valleys, crossing the land from the west to the east and finally emptying into the sea. And so China's four great rivers were formed—the Heilongjian (Black Dragon) in the far north, the Huanghe (Yellow River) in central China, the Chanjiiang (Yangtze, or Long River) farther south, and the Zhujiang (Pearl) in the very far south.

Quoted from *Dragon Tales: A Collection of Chinese Stories* (Beijing: Chinese Literature Press, 1988)

A Christian principle taught by Jesus is to "lose one's life" for Jesus' sake and the kingdom. How is this principle repeated in this story?

As you can decipher from the chapter title, the study of Chinese religion is different from other religions previously covered in this text. "Chinese religion" does not connote one religious tradition. Rather, Chinese religion is a combination of folk religion,[2] Taoism, Confucianism, and Buddhism. Elements of each of these religious traditions can be found in Chinese culture, especially prior to the Communist takeover in 1949. Now, as freedom and western culture make their way back into China, the elements in these religions and the religions themselves can hope for a rebirth. This chapter provides a sketch of religion in China through the centuries and explains how these various religious expressions have co-mingled and yet stood apart through these many years.

BCE

1027	Chou Dynasty Begins
604	Lao Tzu's birth
551	Confucius's birth
300s	Chuang Tzu
200s	Han Dynasty
	Hsun Tzu

CE

65	Buddhism in China
581	Beginning of Sui Dynasty
845	Persecution of Buddhists
900s	End of T'ang Dynasty
	Neo-Confucianism
	Beginning of Sung Dynasty
1600s	Beginning of Qing Dynasty
1949	Communist takeover of China
1966	Cultural Revolution in China

I. A BRIEF HISTORY OF CHINESE RELIGION

This study of Chinese religion begins within the political and social setting of China just as Lao Tzu and Confucius, promulgators of what are now called Taoism and Confucianism, came onto the world scene in the sixth and fifth centuries BCE. Though there is a question as to whether Lao Tzu was a historical figure at all, there is no doubt that the historical period ascribed to him and Confucius paralleled the Warring States Period (475-221 BCE) when the long-standing Chou dynasty had disintegrated to the point of not only political and social disarray, but also moral decline.

Ancient Folk Religion

Popular Chinese religion—called folk religion—before the establishment of the organized religions of Confucianism, Taoism, and Buddhism, was rich in its breadth of religious experience. Like most ancient cultures, the Chinese culture did not distinguish between religious and secular practices. All aspects of life were totally integrated.

Under the heading of folk religion, *ancestor worship*[3] played an integral part from the beginning of the Chou Dynasty. Ancestors were not so much worshipped as deities but revered as older, wiser members of the family unit. The older a person was at the time of death, the more honored. It was believed that ancestors had two souls. One soul would disappear at death while a second one was immortal. This second soul was the object of reverence. It was the responsibility of the male head of the household to make sure ancestors received proper care. Failure to offer proper reverence to ancestors could anger them to the point that they might destroy crops, send illnesses, or cause mental distress, including nightmares.

Ancestors were not the only ones who were reverenced by the ancient Chinese. There was also an elaborate pantheon of gods and goddesses. *Heaven* was the highest god over a number of lower gods and goddesses. Heaven also was intrinsically connected to human nature as a source of goodness, and governed the destiny of the rulers and people. Kings and emperors of China claimed to be Heaven's representative on earth. The Chinese also believed in lesser gods. For example, T'u-ti was a type of Chinese god or goddess that was connected to a specific location like a home, village, temple, field, or even a street or bridge. All the deities received sacrifices. The ruler would offer sacrifices to the high god Heaven, while local people would offer sacrifices to their agricultural gods or household gods.

Divination[4] was a common practice in ancient China for reading messages from the gods. The Chinese would attempt to read signs from nature—like a cloud formation or the cracks in a tortoise's shell—to determine what would happen in the future. It was quite common for temples to have a place to throw crescent shaped sticks. A divine specialist would then be consulted as to the meaning of the configuration of the sticks.

Astrology was also a common form of divination. The configuration of the stars and planets were omens for either good or evil. Solar eclipses were usually a particularly bad sign, for the covering of the sun created darkness, an evil omen.

You may be familiar with the Taoist symbol for *yin and yang*,[5] half of which is dark with a light spot while the other

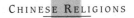

half is light with a dark spot. This symbol and the idea yin and yang itself predates Taoism. Yin and yang originally referred to the shaded and sunny sides of hills and valleys. They later came to symbolize the complementary, harmonious play of pairs of opposites in the universe. They are interdependent in the sense that one has no

Yin and yang symbol

meaning without the other. For example, good has no meaning without evil, light has no meaning without dark, and cold has no meaning without hot. One defines the other. There is no antagonism between the pairs for both are needed. Each contains a little of the other, as the light and dark spots indicate. Good has an element of evil, light has an element of dark, cold has an element of hot, and vice versa. For the Chinese, nature is in a continual dance to remain balanced between the yin and the yang.

Confucius and Confucianism

Confucius is the Latin version of K'ung-Fu-Tzu, meaning "Master K'ung." Confucius was born in 551 BCE in the small feudal state of Lu, the product of the union between his seventy-year-old father and one of his father's teenage concubines. Tradition says Confucius's father was a great military hero who was granted a small piece of land upon retirement from the military. After his father died when Confucius was three, Confucius and his mother were shunned by his father's family. Poor and without social ties, they moved to a nearby town where his mother worked and taught the eager Confucius.

As a teenager Confucius took a minor government post of keeping books for granaries. He married at age nineteen and his beloved mother died when he was twenty. However, nothing could get in the way of Confucius's education. For Confucius, learning was not merely an accumulation of knowledge, but an important means to build character. As he continued his studies, Confucius began teaching groups of young men all he knew, though teaching was not his first love. Rather, Confucius spent his entire adult life aspiring for public office. He even went on a twelve-year search with a few of his students for a feudal state that would hire him as a public official. However, since Confucius held the political position that governments were in much need of reform, existing governments saw him as a

Confucianism symbol

threat to their administration. Confucius spent the last years of his life teaching and compiling some Chinese ancient texts. Included in his writings were the Analects, the "sayings of Confucius." Though slow to catch on, Confucius's teachings were eventually widely read.

Confucius died in 479 BCE, believing himself to be largely a failure. He was very wrong about that.

When was a time when someone else held you in greater esteem than you yourself did?

143

Confucius's writings revealed that he saw chaos all around him. He believed that if society would return to the values of the ancients, chaos would disperse. Confucius was especially interested in those values that were transmitted through rituals such as ancestor worship, worship of the high god Heaven, and death rites. He believed that it was his duty to recapture these lost elements of ancient civilization and reintroduce them into his world. Proper ritual observance and moral persuasion were Confucius's formula for success.

Though Confucius is considered the founder of Confucianism, he is not a founder in the same sense as Siddhartha Gautama is of Buddhism or Jesus of Nazareth is of Christianity. Confucius regarded himself as a transmitter of ancient Chinese social values rather than as a founder of a religion or a philosophy. He studied ancient Chinese scriptures and attempted to revive their wisdom in his society. Confucius was not inventing anything new. He was simply putting his contemporaries in touch with their ancestors.

It wasn't until two centuries after Confucius's death that two of his disciples, Meng Tzu (c. 371-289 BCE) and Hsun-Tzu (c. 298-230 BCE), were able to make significant inroads in communicating Confucian teachings to the political elite. However, they promoted completely opposite reasons for adopting Confucius's ideas. Meng Tzu advocated the intrinsic goodness of human nature, teaching that by not cultivating one's good nature, evil would slowly take over. Meng Tzu maintained that by following the Confucian teachings of self-cultivation, a person could again manifest his or her intrinsic goodness. Hsun-Tzu, on the other hand, asserted the intrinsic evil of human nature. Hsun-Tzu taught that it was necessary to learn how to live morally in order to avoid evil and become good.

During the Han Dynasty (206 BCE—220 CE), the teachings of Confucius became, by imperial decree, the state ideology. (This may be a major reason the Han Dynasty lasted longer than any other Chinese regime.) Confucianism was taught in all the schools and the *Confucian Classics* were required reading for all who aspired to public office. The Confucian ideal of education being not merely for the accumulation of knowledge but also for the building of character took hold. Confucianism began to move toward egalitarianism by its claim that a person was not made noble by birth, but by character. Character-building was a lifelong process of education and self-discipline. By the beginning of the Common Era, the moral idealism of Confucianism could not be separated from the overall Chinese society. Around this time, a cult honoring Confucius as a semi-divine figure emerged. (By the sixth century CE temples to Confucius dotted the land.)

The influence of Confucianism decreased with the collapse of the Han Dynasty (third century CE) while the influence of Taoism and Buddhism increased. By the tenth century however, Confucianism was again gaining prominence. This resurgence was called *Neo-Confucianism*, and it integrated elements of Buddhism and Taoism. Scholars of

Neo-Confucianism were well versed in all three religious traditions and sought to integrate the Taoist beliefs on the universe with the Buddhist beliefs about human nature in the midst of the Confucian scholarly tradition.

This trend reversed itself again during the Qing Dynasty (1644-1911 CE) when there was a move to return to the more "pure" Confucianism of the Han Dynasty. Yet, because of the introduction of many European elements into Chinese society during this time, the reform of Confucianism was unsuccessful. In addition, there was a check on the cult of Confucius in the sixteenth century. Statues of Confucius were replaced with plaques with inscriptions of some of his teachings. Though there was another attempt to form a Confucian cult in the twentieth century, the advent of communism in China put a stop to it.

The Chinese communist revolution of 1949 placed Confucianism in disfavor all around. The Chinese monarchy and traditional family structures and rituals, which helped support Confucianism, were gone. After Mao Tse Tung and the communists came to power, Confucianism, along with all other religions in China, was officially banned from the nation. All religion was considered elitist, out-dated, and a threat to personal freedom.

Presently, Confucianism is again stirring interest among the Chinese elite. Attempting to counter the westernization of China, Confucianism is being regarded as an important part of the Chinese heritage. In fact, to many, Confucius is known as the "father of Chinese culture."

What is your experience of how traditional family structure, rituals, and government can support and foster successful religion?

Words of Confucius

At fifteen, I bent my will to study.

At thirty, I stood firm.

At forty, I did not doubt what was correct.

At fifty, I knew the decrees of heaven.

At sixty, my ears became docile towards truth.

At seventy, I could follow the mind's longings without stepping beyond the strict confines of a carpenter's square.

(Analects 2:4)

Lao Tzu and Taoism

Lao Tzu is traditionally known as a Chinese philosopher who may have lived around the fifth century BCE. He is credited as the founder of Taoism,[6] a religion with roots to 2000 BCE but not expounded officially until around 500 BCE. What little we know was written by Ssu-ma Ch'ien in his *Historical Records* around 100 BCE. According to this account, Lao Tzu's family name was Li and his given name was Erh. Lao Tzu was in charge of sacred books at the court of the Chou dynasty where he may have met up with Confucius, his younger contemporary.

Taoist shrine

known as the *Tao Te Ching*, or "The Way and Its Power," addressing it to sage-kings.

By the third century BCE, Taoist writing emphasized more concern with the individual than with rulers. A follower of Lao Tzu, Chuang Tzu (368-286 BCE), wrote a text rejecting participation in society. In 142 CE, Chang Tao-ling claimed to have received a revelation from "Lao the Most High." Chang Tao-ling was named the first "celestial master" of Taoism. His successors were the spiritual leaders for Taoist priests who ministered in Taoist "churches." The period of celestial masters emphasized both political renewal and self-perfection. In the third century CE after the fall of the Han Dynasty, Chinese rulers began to turn to Taoist leaders for advice in temporal and spiritual matters. Yet, like Confucianism, the ritual aspects of Taoism tended to focus on the elite and not attract common people, until the fourth century when Taoism began to include some elements of folk religion.

In the centuries since, Taoist priests have continued to encourage methods of self-perfection and help individuals control the forces of yin and yang. As with every other form of religion in China, Taoism was discredited by the communist rulers of the twentieth century. However, elaborate Taoist rituals are still conducted in Taiwan and elements of Taoism continue to impact all of Chinese religion and culture.

Disillusioned with the political and moral decline, Lao Tzu rode west to the Chinese wilderness. It is said that the guardian at the frontier pass, Yin His, asked Lao Tzu to write down his words of wisdom. Lao Tzu wrote what became

Both Confucius and Lao Tzu were deified by their followers after their death. Who is a contemporary person who has gained in esteem since his or her death?

Buddhism in China

Buddhism came to China in the first century CE, though it lay rather dormant until the fall of the Confucianist Han Dynasty in 220 CE. At that time, Buddhists began to build temples, monasteries, and orphanages. Mahayana Buddhism dominated, though Vajrayana Buddhism could be found in Mongolia and Tibet by the eighth century CE. Rather than teaching the Buddhist doctrine of *anawa* or "no-self," Buddhists in China taught about the indestructibility of the soul. Also, Buddhists tied the teaching of nirvana to the concept of immortality. In its early stages, Buddhism was closely tied with Taoism, with its various ascetical practices, the use of magic, and the emphasis on the attainment of immortality. In fact, there were some who believed that the Buddha was a reincarnation of Lao Tzu. Temples could be found where the Buddha and Lao Tzu were worshipped together. Translation of the sacred Buddhists scriptures into Chinese began in earnest in the fifth century CE, helping Buddhism to enjoy recognition from both the elite and the peasantry alike. During the Sui Dynasty (581-618 BCE) Buddhism was established as the state religion in China. But it was under the T'ang Dynasty (618-907 BCE) that Buddhism flourished the most.

Under the T'ang Dynasty the number of Buddhist monasteries increased greatly, but the ordination of monks came under control of the state. Buddhism could not lose the perception that it was a "foreign religion." As the monasteries accumulated wealth through land holdings, eventually there was a backlash against Buddhism which accumulated to the point of persecution in 845. Buddhist temples, monasteries,

and shrines were destroyed. Over the next couple of centuries, Buddhism united even more closely to Taoism and those two religions converged with Confucianism and folk religion to form the underpinnings of Chinese religion. Though the Buddhist and Taoist scholars tended to remain separate, Chinese culture as a whole experienced a multi-tradition religious landscape.

Chinese history contributed to a blending of religions. How has American history contributed to a blending of various religious traditions?

SECTION 1 SUMMARY

✤ Chinese religion is a generally a combination of folk religion, Confucianism, Taoism, and Buddhism.

✤ Chinese folk religion includes ancestor worship, divination, astrology, and the principles of yin and yang.

✤ Confucius attempted to revitalize society through the wisdom of the ancients. He was especially interested in values transmitted through ancestor worship, worship of the high god Heaven, and death rites.

✤ Taoism developed in response to Confucianism.

✤ Buddhism had to acculturate to Chinese society before it could find acceptance. Eventually it united with other Chinese religions to form the multi-tradition Chinese religious landscape.

✤ Though Confucianism, Taoism, and Buddhism were all part of Chinese culture, typically only the educated scholars in each tradition were aware of the distinction.

SECTION 1 REVIEW QUESTIONS

1. Briefly describe these elements of Chinese religion: ancestor worship, divination, astrology, and yin and yang.

2. What was the Confucian ideal of education?

3. What did the celestial masters of Taoism emphasize for temporal and spiritual matters?

4. In what ways was Buddhism originally closely tied with Taoism?

II. BELIEFS AND ACTIONS

Since both Confucius and Lao Tzu were contemporaries, it is not surprising to find that they had some of the same ideas about human nature, society, sovereignty, Heaven, and the universe. The difference was their emphasis. While Confucianism emphasized the cultivation of a virtuous life, which in turn would spawn political leaders who could help create an ideal society, Taoism was more concerned with "the way life is." Recall that *Tao* means "way."

Confucianism

Confucius believed in the high god Heaven and the various other Chinese deities. Confucius also engaged in other folk rituals and practices of his time. In other words, one might call Confucius a "practicing Chinese." However, Confucius was also wary of the various cults that were part of Chinese society. Though he did believe in the various gods and goddesses, he also believed that they should be kept at a distance. As the high god Heaven was perfect, so humans should strive for perfection. For

Confucians, that perfection came not from relationships with the gods, but through people's relationships with one another. In many ways, Confucianism was a form of character indoctrination. The one who attained perfection was a *chun-tzu*, the "superior one." In Confucius's time, only aristocratic men were educated, but Confucius chose to teach any male he considered intelligent enough to engage in the process of

Emperor to subject—An emperor was to be an example to his subjects, calling them to live the same virtuous life as he did.

Father to son—A father was to be a model to his son who was, in turn, to honor his parents in this lifetime and revere them in the next.

Husband to wife—The husband was to head the household and preserve

The relationship of a husband to his wife is covered under li.

learning and character building. The period of formation included the principles of *li* and *jen*—though not specifically religious, they are nevertheless representative of Chinese culture and thought.

Li

Li had to do with the proper way to live, calling for courtesy, etiquette, formality, and respect. Li also called for sincerity in these gestures, teaching that they should flow from the basic goodness of the person. Li focused on an ideal way of behaving for five common relationships in Chinese society:

the memory of his family's ancestors; the wife was to bear sons and to obey her husband.

Elder brother to younger brother—The younger brother was to respect his older brother, for the older brother was responsible for carrying out the family rituals in ancestor reverence.

Friend to friend (males)—Friends were to respect each other, with the junior friend showing deference to the elder one.

Jen

Jen refers to "humanity" or "benevolence." While li pointed outward toward behavior, jen pointed inward to one's heart. According to Confucian thought, a person should be transformed from a life ruled by passions to one ruled by enlightened wisdom. Religious and ethical rituals helped a person achieve jen.

A person who combined li with jen was in position to be a *chun-tzu*, a superior one. A person cannot fake being *chun-tzu*. Being *chun-tzu* means having jen be so much a part of one's self that benevolence flows into action in any situation.

Confucian character formation would prohibit someone from being phony or "two faced." How so?

Taoism

Though the word Tao can be defined as the "way, path, or course," really any definition falls short. Taoism can be thought of as the way or the nature of things. The goal of humanity, then, is to move in harmony with Tao. A "go with the flow" attitude permeates all creation, so creation flows with Tao. Taoism is a return to simplicity and harmony with all creation, for Tao is the ultimate source of all creation—an impersonal God, so to speak.

Experiencing Taoism

In order to go into Taoism at all, we must begin by being in the frame of mind in which it can be understood. You cannot force yourself into this frame of mind, any more than you can smooth disturbed water with your hand. But let's say that our starting point is that we forget what we know, or think we know, and that we suspend judgment about practically everything, returning to what we were when we were babies, when we had not yet learned the names or the language. And in this state, although we have extremely sensitive bodies and very alive senses, we have no means of making an intellectual or verbal commentary on what is going on.

You are just plain ignorant, but still very much alive, and in this state you just feel what is without calling it anything at all. You know nothing at all about anything called an external world in relation to an internal world. You don't know who you are, you haven't even the idea of the word you or I—it is before all that. Nobody has taught you self control, so you don't know the difference between the noise of a car outside and a wandering thought that enters your mind—they are both something that happens. You don't identify the presence of a thought that may be just an image of a passing cloud in your mind's eye or the passing automobile; they happen. Your breath happens. Light, all around you, happens. Your response to it by blinking happens.

So, on one hand you are simply unable to do anything, and on the other there is nothing you are supposed to do. Nobody has told you anything to do. You are completely unable to do anything but be aware of the buzz. The visual buzz, the audible buzz, the tangible buzz, the smellable buzz—all around the buzz is going on. Watch it. Don't ask who is watching it; you have no information about that yet. You don't know that it requires a watcher for something to be watched. That is somebody's idea; but you don't know that.

Lao Tzu says, "The scholar learns something every day, the man of Tao unlearns something every day, until he gets back to non-doing." Just simply, without comment, without an idea in your head, be aware. What else can you do? You don't try to be aware; you are. You will find, of course, that you cannot stop the commentary going on inside your head, but at least you can regard it as interior noise. Listen to your chattering thoughts as you would listen to the singing of a kettle.

We don't know what it is we are aware of, especially when we take it altogether, and there's this sense of something going on. I can't even really say 'this,' although I said 'something going on.' But that is an idea, a form of words. Obviously I couldn't say something is going on unless I could say something else isn't. I know motion by contrast with rest, and while I am aware of motion I am also aware of at rest. So maybe what's at rest isn't going and what's in motion is going, but I won't use that concept then because in order for it to make sense I have to include both. If I say here it is, that excludes what isn't, like space. If I say this, it excludes that, and I am reduced to silence. But you can feel what I am talking about. That's what is called Tao, in Chinese. That's where we begin.

Quoted from an article by AlanWatts (http://www.alanwatts.com/Taoism.html)

Action Without Action

Taoists believed that the force through which Tao acts is *wu-wei*,[7] or non-action. Wu-wei may be more precisely explained as "action without actions." It is paradoxically the power of action through non-action. For example, the emotions a painting can evoke just by hanging in a gallery are a form of wu-wei. The government leader who purified himself in order to purify society is wu-wei. Or, wu-wei is the non-action of a newborn whose various needs are nevertheless taken care of. The non-action evokes action. That is the way of Tao.

Immortality

While the goal of a Confucian was to be a chun-tzu, the goal of a Taoist was immortality. Taoists believed that actual physical immortality was a reachable goal. Immortality was expressed through union with Tao. To attain immortality a Taoist would engage in several practices. Breath control, good hygiene, certain elixirs, meditation, and proper rituals all contributed to immortality. Taoists often refrained from eating certain foods, like grain and meat. To Taoists, life was a delicate balance between yin and yang. If that balance could be maintained, death could be avoided and immortality achieved.

Deities and Other Spirits

By the ninth century CE, Taoists believed in a whole pantheon of gods, including, eventually, Lao Tzu. The high god of the pantheon was known as Yu Huang, the Taoist "sky god" or "Heaven" as known by the Confucians. Taoists were known for their celebrations, lavish costumes and temples, and complex rituals. Those who were believed to have reached immortality were known as *hsiens*.[8] They too were worshipped as gods, along with Buddha, bodhisatvas, and gods of other Chinese religions.

How does "go with the flow" aptly describe one of the tenets of Taoism?

Scriptures

Neither Confucius nor Lao Tzu considered themselves founders of a religion. Confucius drew from the ancient sages while the *Tao Te Ching* ("Book of the Way") is not believed to be the work solely of Lao Tzu but also of several persons living after Lao Tzu who drew from centuries-old writings. (For this reason it is accurate to say that Taoism predates Confucianism.) Neither Confucius nor Lao Tzu ever claimed that they received revelations from any deities. So, too, their scriptures are not documents of revelation such as the Bible or the Qur'an. Confucius is credited with compiling and creating several volumes of Chinese literature to add to what was already in place. After his death, a large body of Confucian and Taoist scriptures became sources of inspiration for centuries and the means to train students in Confucianism.

Confucian Classics

The Confucian sacred writings are commonly called the *Confucian Classics*, though some of them are writings that predate Confucius. The *Confucian Classics* can be divided into two main groups:

The Five Classics are classics of an ancient age considered by Confucius to be golden. These were the main documents used by Confucius to teach his students and included historical documents, an anthology of poems, a manual for divination, records of the state of Lu where Confucius was born, and three works on the principles of li, that is, proper conduct.

The Four Books were compiled by Confucius's followers. They are texts of wisdom inspired by Confucius and

Meng Tzu, Confucius's disciple. The Four Books include the *Analects* (sayings of Confucius), *The Great Learning* (which details how perfection can benefit society), *Doctrine of the Mean* (philosophical utterances systematically arranged with commentaries by the compilers of the text), and *Book of Meng Tzu* (sayings of the great follower of Confucius).

Eventually a student had to master these nine texts in order to pass exams and secure employment in the government.

The Great Wall

Tao Te Ching

The *Tao Te Ching* is one of the most widely read pieces of Chinese literature in the world. It is the main piece of sacred writings of the Taoists. The *Tao Te Ching* has been translated into a number of languages. Though its authorship is attributed to the sixth century BCE sage, Lao Tzu, it is more likely that a group of people authored it several centuries after his lifetime. The *Tao Te Ching* is the source of the Taoist beliefs discussed earlier, that is, Tao is the nature of things, all that emanates from Tao returns to Tao,

the power of wu-wei (non-action), and the call to live a life of simplicity in harmony with Tao. The following are excerpts from the *Tao Te Ching* on the Tao itself:

The tao that can be told
is not the eternal Tao.
The name that can be named
is not the eternal Name.
The unnameable is the eternally real.
Naming is the origin
of all particular things.

The Tao is like a well:
Used but never used up.
It is like the eternal void:
filled with infinite possibilities.

It is hidden but always present.
I don't know who gave birth to it.
It is older than God.

The Tao is called the Great Mother:
empty yet inexhaustible,
it gives birth to infinite worlds.
It is always present with you.
You can use it any way you want.

The Tao is infinite, eternal.
Why is it eternal?
It was never born;
thus it can never die.
Why is it infinite?
It has no desires for itself;
thus it is present for all beings . . .

(*Tao Te Ching* 1:1-2, 4, 7)

Chinese Living

For the average Chinese, the religions discussed in this chapter are not distinguishable within his or her religious experience. For example, it is not unusual to see statues of both Lao Tzu and the Buddha in the same temple and equally revered.

Confucius assured that the best way to live was as a superior person who combined li with jen. Taoists and Buddhists would say that the most virtuous person practiced wu-wei, or action without action. Both jen and wu-wei are a part of the fabric of Chinese culture. It is likely that the average Chinese person who practices them is unaware of whether one religion is being emphasized over the other.

One would think with such diverse practices and beliefs, the idea of forming a community rooted in religious beliefs would not be possible. For example, Chinese society has long been rooted in family structures, including the practice of ancestor worship, yet monasticism was an important part of Buddhism and Taoism. How could these three very different religious traditions combine and merge to form one Chinese community? A famous cliché may help to explain. It goes like this: Chinese are Confucian in public, Taoist in private, and Buddhist with regard to death. Chinese have a broad spectrum of beliefs and practices that are woven so tightly into Chinese culture that the only way to make distinctions is to take the threads out piece by piece. However, systematically removing the threads would weaken the fabric of society. That is why only in a course of study like this one are these distinctions usually pointed out.

How are traditions from various religions blended into the American culture?

SECTION 2 SUMMARY

✤ Confucianism is concerned with character formation. In Confucianism, li ("proper way of living") and jen ("benevolence") are two of the most important virtues leading to perfection.

✤ Tao permeates all creation—it is an impersonal God, so to speak.

✤ Wu-wei is "action without action," the force through which Tao acts.

✤ Taoists believe that actual physical immortality is a reachable goal.

✤ The Confucian Classics are a set of nine works—divided into two sections—that make up the Confucian scriptures. Some of the writings predate Confucianism.

✤ *Tao Te Ching* is the main sacred writing of the Taoists. It means "the way and its power."

✤ Both the jen of Confucius and the wu-wei of Taoism and Buddhism form the fabric of Chinese living.

✤ The average Chinese person does not consciously make a distinction between the various Chinese religious traditions.

SECTION 2 REVIEW QUESTIONS

1. Explain li and jen. How do they compliment one another?

2. What is the meaning of Tao?

3. Explain wu-wei by giving at least one example.

4. What are some steps a Taoist might take to achieve immortality?

5. What makes up the Analects?

6. Who likely authored the *Tao Te Ching*?

7. How does the saying "Chinese are Confucian in public, Taoists in private, and Buddhist with regard to death" help to describe the Chinese integration of religion?

III. SACRED PLACES

Whatever the number of "sacred spaces" in China prior to 1949, the number has diminished since the communist revolution. In the past fifty years many Chinese temples have been either destroyed or turned into government facilities. Those temples left for religious practice are heavily regulated. The government also monitors the selection of religious leaders in the various traditions.

Temples

China has a number of different kinds of temples. There are Taoist and Buddhist temples, and even some Confucian temples. Temples are further defined as local or state temples. Local temples are places for people to make offerings to the gods and to the local ancestors. Before this century, the state temples were places where the emperor would make sacrifices on behalf of his subjects, usually to Heaven, other lesser deities, and to Confucius.

Shrines of Ancestors

Within the Chinese temples are typically shrines to local gods and to ancestors of the local family or families. Also, most Chinese maintain an ancestor shrine at home where offerings of food and incense are made to one or more ancestors, sometimes even on a daily basis.

Ancestor Graves

For the Chinese, the world of the dead is a mirror image of the world of the living. This means that the needs of the deceased are similar to the needs of the living. Choosing a burial site is taken very seriously by the Chinese. A wrong

gravesite would be one inhabited by evil powers and bad spirits. *Feng-shui* is the art of divining a place or date that has a positive spiritual aura. Feng-shui has become popular recently in the United States as an aspect of interior design.

Ch'u Fou is the burial place of Confucius. As Chinese reverence their familial ancestors, they also revere their spiritual ancestor, Confucius.

As China's government permits more religious freedom, what do you think will be the reaction of the general Chinese population?

SECTION 3 SUMMARY

✤ Many Chinese temples were destroyed or turned over to the government after the Chinese revolution.

✤ Chinese honor their ancestors at local temples, home shrines, and graves.

✤ Ch'u Fou is sacred because it is the burial place for Confucius.

SECTION 3 REVIEW QUESTIONS

1. Why are there fewer Confucian temples in China now than there were prior to 1949?

2. Define *feng-shui*.

IV. SACRED TIME

Chinese religions operate on a lunar calendar unique to their traditions. Like the other lunar calendars, the Chinese lunar calendar has 354 days. The Chinese name their years by combining one of the ten celestial stems with one of the twelve terrestrial branches. The stems and branches are arranged in such a way that the name of a year will recur only once every sixty years. The twelve terrestrial branches also have animals associated with them. It is with the animal name of the year that westerners are most familiar, such as "the Year of the Dragon."

Celestial Stems	Terrestrial Branches	Animals	Gregorian Calendar
Chia	Tzu	Rat	2008
Yi	Chou	Ox	2009
Ping	Yin	Tiger	2010
Ting	Mao	Hare	1999
Wu	Chin	Dragon	2000
Chi	Ssu	Snake	2001
Keng	Wu	Horse	2002
Hsin	Wei	Sheep	2003
Jen	Shen	Monkey	2004
Kwei	Yu	Rooster	2005
Chia	Hsu	Dog	2006
Yi	Hi	Boar	2007

Festivals

Many traditional festivals are a part of Chinese heritage. Recently, there has been some resumption of the festivals in communist China, though each has been celebrated outside of mainland China on a regular basis. Descriptions of the main Chinese festivals follow.

Chinese New Year

The Chinese New Year is the most important of all Chinese festivals. It takes place sometime between late January and late February, depending on behavior of the humans for the year. Tso Kwan means "Stove Master." He is the kitchen god of China. On New Year's Day itself family members exchange small gifts, often money wrapped in a

Chinese New Year

the lunar (moon) calendar. Major celebrations occur in Hong Kong, until recently under British rule. A few weeks before the New Year, the Chinese prepare by thoroughly cleaning their homes and purchasing items like tangerine plants, flower displays, Chinese paintings, and calligraphy. Hong Kong is laden with brightly colored decorations and stores are packed with shoppers.

On New Year's Eve, Chinese say prayers and pay homage to Tso Kwan, who returns to heaven to report on the red packet. Another traditional part of the festival is Kai Nien or "Squabble Day," so called because it is believed that if you argue on this day, many arguments will follow during the rest of the year. On the fourth day of the festival Tso Kwan is welcomed back and a new picture is hung in the kitchen. On the fifteenth day of the festival, a three-day lantern celebration begins. Lanterns are hung in homes promoting good fortune, health, and happiness. The celebration of lanterns ends the New Year's festivities.

Ching Ming

Ching Ming means "Remembrance of Ancestors Day." It is celebrated in April and is a day devoted to honoring deceased relatives. Chinese flock to cemeteries to clean and care for the graves of their relatives. Also, willow branches are hung in doorways to ward off evil spirits. Legend has it that those who don't hang the willow will appear as dogs in their next life.

The legend dates from the eleventh century CE when Tin Hau had a dream that her brothers were drowning. She flew over the waters on clouds and rescued her family.

There are numerous shrines and temples dedicated to Tin Hau. Chinese boat people, sailors, and those who live on the waterfront sail to Da Miao (the Great Temple) in Joss HoUse Bay on Tin Hau's birthday, paying respect to the goddess and asking for safety in the coming year.

River market

Tin Hau

The Tin Hau festival is celebrated on the twenty-third day of the Third Moon (late April, early May). The day is set aside to honor a young girl known as Tin Hau, the "Queen of Heaven." She is the mother of boat people and sailors.

Tuen Ng (Dragon Boat) Festival

Tuen Ng, or the "Dragon Boat Festival" is held in late spring. The day honors Wut Yuan, a famous Chinese patriot who wrote many classical poems espousing Chinese nationalism. At the end of his life, Wut Yuan became disillusioned and drowned himself in the Milo River. The local people were so upset by this that they went out on the river in boats and began to beat the water with their paddles to keep the fish from eating his body. They also threw rice in the water to draw the fish away.

The Dragon Boat Festival consists of a variety of decorated, colorful boats, all including the fierce head of a dragon. The dragons symbolically search the waters for Wut Yuan's body.

Mid Autumn Festival

The Mid Autumn festival is second in popularity to New Year's. It recalls a time during the Tang Dynasty when Chinese rulers carefully studied the moon. Today, to celebrate this festival, Chinese people, and citizens of Hong Kong especially, travel to high places in the region to make sure they have a good view of the moon. The hills of Victoria in Hong Kong, as well as the area beaches shimmer in the glow of lantern lights.

Life Cycles

In Chinese culture the birth of a boy is preferred over the birth of a girl. It is a boy who carries on the family name,

takes care of the parents in old age, and sees to it that ancestors are cared for. Today there is a government policy in China limiting births in an attempt to slow population growth. In this case, the birth of a girl is seen as particularly misfortunate as the couple often has no chance for a second child. Because of this, many Chinese women determine the sex of the child before birth and abort the fetus if it is a girl.

After the birth of a child, the mother is to rest for a one-month period, allowing other family members to care for her and her child. At the end of the month there is a celebration in which the newborn is given symbolic gifts representing good health and prosperity. People eat eggs on that day as a sign of good luck.

Food also plays a part in the celebration of the "coming of age" of a child in the beginning of his or her teenage years. The celebrants eat chicken as a main course, believing chicken to be a sign of maturity. Chinese also mark other traditional times and events, including marriage and death.

Marriage

There are six stages to a Chinese marriage:

Proposal—A determination is made of whether or not the man and woman are a good match. There is the exchange of the "eight characters" of the man and woman to check the Chinese horoscope. The eight characters are the year, month, day, and hour of the birth of each person. Also, if any inauspicious event occurs in the family of the bride-to-be during the three days after the proposal, it is taken as a sign that the proposal has been rejected.

Engagement—After the wedding date is determined with the help of the Chinese horoscope, the woman's family announces the engagement with invitations and the gift of cookies made in the shape of the moon.

Dowry—The woman's family delivers the dowry in a procession to the house of the groom-to-be. The man sends gifts equal in value to the dowry to the woman.

Procession—The man goes to the family home of the woman to escort her to his home.

Wedding—On the wedding day vows are exchanged and a great banquet takes place.

Morning After—The day after the wedding the new bride serves her parents-in-law breakfast and they reciprocate. Gifts of dried fruit are given to the newly married couple as a symbol of a good marriage and fertility.

Death

At death, the body is washed and placed in a coffin. Food and objects significant to the deceased are placed in the coffin to help the deceased enter the next world. Family members cry out to inform the neighbors of the death and put on clothes made of coarse material. Mourners bring incense and money to help with the funeral expenses. A Taoist or Buddhist priest performs the funeral rites. Sometimes a Christian minister assists. Mourners follow the coffin to the cemetery carrying willow branches, which symbolize the soul of the person who died. The branch is then carried to the family ancestral altar and placed there in honor of the spirit of the deceased.

SECTION 4 SUMMARY

❖ The Chinese year is most familiarly known by the name of the animal associated with the twelve terrestrial branches.

❖ Though there are numerous traditional Chinese festivals, few are celebrated on mainland China.

❖ The Chinese New Year is the most important Chinese festival. The Mid Autumn festival is second in importance.

❖ The Chinese mark important life cycle events with traditions encompassing a variety of religions.

SECTION 4 REVIEW QUESTIONS

1. Describe the Chinese New Year's celebration.

2. Why is the birth of a boy preferred over the birth of a girl in Chinese culture?

3. Name the six stages of a typical Chinese marriage.

Who Is My Neighbor?

CHINESE AMERICANS IN LOS ANGELES

Today in Los Angeles County there are nearly a half a million Chinese Americans, making the Chinese Americans one of the most populous and influential ethnic groups in the region.

In the late nineteenth century, a Chinatown was established in the heart of Los Angeles, occupying three sides of the El Pueblo Plaza. Old Chinatown had eight streets, hundreds of buildings and stores, several restaurants, three temples, eight missionary churches, a Chinese school, and a theater for Chinese operas. Chinatown was the center for laborers and farm workers. (Chinese of that time were also the dominant group in Los Angeles in agricultural produce as growers, vendors, and market proprietors.)

In the 1930s the city of Los Angeles built its Union Station in the midst of Chinatown, forcing a relocation to the north and west. New Chinatown still exists today, just blocks from city hall and the Music Center, and just down the hill from Dodger Stadium, home of the local baseball team. New Chinatown is still the home to many old time residents and merchants, as well as more recent settlers.

The Chinese in the United States have faced their share of discrimination. The most serious incident in Los Angeles was the murder of nineteen Chinese by a mob of 500 locals in 1871. Laws restricted Chinese immigration to the United States for many years. Local restrictive covenants on the ownership and use of property required Chinese immigrants to live in and around the inner-city Chinatowns.

Los Angeles relaxed such covenants in the 1950s and Chinese Americans began to live in other neighborhoods around Los Angeles. New immigration laws in the mid 1960s resulted in a great increase in the Chinese American population. The Chinese origins of these people are Quongdong, Chieu Chow, Amoy, and Fukien. There are also many arrivals from Hong Kong, Taiwan, and all parts of China. Many have low incomes and are elderly. These immigrants tend to use Chinatown as their entry point and place of residence. However the more affluent of the Chinese immigrants have settled and do business in the suburbs, especially the San Gabriel Valley and parts of Orange County. However, even among these suburban Chinese immigrants is a respect for New Chinatown as a social, spiritual, and cultural base of their heritage.

Asian farmer

Conclusion

Chinese religion received its name from the place where it began. However, the overt practice of Chinese religion in mainline China today is almost non-existent. It survives with those of Chinese origin or ancestry who live out-side mainline China in places such as Taiwan, Korea, Indonesia, Europe, and North America. Though there has recently been some loosening of regula-tions from the Chinese government, reli-gious practices are rare. Even where Chinese religions are practiced there is a great integration especially among Confucianism, Taoism, and Buddhism. The average Chinese person has little knowledge of the origins of his or her religion, nor how the different traditions vary. Religious observance often involves ancestor worship and a respect of older, wiser family members. Oftentimes it also involves superstitions, offerings, and rituals designed to temper the evil spirits and reward the good ones.

In these days of increasing western influence in China it remains to be seen if other religions that demand more rigid control of mind, body, and spirit will have success in gaining a following there.

Hong Kong Harbor

Buddhist nun

CHAPTER 7 IN BRIEF

❖ Chinese religion is a multi-religious tradition of folk religion, Taoism, Confucianism, and Buddhism.

❖ Through much of its history there has been a close relationship between Chinese religion and the state.

❖ Confucianism is a form of character indoctrination; the one who attains perfection is Chun-tzu, the "superior one."

❖ Taoism is the "way" or "nature of things." It involves a "go with the flow" mentality.

❖ Chinese living is greatly influenced by Confucian teachings of li ("courtesy, etiquette") and jen ("benevolence").

❖ Taoists believe that the force with which Tao acts is wu-wei, or nonaction.

❖ Temples, homes, shrines, and ancestor graves are sacred spaces for the Chinese.

❖ All of the traditional Chinese festivals in some way have to do with appeasing the gods, spirits, or ancestors.

CHAPTER 7 REVIEW QUESTIONS

1. Why are ancestors so important to the Chinese?

2. Explain wu-wei.

3. What are two common relationships on which li is focused?

4. How has Buddhism influenced Chinese religion?

5. What would a person who kept a balance between yin and yang achieve?

6. How does the ultimate goal for a Confucian compare with the ultimate goal of Taoist?

7. Why is it believed that Taoism predates Confucianism?

8. What is the *Tao Te Ching?*

9. In the feature "Who Is My Neighbor?" what were examples of Grand Aunt's feng shui?

10. Explain why most Chinese may not be able to explain the origins of their religion or the differences between it and another religion.

RESEARCH AND ACTIVITIES

1. Read an Amy Tan novel (e.g, *The Joy Luck Club, The Kitchen God's Wife*), and write an essay on how Chinese religion is portrayed in it.

2. Watch the Disney animated film *Mulan* and participate in a class discussion on

its portrayal of Chinese religion. Note whether or not there is one religious tradition that seems to be more emphasized than others in the film.

3. Create a multi-page portfolio that contains Confucian sayings and Chinese art.

4. Read *The Tao of Pooh* or *The Te of Piglet*, both by Benjamin Hoff. What does Hoff teach about Taoism?

5. Write an essay on one of the following topics:

"American Society Needs to Put More Yin in Its Yang."

The Chinese custom of female foot binding

Christianity in China

Urban United States Chinatowns

SELECTED VOCABULARY

Chuang Tzu	Jade Emperor
chun-tzu	Jen
Confucian Classics	Lao Tzu
Confucius	li
divination	Tao Te Ching
feng-shui	wu-wei
folk religion	yang
Heaven	yin

Chapter 8
JAPANESE RELIGIONS

n a traditional Japanese story, the heavenly gods Izanagi and Izanami descend to bring order out of the chaos of the earth, resulting in the creation of Japan:

Many gods were thus born in succession, and so they increased in number, but as long as the world remained in a chaotic state, there was nothing for them to do. Whereupon, all the Heavenly deities summoned the two divine beings, Izanagi and Izanami, and bade them descend to the nebulous place, and by helping each other, to consolidate it into terra firma. "We bestow on you," they said, "this precious treasure, with which to rule the land, the creation of which we command you to perform." So saying they handed them a spear called Ama-no-Nuboko, embellished with costly gems. The divine couple received respectfully and ceremoniously the sacred weapon and then withdrew from the presence of the Deities, ready to perform their august commission. Proceeding forthwith to the Floating Bridge of Heaven, which lay between the heaven and the earth, they stood awhile to gaze on that which lay below. What they beheld was a world not yet condensed, but looking like a sea of filmy fog floating to and fro in the air, exhaling the while an inexpressibly fragrant odor. They were, at first, perplexed just how and where to start, but at length Izanagi suggested to his companion that they should try the effect of stirring up the brine with their spear. So saying he pushed down the jeweled shaft and found that it touched something. Then drawing it up, he examined it and observed that the great drops which fell from it almost immediately coagulated into an island, which is, to this day, the Island of Onokoro [Japan]. Delighted at the result, the two deities descended forthwith from the Floating Bridge to reach the miraculously created island. In this island they thenceforth dwelt and made it the basis of their subsequent task of creating a country.

Quoted from *Reading About the World*, Volume 1, edited by Paul Brians, Mary Gallwey, Douglas Hughes, Michael Myers, Michael Neville, Roger Schlesinger, Alice Spitzer, and Susan Swan (American Heritage Custom Publishing.)

CE

5	Establishment of National Shrine at Ise
552	Buddhism comes to Japan
594	Buddhism commissioned as a state religion
1175	Pure Land Buddhism established
1200s	Rise of samurai
1549	Jesuit missionary Francis Xavier arrives in Japan
1600s	Beginning of Tokugawa Shogunate
1854	Meiji restoration and creation of State Shinto
1945	Japan defeated in World War II

Japanese have long felt their island nation has heavenly origins. In fact, Japanese believe gods inhabited the land and were very much a part of the created world. Like Chinese religion, Japanese religion is an amalgamation of religions. There are the indigenous traditions of folk religion and Shinto as well as Buddhism, Confucianism, and Taoism. Placed in a Japanese setting, these religious traditions have a very thin, often transparent line separating them. Shinto literally translates to "the way of the gods," coming from the Chinese *shin tao*. Shinto has its roots in *animism*, a belief that says there is a spirit, or god, in all things. Japanese are especially in tune to the presence of gods and spirits in nature. Since the other religions have been discussed elsewhere in this text, more emphasis will be placed on Shinto in this chapter and its relationship with other religious traditions of the Japanese.

What is one lesson about God you have learned from examining nature?

I. A BRIEF HISTORY OF JAPANESE RELIGIONS

The exact origin of purely Japanese religion is difficult to determine. The written history begins when Japanese culture meets with Chinese and Korean culture at the beginning of the Common Era. The Chinese introduced the systematic Chinese characters to Japanese writing. Prior to that period, there was no name for the diverse Japanese religious expressions. Japan was organized by clans, and worship and ritual took place through the clan structure. With the influx of new religions, the Japanese found it necessary to name what was purely Japanese religion. Though Shinto was the name given to the indigenous Japanese religion by the Chinese, the word *kami* [1] may actually better describe Japanese religion. There are thought to be eight million kami, divided into either gods of the sky or gods of the soil. The kami are everywhere. At first honored in natural settings, kami eventually became enshrined at various local clan sites. However, kamis did not reside at the shrine, but were called upon during the ritual and then sent away.

In the Japanese creation story, the world and all that is in it is counted as good. After the creation of Japan, Izanagi and his mate Izanami inhabited the island. The couple bore many offspring, of which Amaterasu, the sun goddess, was the chief. Other kami gave birth to the Japanese people. As the story unfolds, Amaterasu was unhappy with the chaos she saw among the inhabitants of the island, so she sent her grandson with a sacred mirror, sword, and jewel to rule. Subsequently, his great-grandson became the first emperor of the island with the mirror, sword, and jewel as the imperial emblems. According to this myth Japan was the center of the world and its rulers were direct descendants of Amaterasu.

In the middle of the sixth century, Buddhism, Taoism, and Confucianism were introduced to Japan. The Japanese imperial court became interested in these new religions because they came from China, a place that seemed superior to Japan. Eager to learn all they could, the Japanese ruling class adopted the Confucian model of education. They also found Confucian social conventions helpful in forging a national identity. Japanese leaders were also attracted to Buddhist philosophy and its elaborate doctrine, well-organized priesthood, art, and literature. In 594 CE Prince Shotoku made Buddhism the state religion and during the next few centuries a number of Buddhist temples, shrines, and monasteries were built. Yet the Japanese indigenous religion did not disappear, for the creation myth that was told and retold made them a divine people.

What is a national myth of the United States? How does it help define the nation, its leaders, and its people?

The Classical Period

During the Heian Period (794-1185), Japan moved from a centralized to a feudal form of government. Buddhism became the prominent religion in Japan. In the ninth century two new Buddhist sects—named Tendai and Shingon—were introduced in Japan via China. Yet, Japanese Buddhism was unique. These were forms of Mahayana Buddhism that saw no problems in claiming kami and bodhisatvas as one and the same thing. Shinto shrines and Buddhist temples stood side by side in Japan. It was not unusual for Buddhist monks to perform rituals at Shinto shrines. This mutual arrangement continued until the nineteenth century when the Meiji government forced a separation between Shinto and Buddhism. It was during the Kamakura *shogunate*[2] (1185-1333) that many sects of Buddhism flourished.

Ch'an Buddhism (a combination of Mahayana Buddhism and Taoism) from China became *Zen Buddhism* in Japan. The two most noted schools of Zen Buddhism are Rinzai and Soto Zen. While Rinzai Zen believes a person can gain immediate enlightenment, Soto Zen believes enlightenment is a gradual process. While Soto Zen emphasized a method of *zazen*,[3] Rinzai placed more emphasis on the *koan*. A koan is a problem with no logical solution that a Zen master presents to a student to solve. Koans are meant to break through logic and intellect in order for an intuitive flash, called a *satori*,[4] to emerge and eventually lead to enlightenment. Three notable koans are:

"What is the sound of one hand clapping?"

"When a tree falls in a forest where no one is present, does it make a sound?"

"What was your face like before your parents were born?"

The heart of Zen Buddhism in both schools is meditation. Zen Buddhists sit in meditation, known as *zazen*, and make no judgments or comments about the insights they receive through their meditation practice. Zen Buddhists compare the mind to a window. The person is to look directly out of the window rather than have someone else explain to them what is outside the window. That other person will inevitably interpret the scene rather than name the person's direct experience.

Zen is more interested in a direct vision of nature than interpretations of nature. Rather than statues and pictures of the Buddha or bodhisatvas, the art of Zen Buddhists is of nature. Gardens, rocks, mountains, and birds are the most popular subjects of Zen Buddhist art. The Zen connection between religion and nature is truly seamless.

How does work deepen your spiritual well being?

The Modern Period

In 1549 the first Christian missionaries (including Jesuit Francis Xavier) came to Japan. These first missionaries, with some government approval, were able to win converts to the faith primarily due to the Japanese interest in things western. However, the work of Christian missionaries did not last long. Fearing the missionaries had a political agenda, an edict banishing all Catholic Christian missionaries was promulgated in 1587. In 1596 twenty-seven European and Japanese Christians were martyred at Nagasaki.

The Tokugawa *shogunate* came into power in 1603. The new rulers (called *shoguns*) had inherited a fragmented government, so they reorganized society in a manner influenced by Confucian values. Particularly important were the five relationships of li (see page 149), especially the relationship between ruler and subject. Also, the Tokugawan reformers required citizens to register with a Buddhist temple which meant that the number of Buddhist temples increased greatly. An overall theme of the reformers was to purify Japan from all outside influences.

Some reformers even attempted to return Japan to a time before the influence of Chinese culture. Motoori Norinaga (1730-1801) was the most famous of these reformers seeking a pure Shintoism, though other religious traditions had become so imbedded in Japanese culture that "pure Shinto" was impossible.

What would it be like if your neighborhood tried to remove the influence that one culture or another has had there?

The Meiji Period (1852-1912) restored some of the imperial power lost under the shogunates. The Meiji opened wide the doors for trade with the west. They believed the centuries of isolation put Japan far behind the industrial west. They also forced a separation between Shinto and Buddhism, and there was a concerted move toward nationalism, restoring Japan to the time when the emperor was a kami and the Japanese people were of divine origin with a divine mission. All Japanese, whatever their religious tradition, were to perform rituals as part of State Shinto, but interestingly, the Meiji decided to declare that State Shinto was not a religion. By doing so, people could practice the religion of their choice and yet remain loyal to the imperial family and to Japan.

What are the advantages and disadvantages of living in a governmental system that separates church from state?

An Eyewitness Account

Lafacdio Hearn was a journalist for *Harper's Magazine* when he was commissioned to write a series of articles on Japan in 1890. While in Japan he married a Japanese woman and became a naturalized citizen of that country. Before his death in 1904 he had written a number of books on Japan and was celebrated in both Japan and the United States. The following is an excerpt from his eyewitness account written at the turn of the twentieth century:

In Izumo, the oldest Shinto province, the customary morning worship offers perhaps the best example of the ancient rules of devotion. Immediately upon rising, the worshiper performs his ablutions;[5] and after having washed his face and rinsed his mouth, he turns to the sun, claps his hands, and with bowed head reverently utters the simple greeting: "Hail to thee this day, August One!" In thus adoring the sun he is also fulfilling his duty as a subject—paying obedience to the Imperial Ancestor. . . . The act is performed out of doors, not kneeling, but standing; and the spectacle of this simple worship is impressive. I can now see in memory—just as plainly as I saw with my eyes many years ago, off the wild Oko coast—the naked figure of a young fisherman erect at the prow of his boat, clapping his hands in salutation to the rising sun, whose ruddy glow transformed him into a statue of bronze. Also I retain a vivid memory of pilgrim figures poised upon the topmost crags of the summit of Fuji, clapping their hands in prayer, with faces to the east. . . . Perhaps ten thousand—twenty thousand—years ago all humanity so worshipped the Lord of Day. . . .

After having saluted the sun, the worshiper returns to his house, to pray before the Kamidana[6] and before the tables of the ancestors. Kneeling, he invokes the great gods of Ise or of Izumo, the gods of the chief temples of his province, the god of his parish-temple also (Ujigami), and finally all the myriads of the deities of Shinto. These prayers are not said aloud. The ancestors are thanked for the foundation of the home: the higher deities are invoked for aid and protection.

Quoted from *The Ways of Religion: An Introduction to the Major Traditions*, edited by Roger Eastman (New York: Oxford University Press, 1993)

After World War II there was a tremendous surge in what were known as "new religions" in either Shinto or Buddhist traditions, but are more properly known as religious movements or societies. Individuals who claimed divine revelation or their own divinity founded these new groups. They were not really new religions, for they integrated elements of the existing religions of Japan into their movement or society. In the twentieth century *Tenrikyo*[7] was an example of one of these so-called "new religions."

The defeat of Japan in World War II was devastating to a nation that believed itself to be at the center of creation. At the end of the war, the Allies forced Emperor Hirohito to renounce his divinity, leaving the Japanese people to practice any religion they chose. Thus, State Shinto and nationalism were weakened. This left room for the "new religions" to advance. Recently, however, the more ancient forms of Shinto and Buddhism have, once again, attracted some Japanese devotees. Surpassing all religious revivals, however, has been the revival of Japanese nationalism. Deprived of building another powerful army by the Allies, Japan has forged an economic power second only to the United States.

SECTION 1 SUMMARY

❖ Japanese religion is an amalgamation of Chinese religion and its various aspects with indigenous Japanese religion.

❖ Shinto, "the way of the gods," is the name given to Japanese religion. Kami (the name for any spiritual or sacred power) also describes Japanese religion.

❖ At various times in its religious history, the Japanese government has supported Shinto or Buddhism as the state religion.

❖ Zen Buddhism with its major schools—Soto and Rinzai—became popular in Japan.

SECTION 1 REVIEW QUESTIONS

1. What role does the Japanese creation myth play in Japanese identity?

2. Why might kami be a better word to describe Japanese religion than Shinto?

3. What was the traditional role of the emperor in Japanese religion?

4. Describe the differences between Soto Zen Buddhism and Rinzai Zen Buddhism.

5. What did the Meiji government restore?

6. What happened to Emperor Hirohito after World War II?

II. BELIEFS AND ACTIONS

Most of the remainder of the chapter will focus on Shinto beliefs and scriptures that are mostly unique to the religious experience of the Japanese. Many other Shinto beliefs have been covered in sections dealing with Chinese religions.

Kami

Kami is most easily understood as the Shinto gods, the gods that dwell in heaven, on earth, and under the earth. However, kami refers to more than just gods. They are not gods in the sense that they are transcendent or all-powerful. Kami has to do with whatever is sacred or powerful. Nature, such as mountains, rivers, trees, or rocks, can be kami. Human beings can be kami. The emperor,

Pagoda and Dragon Snow Mountain

as representative of sun goddess Amaterasu, great warriors, poets, scholars, and wise ancestors are kami. The main focus of kami is to aid and protect. There are creative as well as destructive kami. For example, an erupting volcano is destructive kami.

The kami inhabit this world in trees, mountains, holy people, the emperor, and anything else deemed sacred or powerful. Hence, Japanese religion sees the natural world as good. Redemption is possible because the world is imbued with goodness. Redemption comes not through good works of helping others, but through proper rituals associated with the kami or the compassion and mercy of a bodhisatva like Amida (one of the five buddhas of Mahayana Buddhism). The imperial leader of Japan manifested kami, and his presence reminded Japanese that all was well in this world.

Shinto Scripture

Shinto does not have any sacred texts considered to be revealed by its gods. However, there are two texts that are considered authoritative and significant for both the religious and historical heritage of the Japanese. In the eighth century CE, the Japanese government commissioned the compilation of the oral myths and legends of the Japanese people. Written in Chinese, the *Kojiki* (*Record of Ancient Matters*) was completed in 712 CE. It includes the creation myth of Japan and concludes with a genealogy of the emperors to Emperor Temmu who commissioned the work. A second writing—*Nihonshoki* (*Chronicles of Japan*) was commissioned to chronicle the history of Japan. It begins with the Japanese creation myth and covers all the history through the end of the seventh century CE.

As with so many documents written in ancient times, these writers portray the elite classes, not the ordinary people. These documents were written to legitimize the imperial government as the direct descendant of the sun goddess Amaterasu so that the imperial leader could claim a form of sacred kingship.

173

Japanese Living

As the indigenous Japanese religion made no distinction between religion and politics, nor between religion and nature, "harmony" is an apt word to describe Japanese living. This virtue is further pointed out in the fact that for possess any rigid system of doctrines which might bring it into conflict with them. From this point of view democracy is a method of defusing gifts, especially between religious groups, in so far as the separation of religion and the State gives a peaceful basis for the volun-

Harmony in all relationships is an important virtue to the Japanese.

the Japanese, people and kami dwell together. As Professor Ninian Smart writes:

> If there is a central perception which prevails, it is probably that of *harmony*. A number of the new religious movements are keen to stress the unity of the world's religions; and, though the Nichiren Shoshu is aggressive, most Mahayana Buddhist groups seek harmony. Shinto too, has an interest in maintaining its harmony with other religions, partly because it does not

tary pursuit of values. It also is in consonance with the Japanese ideal in gaining consensus before any serious line of policy is undertaken.

Quoted from *The World's Religions*, by Ninian Smart (Englewood Cliffs, NJ: Prentice-Hall, Inc., 1989)

Besides harmony, another strong virtue important to the Japanese is loyalty. The Confucian value system is very strong in the Japanese culture. In those five relationships of li, loyalty is the glue. Though it is clear that the subordinate is to be loyal to the superior, in Japanese life the superior is also responsible to the subordinate, and thus, exhibits a certain loyalty to him or her. The virtue of loyalty is still exhibited in corporate Japan where loyalty to the clan until death has been replaced with loyalty to the corporation until retirement. Loyalty went to the extreme when samurai warriors were willing to commit suicide or *harakiri*[8] rather than bring shame upon the ruler.

Community

The clan or extended family is the most important social structure for the Japanese people. The Japanese people

themselves have been called the national clan. At one time the emperor was the head of the clan and made offerings at the national shrine at Ise on behalf of the Japanese people. Though initially a kami for the imperial family, the sun goddess Amaterasu became the national kami. Thus, because of their divine origin, the Japanese people understood themselves as a divine people.

Do you consider yourself preordained to accomplish something worthwhile with your life? What is it?

Three Types of Shinto

The are three types of Shinto: Shrine Shinto, Sect Shinto, and Folk Shinto. Shrine Shinto is the most institutionalized with an ordained priesthood. More information on each type follows.

Shrine Shinto is the most common of the three Shintos. It is present throughout Japan through its system of local Shinto shrines. Within Shrine Shinto the myriad Japanese festivals play a major role.

Sect Shinto was established in the nineteenth century when there was a major surge in "new religions," each with its own founder. The government organized them together and called them Sect Shinto as opposed to the Shrine or State Shinto the government supported. Many of these original sects have undergone major transformations and have subdivided into still other sects.

Folk Shinto is generally the religion of rural Japan. With few priests and shrines in the countryside, the home observances are the most important in Folk Shinto. The rite of purification is more elaborate and superstition, magic, and shamanism[9] are much more prominent in Folk Shinto.

SECTION 2 SUMMARY

❖ The major focus of Japanese religion is on the kami.

❖ Japanese religion finds all life, all creation, and human nature intrinsically good.

❖ There are no sacred Japanese writings revealed by the gods, though two ancient texts do contain myths and legends of ancient Japan.

❖ Harmony is a most valued virtue in Japanese life.

❖ Three types of Shinto have been present since the nineteenth century: Shrine Shinto, Sect Shinto, and Folk Shinto.

SECTION 2 REVIEW QUESTIONS

1. Besides being a name of Shinto gods, what does kami refer to?

2. Why are harmony and loyalty valued virtues in Japanese religion?

3. Name the greatest distinctions between the three types of Shinto.

III. SACRED PLACES

As it lacks a formal scripture, doctrine, and ethical code, the Japanese religion places great emphasis on ritual. These rituals take place at home shrines, local shrines, or national shrines. Since there is no specific day of the week for worship, devotees generally perform their home ritual on any morning they wish, either as an individual or as a family. They can also go to the local shrine any day of the week to honor the local kami. There are thousands of Shinto shrines in Japan, though only a very few have priests.

Most Japanese homes, as well as many places of business or work, have both a kamidana and a Buddhist shrine. While the Shinto emphasize things of life such as birth, marriage, agriculture, or even a new job, the Buddhist emphasis is on the end of life and the afterlife. Offerings are made by the head of the family to the kami or Buddhist deity seeking blessings and protection for the family from evil.

The local Shinto shrine is a familiar piece of architecture in the Japanese landscape. Since it is believed that kami exist in nature, the Japanese people found it important that the shrines be surrounded by nature. Even in the most urban cities of Japan, the Shinto shrine is an oasis of tranquillity and beauty, an environment fit for a kami. Also, since Shinto and Buddhism are so closely connected in Japan, a Shinto shrine is generally located near a Buddhist temple.

The most distinctive element of the Shinto shrine is the *torii*, an entrance gate made of two timber posts and two timber cross beams. Symbolically the torii separates the profane world outside from the sacred residence of the kami inside. Those shrines with a strong Buddhist influence tend to have the torii painted red or black while the toriis that are decidedly Japanese are left unpainted.

The format for worship at the shrine is simple both for individual and communal worship. Devotees first perform a purification rite where they wash their hands and face and rinse their mouths. They then enter a hall where the offering is made. Today the offering is usually money, but when Japan was much more agricultural, the offerings were the fruits of the harvest. Next, there is a small chamber where the kami body[10] is kept. Even though the kami body is normally something quite simple like a mirror or a pebble, it is considered so sacred and emits so much spiritual power that a priest rarely looks

Shinto Shrine, Sakurayama Hachiman
Shrine

Torii Gate

Heian Jingo Shrine

inside the chamber. Even if the door to the chamber is opened, a screen blocks the kami body. The occasion for opening the chamber is usually a festival in which the kami is invited to participate.

Whether the worship at a shrine is done individually or as a community at a festival, the elements are similar. There is the rite of purification, the offering, and the prayer. Offerings at the national shrines bring spiritual benefits to the whole of Japan.

The Grand Shrine at Ise

Ise was the location of the shrine for the imperial family in ancient Japan. Since the imperial family believed they were direct descendants of the sun goddess Amaterasu, they dedicated this shrine to her and placed a bronze mirror as a kami body in its inner chamber. Hence, Amaterasu was the kami of the imperial family. Eventually the shrine of the imperial family became the national shrine of Japan and the emperor acted as the priest of that shrine, making offerings on behalf of his country. Today the Grand Shrine of Ise still has many pilgrims and visitors. It is one of the major symbols of Japanese religious, political, and cultural heritage.

What's in a Mirror?

The mirror is one of the most sacred symbols in Shinto. Legendary beautiful mirrors, noted for their valuable decoration and the accuracy of their images, have been cherished legacies passed from mother to daughter for generations. A good mirror tells us the truth about ourselves and through its illuminating power gives us wisdom, the wisdom that comes with self-awareness and knowledge. Without a true mirror, we cannot know ourselves. And without mirrors we remain in caves of silence.

Quoted from *On Mirrors, Mists and Murmurs in Weaving the Visions: New Patterns of Feminist Spirituality,* by Rita Nakashima Brock (San Francisco: HarperSanFrancisco, 1989)

What truth does your mirror tell you about yourself?

SECTION 3 SUMMARY

❖ It is common for a home to have both a kamidana and Buddhist shrine.

❖ The local shrine is where much of Shinto individual and communal worship takes place.

❖ The kami body is an object—often a mirror or sword—into which it is believed a kami descends during a Shinto worship service.

❖ The greatest shrine in all of Japan is the Grand Shrine at Ise, originally dedicated to the sun goddess Amaterasu by the imperial family.

SECTION 3 REVIEW QUESTIONS

1. Why do many Japanese homes have both Shinto and Buddhist shrines?

2. What is the significance of a torii at a shrine or temple?

3. Name the typical elements in a Shinto worship service.

4. Why is the Grand Shrine at Ise significant for Japanese religion?

IV. SACRED TIME

For calculating times of many of its festivals, the Japanese use a lunar calendar similar to the Chinese lunar calendar. However, during the Meiji period when Japan's interest in competing in the western world heightened, the Gregorian calendar began to be used and is in general use today in Japan.

Japanese Festivals

Matsuri is the name for Japanese festivals. As the shrines and their kami are local or regional, so are most Japanese festivals. Though most matsuri are connected with Shinto, all the religious traditions of Japan participate in the annual cycle of matsuri.

Omisoka is the name for the Year-End Festival. It is the day of preparation for New Year's Day. People clean their homes, especially their Buddhist altars and kamidanas. The local shrines and temples are also purified as well as the graves of the ancestors in preparing for the New Year.

The New Year, called *Shogatsu*, is the most important celebration in Japan. It is a three-day celebration held on January 1, 2, and 3. At Buddhist temples in Japan, eight bells are rung on New Year's Eve and one hundred bells are rung on New Year's Day to purify the people of the 108 sins in Buddhism.

Hina Matsuri is "Girls' Day" and is celebrated on March 3. Though Girls' Day is not a public holiday, most Japanese families with daughters celebrate the occasion. Parents arrange dolls

Celebrating the New Year

that have been dressed in traditional Japanese court costumes on a tier to symbolize a princess wedding. The prince and princess are placed on the top of the tier and the dolls go down in rank to the court musicians at the bottom. Offerings of rice cakes, peach blossoms, and sweet white sake are set before this tier. The daughters themselves dress in *kimonos*[11] and the families celebrate, wishing the girls health and happiness.

Kodomo no Hi or "Children's Day" is a public holiday celebrated by all children. It was once Boys' Day as a counterpart to Girls' Day. The tradition of this day goes back to ancient Japan, but it became a huge festival during the time of feudal Japan when samurai was an estimable career for Japanese boys. On this day kites shaped like carp fly in the skies of Japan. The carp was chosen for its characteristics of courage and fortitude, as a carp can swim upstream and even up waterfalls.

Obon is a three-day festival, celebrated in mid-August, in which the Japanese people believe the ancestral spirits return home for a short time. The families go to the gravesites of their ancestors and light candles, lanterns, and bonfires to give the spirits light with which to see their way home. The highlight of this festival is the folk dances performed at temples or shrines.

Life Cycle

The eclecticism of Japanese religion is illustrated best in the Japanese life cycle. The newborn infant is taken to the local shrine between thirty and one hundred days after his or her birth and presented to the kami. The Japanese traditionally believe the kami watches over the child for the rest of his or her life.

Japanese weddings are traditionally held at shrines. However, an increasing number of weddings are taking place at Christian churches, even if the couple is not Christian. There are still some Shinto elements to the wedding, but more

© Galyn C. Hammond

brides are preferring to wear a white gown on their wedding day than a traditional kimono.

Regarding death rituals, the Japanese people have great respect for their ancestors, so they visit the graves of deceased family members often during the year. Most cemeteries in Japan are Buddhist cemeteries. Generally, after the funeral, there are a series of memorial services held over a period of months and years until the fiftieth year when the deceased is considered to be truly an ancestor in the Japanese tradition.

A Woman's Place in Japan

There is some evidence that early Japan was politically matriarchal, and priestesses and shamanesses[12] played an important role in early Shinto. All this changed when Japan came into contact with China and wholeheartedly adopted Confucian ethics. By the eighth century, women were no longer permitted to rule, and by the fifteenth century they had lost virtually all civil rights. Only during periods of severe crisis were some women politically influential, but only briefly.

Contact with the West during the nineteenth and twentieth centuries has done little to change the rights of women. Modern Japanese males have simply shifted their allegiance from feudal lords to the presidents of corporations and businesses. Husbands still consider their wives to be functional creatures essential to the fulfillment of family life: as mothers of their children and managers of their households. In traditional Confucian style, the ideal Japanese family consists of three generations living under one roof. Marriage provides a line of heirs for the "ancestral house." Marriages are still arranged by parents and a barren woman is promptly returned to her home.

Quoted from *World Faiths, second edition,* by S.A. Nigosian New York: St. Martin's Press, 1994)

SECTION 4 SUMMARY

❖ Matsuri is the name for Japanese festivals. Most matsuri are connected with Shinto, though all religious traditions play a part.

❖ Because the social structure of Japan is based locally, there is a wide variety and number of festivals in Japanese religion.

❖ New Year's Day is the greatest festival in Japan, though it is not strictly a religious festival.

SECTION 4 REVIEW QUESTIONS

1. Why did Japan move to the Gregorian calendar?

2. Describe what takes place on the Girls' Day festival.

3. What happens on the fiftieth anniversary of a Japanese person's death?

Who Is My Neighbor?

JAPANESE RELIGIONS IN AMERICA

On Alpine Avenue in Stockton, California, not far from the University of the Pacific, is the Tsubaki America Grand Shrine. While there have long been Shinto shrines on the islands of Hawaii, where many Japanese have lived for nearly a century, this Shinto shrine is the first to have been built in mainland America. From the street, the house on Alpine Avenue seems to be an ordinary suburban home. Inside, however, at the household altar, called a kamidana, the Shinto priest makes daily offerings to the kami. And behind the house, the distinctive torii gateway marks the path toward the Tsubaki Shrine, which is in the garden. A sign at the gateway reads,

The name of this shrine in the Tsubaki (English translation Camellia) House is Tsubaki America Grand Shrine. It is a branch shrine of Ise District One Shrine, Tsubaki Grand Shrine, located in Japan's Mie prefecture, 300 miles west of Tokyo. Tsubaki Grand Shrine is one of the oldest Shinto Shrines in Japan, with a 2,000-year history.

Each part of the wooden garden shrine was sent by boat from Japan and assembled here in Stockton. The anniversary of its opening is celebrated every year in the early summer. This is one of its three matsuri, or festivals, which include the annual festival, and the fall and spring festivals.

Reverend Iwasaki, one of the first priests of the Stockton shrine, underscores the challenge of building shrines for the kami in America. "In Japan, most of the shrines were there when people were born, so the idea to build a Shinto shrine did not occur to the Japanese," he said. But in America as well there is a spiritual sensitivity to the land, especially among the native peoples and those who cherish the natural environment. "There is something spiritual in places like Yosemite and Tahoe," he said. It is this reverence for the spirits that rest and abide in the whole of the natural world that provides the most fertile soil for the appreciation of Shinto in America.

Conclusion

Shinto is the name given to the indigenous religion of Japan. One cannot speak of "pure Shinto" after the coming of Chinese religion to Japan. Once Chinese religion was introduced to Japan, Japanese religion was influenced forevermore by Buddhism, Confucianism, and to a lesser extent, Taoism and Christianity. Yet the adherents of all the religious traditions were considered, at

percent of Japanese have responded in public polls that they are religious, it seems that the wrong questions have been asked. Most Japanese also responded that they performed rituals at home, at the workplace, at shrines, or at temples. Traditionally, the Japanese did not separate religion from politics or nature, and it seems today that they do not separate religion from any part of their everyday lives.

least until the end of World War II, part of a national clan with the emperor as the head. With the military collapse and economic growth of Japan, a number of new religious movements have emerged, predominantly influenced by Shinto or Buddhism. Though only 30

CHAPTER 8 IN BRIEF

❖ Japanese religious history begins with the Japanese creation myth.

❖ Indigenous Japanese religion is heavily influenced by Chinese religion.

❖ Many sects of Buddhism flourished in Japan and intermingled with Japanese Shinto.

❖ The emperor was the sacred monarch of Japan until the end of World War II.

❖ Shinto believes that the world is overflowing with kami and thus, the world and human nature is intrinsically good.

❖ The Kojiki and the Nishongi are closest to Japanese sacred writings, though neither is considered to be revealed by God.

❖ Most Japanese homes have both a Buddhist altar and a Shinto shrine.

❖ Though kami were originally worshipped in natural settings, they are now worshipped in shrines that are set in natural surroundings.

❖ Most Japanese worship is individual or family based. Communal worship is in the form of religious festivals.

❖ Buddhism, Shinto, and Christianity are all part of the Japanese life cycle rites.

CHAPTER 8 REVIEW QUESTIONS

1. What is the meaning of the term Shinto?

2. Define and give one example of kami.

3. What is the role of the "kami body" in Shinto shrine worship?

4. What is at the heart of Zen Buddhism?

5. Give an example of a koan.

6. What was the overall theme of Tokugawa reformers?

7. Compare and contrast the three types of Shinto in Japan today.

8. What is the purpose of a kamidana?

9. Explain why harmony is an apt word to describe Japanese living.

RESEARCH AND ACTIVITIES

1. Write an essay on one of the following topics:

   The popular appeal of Japanese religions in America

   The various methods and symbols of ritual purification

   The influence of Chinese culture on Japan

   The state of religion in Japan today

   Japanese art, architecture, or literature and its relationship to religion

   The martial arts and Japanese religion

   The history of Christianity in Japan

2. Read one of the following three books and write an essay on the author's portrayal of some aspect of Japanese religion: *Silence* by Shusaku Endo, *Shogun* by James Clavell, or *Zen and the Art of Motorcycle Maintenance* by Robert Pirsig.

3. Create your own koan. (See the examples on pages 169-170).

SELECTED VOCABULARY

Folk Shinto	Sect Shinto
harakiri	shamanism
kami	shogunate
kami body	Shrine Shinto
koan	Soto Buddhism
matsuri	torii
samurai	zazen
satori	

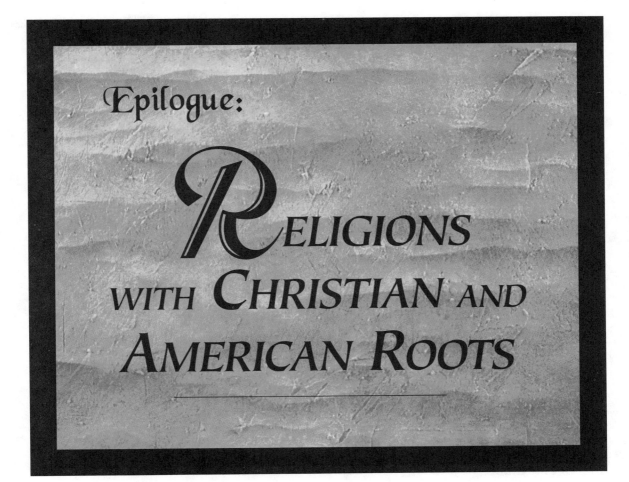

Epilogue:

Religions with Christian and American Roots

 opefully this course has helped you broaden your understanding of some of the world's religions, beginning with a study of those religions more familiar to you (Judaism, Christianity, Islam) before widening the circle to include religions with roots far away in both time and location (Hinduism, Buddhism, Chinese religions, and Japanese religions). In our increasingly close-knit world, even these religions have likely entered your consciousness previous to this class.

In this epilogue, the circle will be drawn more tightly to your own experience as we examine five other religious traditions that have their roots mostly in nineteenth century America and in Protestant Christianity, though they advocate some beliefs that fall outside of traditional Protestant Christianity. They are religions that your neighbors, friends, relatives, or perhaps even you subscribe to. They are also American religious traditions that are often misunderstood. For each of these we will briefly look at some historical background, beliefs, and practices.

Church of Jesus Christ of Latter-day Saints

A Brief History

The Church of Jesus Christ of Latter-day Saints (commonly called the Mormon[1] Church) traces its origins to Joseph Smith, Jr. (1805-1844). At age fourteen Smith was praying in a grove near his family's farm in upstate New York seeking guidance after attending a church revival. There God the Father and Jesus Christ appeared to him and directed him not to claim membership in any church for they had become corrupted. Rather, Smith was told, the church founded by Jesus would be restored to its original purity in teachings and priesthood. Four years later a heavenly being named Moroni appeared to Smith and directed him to a hill where metal plates containing ancient hieroglyphics were buried. Over the next four years Smith translated the plates into what is known as the *Book of Mormon*. This sacred scripture contains religious writings of an ancient American civilization, including an appearance of Jesus on American soil after his resurrection. The Church of Jesus Christ of Latter-day Saints was established in 1830, the same year the *Book of Mormon* was published.

Followers of Smith were persecuted. Finding it necessary to move several times, the new community settled in Nauvoo, Illinois, in 1839, became prosperous, and built their first temple. However, even there the community found opposition. One reason for the persecution was that the Latter Day Saints, or Mormons, practiced polygamy[2] arising from a revelation of Smith's. A more practical reason for opposition was that the Mormons had established a powerful voting bloc in Nauvoo, thereby wiping away the political control of the locals. In 1844 Smith and his brother Hyrum were killed by an

Brigham Young

angry mob after being imprisoned in nearby Carthage.

Brigham Young succeeded Joseph Smith as leader of the Mormons. (Some members of the church believed that only a descendent of Joseph Smith, in this case Joseph Smith III, should head the church. A splinter group of those followers formed the Reorganized Church of Jesus Christ of Latter-day Saints with headquarters to this day in Independence, Missouri.) Because of continuing persecutions, Brigham Young led the Mormons on a 1300-mile journey across the Great Plains and into

Utah and the Salt Lake basin. Salt Lake City, Utah, continues to be the center of the Mormon church.

In the late twentieth century the Church of Jesus Christ of Latter-day Saints is one of the fastest growing religions in the world. There are about ten million members worldwide, with approximately half living in the United States.

If members of a new religion descended on a rural town today, what do you think would be the reaction of the local people?

Beliefs and Actions

Mormons hold that primitive Christianity as founded by Jesus was corrupted through apostasy[3] in about the second century. Hence, to restore the church of Jesus Christ Mormons believe there is a need for new revelation, new scripture, and a new priesthood, all of which are found in the church restored by Joseph Smith. Though Mormons accept that elements of truth are found in all religions, they also believe that they alone are the true Christians. Mormons do not consider themselves Protestants, but Christians in the most pure form as founded by Jesus. Some of the beliefs of Mormonism are:

❖ Mormons believe that salvation is only possible within their church. In order to save ancestors, Mormons hold a type of baptism service that allows for the baptism of dead relatives of those already within the church.

❖ Mormons believe that Native Americans are the ten lost tribes of Israel.

Morman Temple at Salt Lake City

❖ Though Mormons name the traditional Trinity, they do not believe that Jesus is God.

❖ As other millennialists,[4] the Church of Jesus Christ of Latter-day Saints teaches that Jesus will return to earth and set up a new Jerusalem in America and a 1000-year reign.

As Mormons hold that God's revelations did not stop with the last page of the Bible, neither do they cease with the *Book of Mormon*. The President (the name for Mormon leaders) is seen as a prophet in the same way as the biblical prophets are. Mormon presidents succeeding Joseph Smith have received new revelations in the years since. For example, President Wilford Woodruff called for the end of the practice of polygamy at the end of the nineteenth century after receiving a revelation. In 1978 President Spencer Kimball received a revelation to allow males of African descent to be ordained to Mormon priesthood. (Blacks had been denied priesthood because the church had claimed they were descendants of Cain, the murderer of his brother Abel.)

Besides the *Book of Mormon*, the *Pearl of Great Price* (writings and revelations of Joseph Smith) and *Doctrine and Covenants* (writings and revelations since the restoration in 1830) are considered sacred writings of the Mormon church.

The Mormon worship service is simple in nature. There are prayers,

Joseph Smith

singing of hymns, listening to sermons delivered by lay people, and a celebration of the Lord's Supper using bread and water. Water is used instead of wine as Mormons are forbidden to use all drugs, including alcohol, tobacco, and caffeine.

Baptism by immersion happens at the age of eight or older. Proxies are baptized on behalf of dead ancestors. Mormons spend a great deal of time investigating and maintaining family genealogies in order to include relatives in this type of baptism.

The Church is very involved in missionary work. It is common for young people around the age of twenty to participate in two years of missionary work, often in another country. About 50,000 people annually are engaged in missionary work.

In 1833 Joseph Smith received a revelation that became known as the Word of Wisdom. In that revelation Smith learned that God required all to engage in good health habits. People were to be both spiritually and physically fit. Maintaining good health included the stipulation of no alcohol, tobacco, or caffeine.

Why do you think the Church of Jesus Christ of Latter-day Saints is one of the world's fastest growing religions?

CHURCH OF JESUS CHRIST OF LATTER-DAY SAINTS SUMMARY

✤ The founder of the Church of Jesus Christ of Latter-day Saints is Joseph Smith, Jr. Members of the church are commonly called Mormons.

✤ The Church encountered much opposition and persecution and eventually settled in Salt Lake City, Utah.

✤ The beliefs of the Church of Jesus Christ of Latter-day Saints both agree with and deviate from traditional Christian teachings.

✤ Practices of the Church include a simple worship service, baptism, baptism by proxy, and extensive missionary work.

CHURCH OF JESUS CHRIST OF LATTER-DAY SAINTS REVIEW QUESTIONS

1. Where does the term "Mormon" come from?

2. Why is the Church of Jesus Christ of Latter-day Saints not considered a Protestant church?

3. Why were Mormons persecuted in Illinois?

4. Why do Mormons allow baptisms of the dead?

Seventh-day Adventists

A Brief History

Adventists is the name for Christians who believe the Second Coming, or advent, of Jesus is imminent. The Seventh-day Adventist Church emerged from a nineteenth century movement.

William Miller (1782-1849) believed the Bible was very specific about when and how the Second Coming of Jesus would take place. Miller calculated that Jesus would return to earth in a physical form and he also calculated a specific date. Miller gained a number of followers calling themselves Adventists who waited expectantly with him. When Jesus did not come, Miller recalculated the date for seven months later. When the Second Coming did not occur as expected for a second time, it was called the *Great Disappointment* and many left Miller. Some Adventists modified their

This is a 1991 photo of World War II Medal of Honor award Desmond T. Doss with his medal. He is a Seventh Day Adventist and the only conscientious objector to be awarded the honor.

teaching. They said that the Second Coming was to be preceded by an *Investigative Judgment* in which God would judge the living and the dead, pronounce the findings, and then execute judgment. Only after the Investigative Judgment was complete could Jesus return to earth and begin his one thousand-year reign. They did not set a date for the completion of the Investigative Judgment, but believed it was imminent.

The Seventh-day Adventist Church came from this movement and was officially formed in 1863. Ellen White, a follower of Miller, was considered a prophetess among the Seventh-day Adventists. She wrote a number of books and gave lectures throughout much of the nineteenth century English-speaking world. The members of this church strictly followed the Bible for Sabbath and dietary laws, besides looking to the Bible for information about the Second Coming. As the Jewish Sabbath had been Saturday and early Christians also observed it, Saturday, the seventh day, was restored as the Sabbath. Seventh-day Adventists prohibited alcohol, nicotine, and caffeine use because of their harmful effects on the body, the temple of the Holy Spirit.

Beliefs and Actions

The Seventh-day Adventists believe the Bible is the sole source of authority for their members. However, their interpretation of the Bible deviates in many areas from most other Christians. For example, Seventh-day Adventists believe that Jesus' act of redemption was potentially for everyone, but was effective only for those who *truly* believe. They also hold that the righteous will be resurrected to heaven with the Second Coming of Jesus, but that the unrighteous will be annihilated in hell. Hence, they do not believe all souls are immortal.

Seventh-day Adventists are initiated through instruction and baptism by immersion. Saturday, the seventh day, is the day of worship. With regard to creation, Seventh-day Adventists deny the theory of evolution and take a literal approach to understanding the creation stories of the Bible.

Besides abstaining from alcohol, smoking, and caffeine, many Seventh-day Adventists are vegetarians. Some also abstain from dancing, theater going, and any other activity deemed harmful to the soul. Ironically, though Ellen White played a significant role in the foundation of the Seventh-day Adventists, the church does not sanction the ordination of women.

Why do you think some Christians wish to forecast the exact date of Jesus' Second Coming?

SEVENTH-DAY ADVENTIST SUMMARY

✤ The Seventh-day Adventist Church is an outgrowth of the Adventist movement of the nineteenth century in the United States.

✤ The Seventh-day Adventists believe the Second Coming will be preceded by an Investigative Judgment.

✤ Saturday is the Sabbath for Seventh-day Adventists.

SEVENTH-DAY ADVENTIST REVIEW QUESTIONS

1. Summarize the origins of the Adventist movement.

2. What was the Great Disappointment?

3. Why do Seventh-day Adventists worship on Saturday rather than Sunday?

Watchtower Bible and Tract Society

A Brief History

Charles Russell (1852-1916) officially founded the Jehovah's Witnesses, then known as Zion's Watchtower Bible and Tract Society, in Pennsylvania in 1884. Russell had been studying with other Bible students attempting to pinpoint the Second Coming of Jesus. He named the fall of 1914 as the time when Jesus would establish his invisible reign in heaven and expel Satan to earth. Then the battle of Armageddon between Satan and Jesus would begin to take place on earth. When the battle did not begin, other dates were set, but no battle at Armageddon has taken place.

Russell was succeeded by Joseph Rutherford (1869-1942). Rutherford gave further shape to the Society by centralizing it, moving the headquarters to Brooklyn, New York, and refining the missionary work of the followers. Russell had been more democratic in his leadership, but Rutherford believed that the establishment of Jesus' invisible reign was a theocracy[5] and the Society must be ready for Jesus' rule. Rutherford adopted the name Jehovah's Witnesses to emphasize Jehovah (another name for Yahweh), the God of the Hebrew Scriptures, as the one true God. Those who witnessed in the name of Jehovah were the true followers of the one God.

Nathan Knorr (1905-1977), the next president, expanded the publication of Jehovah's Witnesses materials, translated a Bible used by all Jehovah's Witnesses (known as the *New World Translation of Holy Scriptures*) and established the Watchtower Bible School of Gilead in New York for the training of leaders.

Presently Jehovah's Witnesses can be found throughout the world. However, they do not always find a welcome, for their allegiance is not to any government but God's theocracy. Their various forms of publications are translated in numerous languages for worldwide distribution. In Europe their affiliated group is known as the International Bible Students Association.

Beliefs and Actions

Many of the beliefs of Jehovah's Witnesses are similar to traditional Christian beliefs. Jehovah's Witnesses believe the Bible is the word of God and the sole source of religious and moral authority. They believe that Jesus is the son of God, born of a virgin, and the reconciler of humankind to God.

However, there are interpretations of the Bible and even translations that traditional Christians cannot accept as orthodox Christian beliefs. Christian biblical scholars reject the *New World Translation of the Holy Scriptures* as defective, citing that the sources of the translation are not the original Hebrew and Greek biblical texts and that the translation is bent to reflect the teachings of the Society.

Jehovah's Witnesses believe that they are the true Christians in the image of the primitive church and that salvation only comes through the beliefs and works of the Society. Jehovah's Witnesses hold that all others who claim to be Christians are false Christians and those not claiming to be Christian are pagans.

Jehovah's Witnesses do not acknowledge the Holy Trinity. Though they hold that Jesus is the son of God, they believe he is not God, but subject to God. Before his earthly birth, Jesus is believed to have been the Archangel Michael. Nor do the Jehovah's Witnesses believe that the Holy Spirit is God, but instead is merely a way to explain how Jehovah is present to and connects with creation.

Jesus' crucifixion and resurrection is explained in a spiritual sense. Jehovah's Witnesses do not believe Jesus was crucified on a cross. Neither do they believe in Jesus' bodily resurrection. They understand the Greek word for cross to mean one piece of timber like a stake or a pole. There was no crossbeam. Since the cross or crucifix was not used as a symbol by the earliest Christians, Jehovah's Witnesses think of them as pagan symbols.

At Armageddon, Jesus will be victorious over Satan, the earth will be purified, and Jesus will set up a theocracy. In the meantime, Satan is on earth using everything at his disposal. In particular, secular governments and all the world's religions are instruments of Satan. Hence, Jehovah's Witnesses pledge no allegiance to any government but Jehovah's. They do not salute a flag, serve in public office or military service, nor do they vote in public elections. In fact, children of Jehovah's Witnesses who attend public schools are not allowed to celebrate Halloween, Christmas, or any other holiday. In time of war, Jehovah's Witnesses are conscientious objectors.

Jehovah's Witnesses do not believe in a hell that is eternal damnation. When a person dies, the soul dies. At the time of the resurrection of the righteous, Jehovah will create a new, perfect body and reinstate the soul of the person.

Jehovah's Witnesses have great reverence for the Bible. They read and study it on a regular basis. Bible study generally takes place in people's homes.

Besides the Bible, the *Watchtower* and *Awake* are two semimonthly periodicals that are very important to Society members. A common practice is to distribute these and other literature door to door and on street corners.

The place of worship for Jehovah Witnesses is a Kingdom Hall where the congregation is known as the "company." There is no day of rest, for every day is holy. Rather than times of worship, Jehovah's Witnesses have various kinds of meetings each week where there are talks on topics found in a recent *Watchtower* or training for various ministries, especially witnessing door to door.

The average member of the Society is known as a publisher who attends meetings during the week and goes door to door as much as possible, usually on Saturdays. Each person has a neighborhood for which he or she is responsible while each Kingdom Hall is responsible for a geographical area containing several neighborhoods.

The only day celebrated by Jehovah's Witnesses is the Memorial of Christ's Death, because Christ's command to do so is in the Bible. Neither Christmas nor Easter are celebrated because Jehovah did not command it, the first Christians did not celebrate those days, and since they *are* celebrated by other "false" Christians and pagans, they must be pagan feasts. Jehovah's Witnesses do not celebrate individual birthdays for the same reasons.

A controversial belief of Jehovah's Witnesses is the prohibition of blood transfusions, as blood transfusions are interpreted as "eating blood," something forbidden by Jehovah. The controversy often becomes heated when a child is in need of a blood transfusion and the parents refuse. The Child

Kingdom Hall

Protection Agency sometimes attempts to override the parent's decision through legal means.

All the Jehovah's Witnesses' teaching and practice is with one goal in mind: to establish a theocracy on earth. Jehovah's Witnesses hope to purify the earth of all evil before Christ sets up his earthly kingdom.

In your opinion have Christian holidays become too secularized?

WATCHTOWER AND BIBLE TRACT SOCIETY SUMMARY

✦ Charles Russell began the Watchtower Bible and Tract Society with the purpose of informing people about the Second Coming of Jesus, which he said would occur in 1914.

✦ Joseph Rutherford succeeded Russell and coined the term "Jehovah's Witnesses."

✦ Jehovah's Witnesses believe that Satan rules the present age on earth.

✦ The Jehovah's Witnesses have no special day for worship and do not celebrate holidays such as Christmas and Easter, nor do they celebrate birthdays.

WATCHTOWER AND BIBLE TRACT SOCIETY REVIEW QUESTIONS

1. What is the significance of the name "Jehovah's Witness?"

2. What is the goal of Jehovah's Witnesses' teaching and practice?

3. Why do Jehovah's Witnesses not celebrate holidays and birthdays?

The Church of Christ, Scientist

A Brief History

Mary Baker Eddy (1821-1910) of Massachusetts founded the Church of Christ, Scientist in 1879. It is commonly known as Christian Science.

Eddy was raised in a strict Congregationalist home where she grew to love the Christian Bible. She was ill much of her childhood and early adulthood and sought various methods of healing, both conventional and non-conventional. When she was in her forties, she fell on an icy sidewalk and severely injured herself. On reading one of Jesus' miracles from the Bible, she suddenly realized that sickness and suffering are merely illusions and can be overcome by right thinking. She believed that the discovery of this right mind, the mind of God, allowed her to be instantly healed. She spent several years intensely studying the Bible to learn precisely what her discovery meant. Her book, *Science and Health*, which she revised several times, forms the doctrine of the Christian Science religion.

Eddy moved the first Church of Christ, Scientist to Boston where it still exists today. The church expanded rather rapidly during the first half of the twentieth century before membership leveled off. There are approximately 1,600 branch churches throughout the United States. Though self-governing, the *Manual of the Mother Church* written by Mary Baker Eddy sets guidelines for the individual churches. There are also Christian Science churches throughout the world, mostly in predominantly Protestant countries.

Beliefs and Actions

Through her vigorous study of the Bible, Mary Baker Eddy came to believe that the teachings of Jesus, especially those with regard to healing, had been lost over the centuries. It was her intention to recapture such teachings for her generation. Eddy considered both the Bible and *Science and Health* as equally authoritative texts.

God is not a masculine God to Christian Science, but a Father-Mother who is both strong and compassionate. Christian Scientists deny Jesus as God, though they do believe Jesus is the son of God. What is distinctive about Christian Scientists is their belief that physical healing is through spiritual means alone. By discovering the truth, that is, God, Christian Science believes that people can be both healthy and happy. Though the effects of evil—suffering and death—may seem to exist, they are actually illusions a person can rid himself or herself of as he or she forms a union with God. Prayer is the form of treatment for physical ills. Christian Scientists pray to possess the Mind of Christ so that through the healing of the mind and heart, the physical is also healed.

When a person needs healing, he or she turns to a registered practitioner. The church authorizes these practitioners to devote their full time employment to assisting the healing of other church members through prayer. These practitioners are not intercessors. Only God heals through God's laws, so the practitioner prays with the member for guidance. They are paid for their services.

Contrary to popular belief, Christian Scientists do not excommunicate members of their church for seeking medical advice. They encourage their members to adhere to public health laws including immunization requirements. They also seek medical help for the delivery of babies. They visit dentists and eye doctors as well.

Though Christian Science does not have a creed *per se*, there are six tenets outlined in *Science and Health*:

1. As adherents of Truth, we take the inspired Word of the Bible as our sufficient guide to eternal Life.

2. We acknowledge and adore one supreme and infinite God. We acknowledge His Son, one Christ; the Holy Ghost or divine Comforter; and man in God's image and likeness.

3. We acknowledge God's forgiveness of sin in the destruction of sin and the spiritual understanding that casts out evil as unreal. But the belief in sin is punished so long as the belief lasts.

4. We acknowledge Jesus' atonement as the evidence of divine, efficacious Love, unfolding man's unity with God through Christ Jesus the Way-shower; and we acknowledge that man is saved through Christ, through Truth, Life, and Love as demonstrated by the Galleon Prophet in healing the sick and overcoming sin and death.

5. We acknowledge that the crucifixion of Jesus and his resurrection served to uplift faith to understand eternal Life, even the allness of Soul, Spirit, and the nothingness of matter.

6. And we solemnly promise to watch and pray for that Mind to be in us which was also in Christ Jesus; to do unto others as we would have them do unto us; and to be merciful, just, and pure.

The presence of Christian Science Reading Rooms near every Christian Science church highlights the importance placed on study. The public is welcomed into Christian Science Reading Rooms to find out more about the religion. Always available there is the Lesson-Sermon from the Mother Church for the week taken from the "pastor of the church," that is, the combination of the Bible and *Science and Health*. The lessons comprise the sermon that will be read at every Christian Science Church worldwide on Sundays. There are twenty-six rotating subjects. The two readers for a particular Sunday are chosen from the congregation. Sunday service is quite simple. The chosen readers read from the Bible, *Science and Health,* and the Lesson-Sermon from the Mother Church. There may be also testimonials on healing.

CHURCH OF CHRIST, SCIENTIST SUMMARY

❖ Mary Baker Eddy founded the Church of Christ, Scientist, commonly known as Christian Science, in 1879.

❖ Mary Baker Eddy believed physical healing took place through spiritual laws, not natural laws.

❖ The two main scriptures of the Christian Scientists—the Bible and Eddy's book *Science and Health*—are known as the "pastor of the church."

❖ Though the various branches of Christian Science churches are autonomous, they are still to abide by the guidelines stated in the *Manual of the Mother Church* written by Mary Baker Eddy.

CHURCH OF CHRIST, SCIENTIST REVIEW QUESTIONS

1. What did Mary Baker Eddy discover about healing?

2. Why is it incorrect to say Christian Scientists are hostile to the medical profession?

3. What is the role of registered practitioners?

Unitarian Universalists

A Brief History

The Unitarian Universalist Association is a consolidation of the Universalist Church of America and the American Unitarian Association. These groups merged in 1961. Groups associated with these movements are commonly called the Unitarian Church.

The Unitarian Church has its roots in the eighteenth century. It is associated with Christianity, yet denies the doctrine of the Trinity. Unitarians do not consider themselves a Christian church. They believe that spiritual wisdom can be found in all the religions of the world. In its origins, the Universalist movement advocated a belief that all will be saved and no one will suffer eternal damnation.

John Adams

Some very famous Americans have been a part of the Unitarian Universalists, including John Adams, Ralph Waldo Emerson, Clara Barton, and Susan B. Anthony.

Headquarters for the Unitarian Church in the United States is Boston, but there is no central governmental control over the more than one thousand congregations in the United States. Each congregation is autonomous in all matters of government, finance, and communal religious practices. On the international level the Unitarian Universalist Association is connected with religious groups through the International Association for Religious Freedom.

The Unitarian Universalist Association has no formal creed, though it does address a statement of principles (see below). Unitarians are encouraged to form their own beliefs and moral judgments based on experience, science, and reason. Ultimate authority is within the individual. Unitarians believe that wisdom can be found in all the religions of the world and they themselves have no sacred text, for they believe that the various sacred texts of the world contain much wisdom and guidance.

What is your opinion on the Unitarian belief that all will be saved?

UNITARIAN UNIVERSALIST STATEMENT OF PRINCIPLES AND PURPOSES

We, the member congregations of the Unitarian Universalist Association, covenant to affirm and promote:

✤ The inherent worth and dignity of every person

✤ Justice, equity and compassion in human relations

✤ Acceptance of one another and encouragement to spiritual growth in our congregations

✤ A free and responsible search for truth and meaning

✤ The right of conscience and the use of the democratic process within our congregations and in society at large

✤ The goal of world community with peace, liberty, and justice for all

✤ Respect for the interdependent web of all existence of which we are a part

The living tradition we share draws from many sources:

✤ Direct experience of that transcending mystery and wonder, affirmed in all cultures, which moves us to a renewal of the spirit and an openness to the forces which create and uphold life

✤ Words and deeds of prophetic women and men which challenge us to confront powers and structures of evil with justice, compassion, and the transforming power of love

✤ Wisdom from the world's religions which inspires us in our ethical and spiritual life

✤ Jewish and Christian teachings which call us to respond to God's love by loving our neighbors as ourselves

✤ Humanist teachings which counsel us to heed the guidance of reason and the results of science, and warn us against idolatries of the mind and spirit

✤ Spiritual teachings of Earth-centered traditions which celebrate the sacred circle of life and instruct us to live in harmony with the rhythms of nature.

Grateful for the religious pluralism, which enriches and ennobles our faith, we are inspired to deepen our understanding and expand our vision. As free congregations we enter into this covenant, promising to one another our mutual trust and support.

The religious practices of Unitarian Universalists vary from congregation to congregation, though most have regular weekly worship. Some call themselves a society or fellowship rather than a congregation. Unitarian Universalists draw from various sources for their communal worship: the Judeo-Christian heritage, other major world religions, earth-centered religions such as Native American, humanism, prophetic men and women, and direct experience.

UNITARIAN UNIVERSALISTS SUMMARY

❖ The Unitarian Church began in the nineteenth century. It is not a Christian church as it denies the Trinity.

❖ Unitarians believe religious and moral authority comes from the individual.

❖ Unitarians draw inspiration and teaching from various traditions.

UNITARIAN UNIVERSALISTS REVIEW QUESTIONS

1. Why are Unitarian Universalists not considered a Christian church?

2. What are some sources Unitarian Universalists draw on for worship?

RESEARCH AND ACTIVITIES

1. Research the life of one of the following and write an essay on the influence of Unitarianism on his or her life: John Adams, Ralph Waldo Emerson, Clara Barton, or Susan B. Anthony.

2. Research the effects the Seventh-day Adventist Church had on the work of John Kellogg.

3. Investigate the connection between the Branch Davidians and the Seventh-day Adventists.

4. Listen to some music of the Mormon Tabernacle Choir. Research the choir's history and mission.

5. Interview a member of one of the religions discussed in this chapter and write a report based on the interview.

SELECTED VOCABULARY

Adventists	Mormon
apostasy	polygamy
Great Disappointment	proxy
Investigative Judgment	theocracy

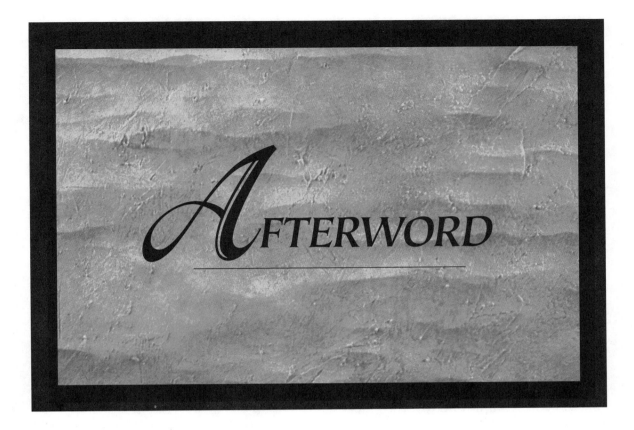

AFTERWORD

 other Teresa may have believed fervently in only one faith, but her deeds made her beloved by many outside it.

"She is regarded as an angel, and not only that, but she is called Mother," said a former president of the Hindu Cultural Society in New York. "Mother in India, in our faith, is as a god. She has the highest honors you could ever give her."

"We consider her a great humanitarian," said Robin Schwarz-Kreger, a Jew. "I don't think Jews have too much pull when it comes to who gets to be a saint, but if anybody is a good candidate, I think it's Mother Teresa."

A lifetime of caring for others, especially the world's poorest people, rendered Mother Teresa like a "bodhisatva" according to a Buddhist minister in San Francisco.

"In our teachings, the ultimate human goal is to become a bodhisatva, someone who cares for people who are in need, poor, sick, and weak," he said.

From her years of tireless work in the slums, Mother Teresa has already profited, said Darui Fazad, a spokesperson for the Islamic Center in Washington D.C.

"She was a very decent, good person who dedicated her life to the poor," he said. "The concept of Islamic charity is that there is no better reward in this life than what she did."

Mother Teresa died on September 5, 1997. Now that she has passed away different religions have different ideas of what her final resting place might be. Catholics, Muslims, and Jews say "heaven." Buddhists say "reincarnated." Their strong opinions acknowledged how Mother Teresa's commitment transcended the boundaries of conventional religions.

Mother Teresa's own sisters in the Missionaries of Charity may have captured it best: "Mother Teresa's spirit is in the work, and the work will go on."

Adapted from an article by Jan M. Faust (ABC News.com, September 12, 1997 © 1997 ABC News and Starwave)

If you recall, one of the tools deemed necessary for a study of the world's religions was empathy. Certainly this is a quality exhibited by and recognized in Mother Teresa of Calcutta.

Empathy is the ability to identify with and understand another's situation—for the purpose of this book, the situation is religion.

How have you done?

Certainly there are many checkpoints for you to gauge your success.

Whereas the early nineteenth century was influenced strongly by Protestant Christianity, and the later nineteenth century and early twentieth century marked by an influx of Roman Catholic and Jewish immigrants to North America, truly the most recent times have expanded our awareness of religions beyond those that are from the Judeo-Christian traditions.

Since the reform of immigration laws in the mid-1960s, many new immigrants from places other than Europe have graced our soil. Muslims, Hindus, Buddhists, and other Japanese and Chinese religions have become part of our consciousness. Today, the media reports not only on Christian festivals, the lives of Christian leaders, and Christian conflicts around the world, but also on these same events and people from a Muslim, Jewish, Buddhist, or Hindu perspective. Ecumenical councils in various regions that were until very recently the places of dialogue between various Christian denominations have now expanded to find commonalties among many of the world's religions.

Just the fact that you attend school on a daily basis provides the opportunity for you to encounter people of various ethnicities, cultures, and religions.

What might be the results of your survey of the world's religions? Perhaps you will report, like other teenagers in Catholic youth programs that emphasize cultural sensitivity, that the study has among other things helped you to be a more religious person, proud to be a Catholic, and to know and live your faith better.[1]

With knowledge and understanding of the world's religions and empathy toward people who profess beliefs other than your own, you can, in the words of Mother Teresa of Calcutta, confidently walk anywhere as a citizen of the world.

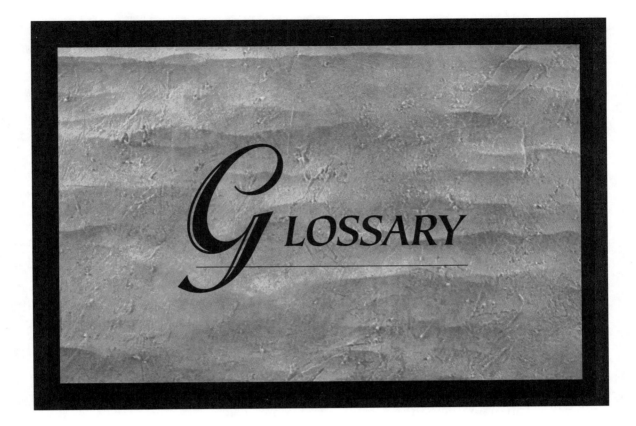

GLOSSARY

Abraham A great prophet of Islam; also a patriarch of Judaism and Christianity.

Abu Bakr Muhammad's first successor; Abu Bakr collected and compiled the revelations of Muhammad into the Qur'an.

adan The Muslim call to prayer.

Adventists Nineteenth-century followers of William Miller who waited expectedly for the Second Coming of Christ; the forerunners of the Seventh-day Adventists.

ahimsa A Hindu term that describes the desire not to harm any form of life. Ahimsa is the basis for the Hindu's belief in nonviolent means as a solution to problems.

Allah An Arabic word meaning "Supreme God" that Muslims use to address God.

anatma The Buddhist doctrine of "not-self" meaning that a permanent, unchangeable, totally independent self does not exist, though people act as if it does. Ignorance of anatma causes suffering.

apostasy A term that describes a situation when a person abandons his or her faith.

arhat A Buddhist term that means "worthy one" and describes someone who has reached nirvana, the ultimate goal of a Buddhist.

ashramas Four stages of life that are general patterns for Hindu males to follow, though most progress through only the first two stages.

Ashura A special date for Muslims. On this date it is held that Allah created the heavens and the earth, Noah left the ark after the flood, and Allah saved Moses from the Pharaoh.

Muslims also believe that this is the date that Allah will judge the people.

atman The Hindu name for the "real self" that is also identical with Brahman. While Hindus taught that self or soul was God (atman), Gautama taught that if the soul was purely God then it is not a soul at all.

avatars In Hinduism the incarnation of gods or goddesses who descend from their heavenly world to earth to rid the world of evil. The two most popular avatars are those of the god Vishnu, named Krishna and Rama.

bodhisatva In Buddhism, one who literally pauses in the door before nirvana to muse over the suffering of those left behind.

Brahma For Hindus, the name of the Creator god.

brahmin The name for the priestly caste of Hindus.

buddha A name for those who have been enlightened according to the Buddhist faith. Buddha with a uppercase "B" refers to Siddhartha Gautama, the founder of Buddhism.

caliph Literally means "to succeed." It is the name given to those leaders who succeeded Muhammad.

caliphate During the classical period, the name for the Islamic empire.

caste The social classes in Hindu society based on a person's position in life that are given at birth. There is no mobility between castes.

Catholic The name for Christians who are in unity with the pope, the bishop of Rome.

Ch'an A Chinese school of Buddhism that emphasizes sitting meditation.

Confucianism A system of beliefs developed by a Chinese philosopher living in the fifth century BCE.

Confucius translates as "Master K'ung" or "Master Teacher."

Confucian Classics A collection of nine books that make up the sacred writings of Confucianism.

covenant Typically understood as a sacred agreement between God and humankind.

Dalai Lama The head of Tibetan Buddhist monastic leaders; the current Dalai Lama is in exile.

dharma In Hinduism, dharma refers to a person's duties in life, especially those related to one's social obligations within one's caste with regard to family and community. In Buddhism, dharma refers to Buddha's teachings.

Divali An autumn festival of Hindus that celebrates the return of Rama, the seventh avatar of Vishnu, from a fourteen-year exile.

divination An ancient Chinese practice of discovering what underlies a present situation or what the future holds through the use of spiritual practices like Tarot card reading or the casting of bones.

Eid al-Adah An Islamic feast that commemorates the willingness of Abraham to sacrifice his son Ishmael in accordance with the will of Allah.

Eid al-Fitr An Islamic festival marking the end of Ramadan.

empathy To identify and understand the situation of another, that is, to "walk in the moccasins of another."

enlightenment In Buddhism, a state in which a person transcends suffering and reaches Nirvana.

feng-shui In Chinese religion, the art of divining a place or date that has a positive spiritual aura.

Four Councils Gatherings of leaders in early Buddhism who were assembled to codify monastic disciplines and unify Buddhist scriptures.

Four Noble Truths Four sacred truths that Buddha discovered; the fourth is that the end of desire will come only if a person follows the Noble Eightfold Path to perfection.

Ganges River The most sacred location of all for Hindus.

Great Disappointment The occasion when many Adventists left William Miller after the second predicted time Jesus failed to return.

Hadith A collection of the stories of Muhammad; the Hadith forms the core of Islamic law.

hafiz An honorary title given to a person who can recite the Qur'an from memory.

hajj The name of a pilgrimage Muslims take to the Ka'bah in Mecca, Saudi Arabia.

Hanukkah A festival that celebrates the victory of the Jews led by Judas the Maccabean over the Syrian Greeks led by Antiochus IV.

harakiri A ceremonial suicide in which a Japanese warrior killed himself out of loyalty to the emperor.

Heaven In Chinese religions, the name for the highest god over a number of lower gods.

hijrah The "migration" in 622 of Muhammad to present day Medina.

Hinduism The primary religion of India.

Holi A Hindu spring festival in which caste differences are often suspended.

imam The name for an Islamic prayer leader.

Investigative Judgment According to Adventists, the time prior to the Second Coming when judgment will take place of the living and the dead.

Islam A monotheistic religion whose adherents submit to the will of Allah.

Islamic creed The Islamic creed names seven beliefs: in Allah, in Allah's books, in Allah's angels, in Allah's messengers, in the last day, in Allah's providence, and in life after death.

Israel Common name of the Jewish homeland, established by the United Nations in 1948.

Jade Emperor The great high god of the Taoists.

Jainism A religion founded in the sixth century BCE by Mahavira as a reaction against Hinduism.

Jen Representative of Chinese thought; it refers to humanity or benevolence.

jinn In Islamic thought, spirits capable of good and bad.

Judaism The religion of the Jewish people.

Jum'ah Friday communal prayer time made by Muslims at a mosque.

Ka'bah The central place for Muslim prayer, located at Mecca, and containing the Black Stone.

kami The Japanese name for any kind of spiritual force or power.

kami body An object, like a mirror or sword, in to which it is believed a kami descends during a Shinto worship service.

karma In Hinduism, the connection between one's actions and the consequences of those actions.

koan A problem with no logical solution that a Zen master presents to a student to solve.

Krishna The principal avatar of Vishnu, often depicted as a handsome young man.

Lao Tzu A possibly legendary figure of the fifth century BCE who is the credited founder of Taoism.

li In Chinese culture, it has to do with the proper way to live, calling for courtesy, etiquette, formality, and respect.

Mahayana A branch of Buddhism; the word literally means "the Great Vehicle," referring to its advocation of liberation for all people.

matsuri The name for Japanese festivals.

Mawlid al-Nabi The day that commemorates the birth of Muhammad.

maya Refers to the illusionary appearance of the world.

Mecca The city in Saudi Arabia where Muhammad was born; a sacred place of pilgrimage for contemporary Muslims.

Medina A holy city in Islam; it was the place where Muhammad migrated to after his preaching was rejected at Mecca.

mezuzah The container that holds a small piece of parchment inscribed with biblical passages, rolled up in a container and fixed to the doors of many Jewish households.

Middle Way Life in a balance between indulgence and asceticism that is central to Buddhism.

minaret A tower at a mosque where the call to prayer is broadcast.

Mishnah In Judaism, the summary of the oral Torah.

moksha Liberation from the Hindu endless cycle of rebirth.

Mohandas Gandhi A Hindu instrumental in India's independence from the British (also known as Mahatma Gandhi).

Mormon The common name for the Church of Jesus Christ of Latter-day Saints.

mosque A meeting place where Muslims pray and worship.

muezzin The person who calls Muslims to prayer five times a day.

Muhammad In Islam, he is Allah's final messenger.

murti A statue, picture, or other image of Hindu gods.

myth A sacred story intended to convey a religious truth.

Nation of Islam An American black Muslim movement founded by W. D. Fard Muhammad.

nirvana The spiritual goal of all Buddhists; it is the release from the life-cycle of suffering.

Noble Eightfold Path The path to ending suffering and thus achieve nirvana offered as the fourth of the Four Noble Truths of Buddhism.

Pali Canon The edited version of the Tipitaka and the final version of the Mahayanan Buddhist scriptures.

Passover The Jewish holiday, also known as Pesach, celebrating the Hebrew's freedom from Egyptian slavery when the angel of death "passed over" the houses of the Hebrews that were marked with the blood of a lamb.

polygamy The taking of more than one spouse in marriage; a practice originally permitted by Mormons.

Protestant Generally refers to Christian churches that follow the reforms of Martin Luther.

proxy In the Mormon church, a person who takes the place of a dead ancestor in a baptism ceremony.

puja Hindu worship of a deity, primarily at a home shrine.

Pure Land A form of Buddhism that emphasizes faith and confidence in a buddha based on intuition and experience.

Purim The "feast of lots," it is a Jewish feast that celebrates the victory of Jews living in Persia in the fifth century BCE over Haman, the prime minister of Persia.

Qur'an The sacred scriptures of Islam.

rabbi A word that literally means "teacher;" they officiate at Jewish synagogue services.

Ramadan The twelfth month on the Islamic calendar in which all healthy Muslims are to fast during daylight hours.

religion Derived from the Latin word religio, meaning "to bind," refers to how a person or community "bound" itself to something that was worthy of reverence or respect.

Rosh Hashanah The name for the Jewish New Year.

Sa'y The Muslim practice of circumambulating the Ka'bah.

sacred Another word for holy.

samsara A name for the cycle of birth, death, and rebirth.

samskaras The name for the various celebrations of events in the Hindu life cycle.

sangha At first just the Buddhist monastic community, now it includes the entire community of Buddhist monks, nuns, and lay people.

Sanskrit The liturgical and scriptural language of Hinduism.

satori An intuitive flash that leads to enlightenment.

satyagraha Passive resistance often advocated as part of Hinduism.

Shabbat The Hebrew word for Sabbath or holy day.

Shahadah The first pillar of Islam; it literally translates as "creed."

Shakyamuni The name his followers called Siddhartha Gautama; it means the "sage of Shakyas."

shamanism The belief that one is possessed by a spirit and can communicate with the spirits in another world.

shari'ah The term for Islamic law.

Shavuot A Jewish harvest festival occurring fifty days after Passover.

Shi'ite A sectarian group of Muslims that form roughly ten percent of the Muslim population.

Shinto Literally means "way of the gods;" it is a Japanese religion with roots in animism.

shofar A ram's horn that is blown during Jewish celebrations.

shogunate A form of military government that ruled Japan until the nineteenth century.

shruti The oldest of the Hindu scriptures.

Sikhism A synthesis of Hinduism and Islam begun in the fifteenth century.

smriti Hindu scriptures not revealed by the gods, yet more popularly read among Hindus.

stupa A dome-shaped monument used to house Buddhist relics.

Sukkot A Jewish fall harvest festival also known as the Feast of Tabernacles or Feast of Booths.

Sunni Along with the Shi'ite, one of two major Muslim groups.

surah Divisions, much like chapters, of the Qur'an.

sutra A word meaning "sacred teaching," these are the main sacred writings of the Mahayana Buddhists.

synagogue A Jewish place of worship; it means "place of assembly."

Talmud A collection of Jewish rabbinical teachings; it is the highest Jewish authoritative writing after the Torah.

Tao Literally means "the way;" it is considered to be the driving force of the universe.

Tao Te Ching One of the most widely read pieces of Chinese literature in the world; it is the main piece of sacred writing of the Taoists.

theocracy A government that is ruled by God or one who is divinely inspired.

Theravada One of three major branches of Buddhism; it literally means "School of Elders."

Three Baskets Refers to the three parts of the Tipitaka, the Theravada Buddhist scriptures.

Three Jewels Considered the core of Buddhism, they are Sangha, Buddha, and dharma.

Tipitaka Central Buddhist scripture that is made up of the "Three Baskets;" the edited version is known as the *Pali Canon*.

tishuvah The repentance Jews strive for between Rosh Hashanah and Yom Kippur.

Torah Literally translates as "law;" the sacred scriptures of the Jews.

torii A symbolic entrance gate made of two timber posts and two timber cross beams for a Shinto shrine.

Ultimate Reality Also called Brahman or Absolute Reality, it refers to that which is real and not dependent on anything else.

ummah A collective word meaning "nation;" it refers to the Islamic community.

untouchables Hindus considered so low that they are not even a part of the caste system.

Varanasi A holy city for Hindus located on the Ganges River.

Vajrayana The prominent form of Buddhism in Tibet; literally the "Diamond Vehicle."

Vedas In the Hindu tradition, a collection of revelations given to the ancient sages by the gods.

Vishnu One of the three great gods of Hinduism.

wudu A ritual washing performed by Muslims before they pray.

wu-wei Literally "without action;" centers on allowing nature to evolve without human action.

yin and yang Opposite but complimentary extremes in Chinese culture; literally yin and yang means "shady" and "sunny."

yoga Disciplines like knowledge, good deeds, and devotion a person can choose to erode the negative karmic effects and move toward liberation; also refers to meditation.

Yom Kippur One of the holiest days of the year for Jews; also known as the "Day of Atonement."

zazen Sitting meditation in Zen Buddhism.

Zionism A Jewish nationalist movement of the late nineteenth and early twentieth centuries designed to return the Jews to their homeland in Palestine.

INDEX

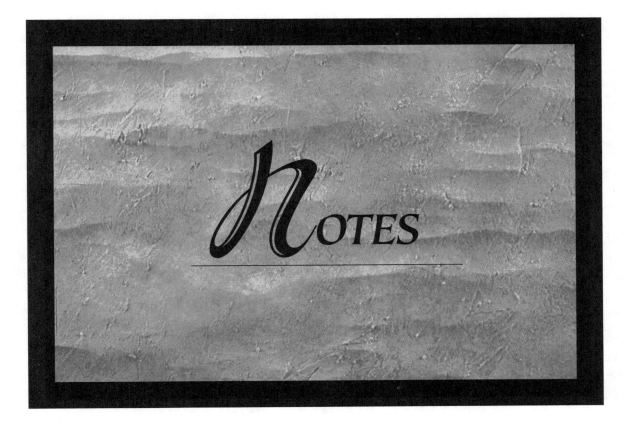

NOTES

CHAPTER 1

1 Both quotations are taken from Declaration on the Relationship of the Church to Non-Christian Religions, *Vatican Council II: The Conciliar and Post Conciliar Documents*. Austin Flannery, O.P., editor. 1975. Northport, New York: Costello Publishing Company.

CHAPTER 2

1 Hellinization refers to the adoption of Greek ways, speech, and culture.

2 Rabbi is a word that literally means "teacher." The rabbi became the Jewish minister in charge of synagogue worship.

3 The Talmud is a collection of rabbinnical teachings. It is regarded as the highest legal authority in Judaism after the Torah. The Talmud consists of interpretations of scripture, rules for hygiene and diet, and directions for synagogue services.

4 The Age of Enlightenment was a philosophical movement of the eighteenth century that emphasized the use of reason to analyze previously accepted doctrines and traditions.

5 Decalogue comes from the word "ten." It is a word for the Ten Commandments.

6 *Shabbat* is the Hebrew word for Sabbath or holy day.

7 *Halakhic* refers to the total body of Jewish law—personal, religious, civil, criminal.

8 A bimah is a raised platform in synagogues from which the Torah scroll is read.

9 A *mezuah* is a small parchment scroll inscribed with two passages from the Jewish scriptures and enclosed in a box. One scroll is fixed on each door

of a Jewish home, except the bathroom. The mezuzah symbolizes the fact that God is present in the home.

10 Tishuvah literally means "repentence."

11 A menorah is a candlestick with seven branches, though synagogue and home menorahs today usually do not have seven branches to avoid exact replication of the Temple menorah.

12 Havadalah is a special Saturday ceremony that literally translates as "separation." It includes a blessing that refers to separations between light and darkness, the holy and profane, and the Sabbath and the rest of the week.

CHAPTER 3

1 A sect is a religious group that separates from a larger religious denomination.

2 Doctrines are principles, beliefs, and teachings of a religion.

3 This date is calculated based on information in Luke 2:2 that Quirinius was governor of Syria and that Roman emperor Caesar Augustus had ordered a census.

4 A word meaning "non-Jew."

5 A self-governing church within the Eastern Orthodox family of churches. Today patriarchates tend to be national churches.

6 "Pope" comes from the Latin word for "father."

7 A series of military expeditions by Christians in the eleventh through thirteenth centuries designed to take the Holy Land back from the Muslims.

8 The doctrine of *transubstantiation* is accepted by Roman Catholics, but is rejected by most Protestants. The Eastern Orthodox Church accepts the bread and wine as Christ's body and blood, but simply says that this is the work of the Holy Spirit and avoids other explanations.

9 Czar is the title of the male monarchs who ruled Russia until the 1917 revolution.

10 Incarnation means literally "to make flesh."

11 An icon is a sacred painting of saints that represents their actual transfiguration in heaven.

CHAPTER 4

1 Caliph comes from the Aramaic *halifah* which means "to succed."

2 A mosque is a meeting place for Islamic prayer and worship.

3 The Haddith are a collection of stories on the teachings of Muhammad, which forms most of the body of Islamic law.

4 Jinn are spirits capable of good or bad. Before Islam began Arabs worshipped jinn as gods.

5 Shahadah translates as "creed."

6 Hafiz means "to memorize" or "to guard."

7 Hajj literally translates "to set out with a definite purpose."

CHAPTER 5

1 The *Vedas* are a collection of revelations believed to have been given to the ancient sages by the gods. Meaning "knowledge," the *Vedas* contained the knowledge the religious leaders needed to perform religious duties. The *Vedas* were memorized and orally transmitted. To this day, there are Hindu religious leaders who have memorized the *Vedas*.

2 Aryans refers to the people who spoke the parent language of the Indo-European languages. Aryans in this sense does not in any way refer to the word used by German Nazis to describe ethnic or racial superiority.

3 Vedic is an adjective refering to the Vedas.

4 Brahmin refers to the priestly class of Aryans and later, Hindus, who were considered the most learned and wise among the people.

5 A guru is a guide or teacher who helps fellow Hindus to achieve salvation.

6 Smriti means "that which is remembered." Smriti deals with more secular day-to-day matters. Though secondary to the shruti scripture, many more Hindus are familiar with smriti scriptures. Smriti scriptures are not revealed by the gods.

7 A mantra is a word, phrase, or special sound, usually from scripture, that has special powers. It is believed that the power comes when the mantra is chanted aloud.

8 Ultimate Reality or Absolute Reality refers to that which is "real" and not dependent on anything else.

9 A Hindu name for the Supreme Being, Ultimate Being, or God. Brahman is the ground of all nature as well as the entire cosmos.

10 Transcendent refers to that which is beyond the material world, beyond what the finite human can know or understand.

11 Karma means "deed" or "action."

12 The cycle of birth, death, and rebirth.

13 Moksha is the ultimate goal for most schools of Hinduism.

14 There are various types of yoga that achieve the purpose of moksha. Yoga can also mean "meditation" or the discipline that prepares the body for meditation.

15 Ashrams are community houses where followers of a guru live.

16 It must be emphasized that Hindus do not believe that the murti itself is the god. Rather, the murti represents the god. However, some Hindus believe the god dwells within the murti during the puja.

17 Granthu is the name for Sikh clergy.

CHAPTER 6

1 Nirvana literally means "to extinguish" or "to blow out," referring to the extinction of suffering, impermanence, delusion, and all that keeps the life cycle (samsara) going. Nirvana is the spiritual goal for all Buddhists.

2 Shakyamuni means "the sage of Shakyas." It is a title of the historical Buddha.

3 At first the sangha was just the Buddhist monastic community. Later sangha came to describe the entire community of monks, nuns, and lay people.

4 Objects venerated because of associating with a holy person that died. Relics often include a bone fragment of that person.

5 Theravada literally means "School of Elders" and is one of three major branches of Buddhism.

6 Literally, "Great Vehicle" because of its advocation of liberation for all people.

7 Later in Japan, Ch'an Buddhism became known as Zen Buddhism.

8 Literally "Diamond Vehicle." Vajrayana Buddhism is the prominant branch of Buddhism in Tibet.

9 Anatma is the Buddhist doctrine of "not-self." This means that a permanent, unchangeable, totally independent self does not exist, though people act as if it does. Ignorance of anatma causes suffering.

10 Tantric refers to texts and practices understood by only a very few.

CHAPTER 7

1 The Jade Emperor is the great High God of the Taoists, a Chinese religion.

2 Folk religion refers to non-institutional religions of a particular culture or group of people.

3 Ancestor worship refers to various ways of showing respect and reverence for family ancestors after their deaths. Worshippers bring offerings to their ancestors in order to obtain protection and guidance.

4 Divination is the attempt to discover what underlies a present situation or what the future holds through the use of spiritual practices like Tarot card reading or the casting of bones.

5 Literally, yin and yang means "shaded" and "sunny." Yin and yang are opposite but complementary extremes in Chinese culture.

6 The word Taoism comes from the root word "Tao," meaning "the way." Tao is considered to be the driving force of the universe.

7 Literally "without action." Wu-wei centers on allowing nature to evolve without human interference.

8 Hsien means "immortal."

CHAPTER 8

1 Kami is the Japanese name for any kind of spiritual or sacred power found in animate and inanimate objects as well as any kind of spiritual force or power.

2 Shogunate is a form of military government that ruled Japan until 1867.

3 Sitting meditation in Zen that integrates the body and mind into watchful stillness.

4 Satori refers to an intuitive realization (rather than analysis or logic) of the real nature of things; a path to enlightenment.

5 Ritual washings.

6 Kamidana means "kami shelf." It is the place where the kami of that household is honored.

7 Tenrikyo is a Shinto sect specializing in faith healing.

8 Harakiri is the name for the ceremonical suicide in which a person used a knife to accomplish the task.

9 Shamanism is the belief that one is possessed by a spirit and can communicate with the spirits of another world.

10 The kami body is an object in which it is believed the kami descends to during a Shinto worship service. Often, the object is a mirror or sword.

11 A long, traditional, richly decorated robe.

12 A shaman is a person who combines the roles of priest, wise man, and magician. A shamaness is the female counterpart.

EPILOGUE

1 Mormon is the name of the prophet who complied the sacred history of the Americas which the prophet Joseph Smith later found and transcribed.

2 Polygamy involves taking more than one spouse in marriage.

3 Apostasy means "abandonment of one's faith."

4 Millennialists are those who believe that at his Second Coming, Jesus and his followers will rule on earth for 1,000 years.

5 A theocracy is a government ruled by God or by one who is divinely inspired.

AFTERWORD

1 *CARA Report*. "New Directions in Youth Ministry: A National Study of Youth Ministry Participants," 1996.

ACKNOWLEDGEMENTS

A textbook of this breadth cannot be written without assistance. While some engendered and kept alive my interest in the world's religious traditions over the years, a number of people read specific chapters of the manuscript.

My gratitude goes to Dr. Ronald Cottle who was my first teacher of the world's religions at Pasadena City College. It was because of his enthusiasm I eventually majored in the study of religion at the University of California, Los Angeles with Dr. Kees Bolle encouraging me on. At the University of San Francisco, Father Paul Bernadicou, S.J., expanded my interest in the world's religions to include the mystical tradition. It was at the University of California, Santa Barbara where much of my education in the world's religious traditions took place. Though I never had a class with him, Dr. Ninian Smart, department chair, author, and consultant for the television series *The Long Search*, was a tremendous influence on the students and his influence is throughout this book. Within the department, Dr. Catherine Albanese, professor of religions in America and Dr. Richard Hecht, professor of Judaism influenced me greatly. However, it was the guidance and continual encouragement of the late Dr. Walter Capps who constantly reminded me that there was a place for me in the field of religious studies.

I am especially extend my gratitude to those who took the time to read specific chapters of the manuscript: Rabbi David Vorspan and Gladys Sturman for the Judaism chapter, Nasreen Haroon and Shabbir Mansuri for the Islam chapter, and Rev. Kusala for the Buddhism chapter. My parents, Robert and Shirley Clemmons, were very helpful in their critique of the first four chapters as well as with their love and encouragement.

As a full time minister in a very large parish and as one who is visually impaired, the support I received from family, friends, and colleagues is invaluable. I thank my community, the Sisters of the Holy Names of Jesus and Mary of the California Province, my ministry partners at St. Monica Parish Community, my colleagues at Westside Interfaith Council and the Catholic-Jewish Women's Committee of Los Angeles. I especially thank Helen Markov, SNJM and Judy Zielinski, OSF who walked with me every chapter of the way. I will be ever grateful to my editor at Ave Maria Press, Michael Amodei, who sought me out to write this textbook and then journeyed with this novice author with the patience of a saint.